The results of British elections depend increasingly on what happens during the intensive four-week campaign, a period shaped not simply by what politicians do and say, but by how the campaign is reported to the public through the mass media. This book, the fourth such collection on each election since 1979, examines the dialogue conducted via the press, television and the opinion polls between politicians and the people in the 1992 campaign. A mixture of academic research, expert experience and personal reflection, the chapters are written by academic scholars and by professionals from the worlds of television, newspapers, polling and party organisation. The book will be of great interest not only to academic political scientists, but to politicians, journalists, market researchers and party workers – indeed, to all with an active interest in elections and the mass media.

Political communications: the general election campaign of 1992

Political communications:
the general election campaign of 1992

Edited by

IVOR CREWE

Professor of Government, University of Essex

and

BRIAN GOSSCHALK

Managing Director, MORI

CAMBRIDGE
UNIVERSITY PRESS

Published by the Press Syndicate of the University of Cambridge
The Pitt Building, Trumpington Street, Cambridge CB2 1RP
40 West 20th Street, New York, NY 10011–4211, USA
10 Stamford Road, Oakleigh, Melbourne 3166, Australia

First published 1995

Printed in Great Britain at the University Press, Cambridge

A catalogue record for this book is available from the British Library

Library of Congress cataloguing in publication data

Political communications: the general election campaign of 1992 / edited by Ivor Crewe
and Brian Gosschalk.
    p.   cm.
Based on a conference held at the University of Essex in September 1992 – Pref.
ISBN 0 521 45396 8 hbk; 0 521 46964 3 pbk
1. Elections – Great Britain – Congresses. 2. Great Britain. Parliament – Elections,
1992 – Congresses. 3. Communication in politics – Great Britain – Congresses.
I. Crewe, Ivor. II. Gosschalk, Brian.
JN956.P65 1994
324.941′0859–dc20   93–47235   CIP

ISBN 0 521 45396 8 hardback
ISBN 0 521 46964 3 paperback

Contents

Illustrations

Figures 12.1, 12.2, 12.3 and 12.4 are reproduced by kind permission of News International plc.

Tables

Preface

This is the fourth book in a continuing series examining political communications in British general elections. Like its predecessors for the 1979, 1983 and 1987 elections, it has a dual purpose: first, to provide an analysis of the media, the parties and the opinion polls in the campaign and, second, to make available the reflections of some of those who participated in it.

The book is based on a conference held at Essex University in September 1992 which brought together, for a weekend's intensive review of the campaign, academics, politicians, journalists, pollsters and many other practitioners of political communication.

Given the size of the conference – 36 contributions and 130 participants – it was unfortunately not possible to publish all the papers and talks in this volume. Many that do not appear here have been published in David Denver *et al.* (eds.), *British Elections and Parties Yearbook* (1993). We are grateful to all the contributors to the conference.

The conference was held under the joint auspices of the Political Communications Group and the Elections, Public Opinion and Parties Group of the Political Studies Association. We wish to acknowledge the generous financial support received from the PSA, the Nuffield Foundation and the University of Essex and the office facilities provided by Lancaster University and MORI. We are grateful to Deborah Crewe, Louise Melly, Caroline Morris and Harriet McGarry for helping to organise the conference. A special debt of gratitude is owed to David Denver, our co-organiser, and to Bob Worcester, for helping to arrange the programme.

'I would very much like to have a re-run of the Spring general election', Robin Cook commented wistfully in his address to the conference in September. We cannot arrange for re-runs of elections but we hope to organise another such conference after the next general election.

Ivor Crewe
Brian Gosschalk

Part I
The politicians

1 The Conservative campaign: against the odds

Lord Wakeham

Many will not find my analysis of the 1992 election campaign very comfortable. In my view, and I was clearly on the record at the time during the election campaign, we were at all times going to win. Of that I had no doubt.

Nevertheless, the Conservative election victory was won against the odds. The margin of victory in parliamentary seats was small; but in terms of the popular vote it was large. In 1992, the Conservative Party polled more votes than any party had ever done before. A fourth election victory in a row is unprecedented in modern British electoral history. It was achieved with economic recovery stalled as the world economy turned down. It was achieved by a new party leader fighting against an experienced opponent, free now of the strong centre-party challenge of 1983 and 1987, and whose control over his own party had become complete. He was widely believed to have done everything needed in rehabilitating his party to secure victory. How did this remarkable outcome occur?

Unlike my predecessors in 1987 and 1983, my task is not simply to add colour and insight to a familiar story. The story of the general election of 1992 has been told thus far in terms which convince the participants rather less than recent preceding elections. Throughout, the media focus was on a campaign largely of their own making. They looked to the presentation, not the politics, to the headlines and the polls, not the underlying movements, to the 'beltway' issues, as they say in America, but not to the doorstep issues.

In the months leading up to the election, and in the days of the campaign, we had a party leader who never wavered in his conviction that we would win, and win well. That was a conviction born of evidence and analysis.

We knew, as much as two years before the election, that the essence of the debate would be simple: 'time for a change' versus 'trust'. And from the local government elections in 1990, we knew that there was every chance of high spending and high-taxing Labour candidates losing votes.

Following the leadership election of late 1990, we had every hope that Labour's weaknesses would drag them down. They were socialists, in a world that had turned against socialism; union-dominated when unions are demons from the past, and widely seen as a party that was still unable to be trusted on Europe, defence, and nationalisation; led by a man whom it appeared the electorate neither trusted nor respected; and, most of all, a still thinly disguised party of tax and spending addicts.

From November 1990, John Major was the principal change-agent in British politics. In his hands, Conservative government, policies and prospects were renewed. Not without some difficulty; for too long there were elements in the Conservative Party and in the media that wanted always to compare John Major with his predecessor and not with Neil Kinnock, which was the only relevant comparison.

In the last eighteen months of the last parliament, the pace of policy innovation matched that of any recent incoming government. The impetus of the Citizen's Charter process forced the system of government to review, to explain, and to embrace reform. By early 1992, that process left Labour Party policy, by contrast, looking tired and out-of-date, lacking in imagination and innovation. But, from our point of view, Labour Party policy documents had one saving grace – they were long and detailed.

A general election could have been held at any point after April/May 1991. And at any time, I believe, the Conservatives would have won. At no point, admittedly, did the polls – private and public taken together – deliver a clear indication that it was right to go. Even so, polls were a second-order factor, since John Major, keen as he was to win his own mandate, set himself key tasks on taking office, and found others thrust on him, including the Maastricht negotiations, all of which had an influence on the choice of date. In the end he felt obliged to defer the date until April.

Unusually, therefore, the timing of the election offered no strategic benefit to the incumbent party. Some small tactical benefit was, however, certainly available. The conjunction of the Budget, a major party meeting in Torquay and economic statistics at the outset of the campaign directly contributed to setting the campaign arguments along a set of tracks from which they made only limited detours. This was not a coincidence. The timing of the election, and Norman Lamont's well-judged Budget, supplemented by John Smith's response, let the tax argument, so skilfully begun in January, re-emerge as the dominating subject for argument between the parties.

Frankly we were surprised at the ease with which our opponents let us get onto our favoured issues. We drew Labour into a debate about 'where's the money coming from?' Time and again, that question was allowed to run. Then, when they attempted to answer this, they left loose ends for us to pull and they delivered confused tax threats of their own; and they failed to inoculate their manifesto against our calculations of the tax implications of their spending plans. I can well believe that, as some in the Labour Party now bitterly complain, the politicians played too small a part in their campaign, the designers too big a part.

If I may dwell on this for a moment, may I just pay credit to Saatchi and Saatchi, once more at this election acting as our advertising agency. To say that advertising – or pollsters, for that matter – should not run a campaign is in no sense to underplay their importance. The key elements of our message were all part of the brief to our agency, not suggestions from them. But then they delivered. Their creative contribution was, in my view, the best since 1979. Posters like the tax bombshell and the 'double whammy' will live with us for a long time.

Once again, we received terrific support from a number of newspapers, although they were also critical of our campaign and full of praise for Labour's efficiency. I am bound to say I think that was more to do with nerves that we would actually lose, than deeply held views. They were, after all, running the opinion polls that Bob Worcester later referred to as 'the worst results for the opinion polls since they were invented'. The sharpness of the pro–Conservative newspapers' comments and the depth and breadth of their reporting undoubtedly helped to ensure some of the movement towards us in the last weeks of the campaign.

There is one aspect I find quite interesting about the comparison between the 1987 and 1992 elections. In 1992 most predictions were overcome in the last week and there was a significant surge to the Conservatives. We have perhaps forgotten that in 1987, up until the last few days, most people were predicting a victory by 50 seats; in fact, we won by 100 seats. Maybe there is something we should all be learning about how elections work in this country. It seems clear that opinion polls under-estimate the Conservative share of the vote and that the final outcome really only starts to be decided in the last few days.

When I speak of the election campaign, I confess that in my mind I now speak not just of four weeks but of a period beginning on 6 January and ending on 9 April.

I look forward to the Nuffield election study which will tell the story in detail, but I should tell you that never before has a British general election been preceded by so intense and so sustained a period of political campaigning even before the starting pistol was officially fired.

We began on 6 January. Labour woke up only slowly but they, too, were campaigning hard during February. But the Liberal Democrats never seemed to get going or, if they did, had little ammunition to fire. Labour were forced to take ammunition out of their election chest. We did not, even though we published over twenty-five party political documents *before* 3 March.

One could argue that during the 'near-term' campaign, as the period from 6 January to 10 March is called, nothing much changed. Voting intention held steady. Several other polling indicators showed the electorate's perceptions of Labour changing only marginally. But I have no doubt that the near-term campaign substantially contributed to the final result. Tax, policies for economic recovery, law and order – all these were brought to the fore. Labour's agenda slipped away. All the while that William Waldegrave and Virginia Bottomley were publishing good news on the health reforms, Robin Cook was supposed to be keeping his powder dry but, in the event, the issue never re-emerged for them in the way some people expected.

In early speculation on the election timing, the dangers of going through to 1992 and being subject to the vagaries of events were always stressed. To counter those dangers, we sought to grab hold of the agenda and control it. That was the role of the 'near-term' campaign.

I want now to turn to the four weeks of the election itself. Space does not permit a blow-by-blow account. I will confine myself to several overall conclusions.

When I arrived at Conservative Central Office at the start of those hectic weeks, I talked to the CCO professionals. Their view was that it would be extremely difficult to hold our position in thirty-nine seats. In another thirty it would be too close to call. Through the campaign, that assessment did not change significantly. It was never seriously undermined by reports. We came out at the top end of our range. We exceeded our expectations in share of the vote terms. We were always sure we would continue to be in government after the election but possibly in rather more difficult circumstances.

I will confess to the occasional flutter of nerves. Anything less would hardly be human. Only John Major seemed entirely free of doubt. But in the run-up to polling day, these thoughts led me to call Willie Whitelaw. I said I would tell him the advice we would give the Prime Minister on the election outcome. But could he – with all his experience – tell me whether, when all the chips are down, the CCO gurus tell us, the politicians, the truth. Willie's answer – typically delphic as to prophecy – was that they may be right or wrong, but they do tell the truth.

Throughout the campaign, I got the impression that Labour's assessment of the likely outcome did not violently disagree with our own. The best they were bidding for was a hung parliament. I will say one thing for Neil Kinnock under these circumstances – it took considerable guts to appear so confident and to be so cheerful.

So, despite my argument that the result was predictable, debate on the 'why' and 'how' of the 1992 election continues. The interpretation of the 1992 election will fill volumes, but I think that the essence of what happened is quite simple.

The Conservatives got the strategy more or less right, even if some detailed implementation was not perfectly delivered here or there. That was hardly surprising, since we accepted that as the price of giving ourselves greater flexibility to respond to events. But, we decided on a political strategy and stuck to it. Tax, John Major, and Labour's unfitness to govern; these were the simple messages. Fewer messages, fewer messengers. Labour's strategy seemed to be to wait for the economy to deliver us into their hands. It did not oblige. Their presentation and tactics seemed determined beforehand and without sufficient flexibility. Even so, this discipline let mistakes through: 'Jennifer's Ear', the Sheffield rally, Neil Kinnock on PR, not costing the manifesto, not even putting 'as resources allow' into the text of their manifesto.

Why, then, did the media so exalt Labour's campaign over ours? I do not complain of media bias, but I do complain of media trivialisation and a fixation on polls and personalities and how the campaign was going, rather than on the issues. In the event, later in the campaign, we cashed in on all of these, turning the Labour lead in the polls against them, using the media obsession over a hung parliament and PR, and giving a powerful, new broadcast image of John Major on his soapbox to capitalise on his popular personality. All powerful tools – none premeditated.

Was it a negative campaign? Certainly not, if that means lacking in positive content. The manifesto was positive and substantial. The same was true of the Prime Minister's campaign speeches. But early on too much positive content was obscured by negative images. Later on, attacking material was still being delivered, but other images, at press conferences, and in PPBs, balanced the whole. It was undoubtedly an aggressive campaign – it had to be to get over the 'You can't trust Labour' message. But it was not the dirty campaign of which some warned.

Did the campaign make a difference? Yes, but not all the difference. I am sceptical of the argument that it was all a late surge, but we were always conscious of Norman Tebbit's view, expressed in the equivalent talk to this conference in 1987, and I quote, that 'timing was important, as in my view it took at least a week from raising the profile of the issue to seeing an effect in the published opinion polls'.

We delayed the strongest part of our campaigning to the end. We were hitting at our hardest from Tuesday, 31 March, D-Day minus 9. Our press advertising began on Friday, 3 April. Again, the Prime Minister's media appearances were skewed to the end of the campaign. By contrast, Labour's campaign seemed to us to peak on D minus 8. In politics, timing is all.

Could Labour have won? The margin in terms of seats suggest they could, but I believe victory in terms of votes was always well out of their grasp. 'Time for a Change' against 'You can't trust Labour' became an unequal struggle, especially once Labour, by their policy review, felt constrained as to what new commitments they could make. Part of our confidence was based on the clear and strong intention of our people to turn out and vote. Only tactical voting, stronger than anticipated in many marginals, upset such calculations. In the collapse of the Liberal Democrat vote lay Labour's only chance. In the event, the Liberal Democrat advance split the opposition vote in many seats once more and a Liberal surge gave us a new and appealing target of undecided voters, whom the Prime Minister brought over.

Our pre-election projections had long put our central estimate of Liberal Democrats share of the vote at 19 per cent. In the event it was 17.8 per cent. The difference represented several key marginals in which our vote increased but Liberal collapse let Labour in.

Did Labour lose or did the Tories win? Some of both. I believe we took the initiative on 6 January and held it throughout, except for a few days between 16 March and 21 March, but even in that time Labour stayed on *our* agenda. When they tried to shift the agenda in the following week, they failed. So, in short, we took victory for ourselves, but Labour must blame themselves for lost opportunities.

Finally, no account of the campaign is complete without an appreciation of two men. First, Chris Patten, whose benign and skilled control of our press conferences and campaigning presentation, and his political feel, were both a vital benefit to our campaign, bought at the cost of personal sacrifice.

And, most of all, John Major. He had never fought an election as party leader before. By Saturday, 28 March, the transition from Prime Minister to consummate campaigner was complete. From then, he dominated the media, he put his own ideas into practice, he controlled the political debate and he won the election for himself.

Historians will look back on the 1992 general election as John Major's personal triumph. They will be right.

2 The Liberal Democrats' campaign

Richard Holme

Liberal Democrat strategy

A comprehensive account of the Liberal Democrats' campaign is provided by Des Wilson in a later chapter. I shall therefore confine my comments to the underlying strategic opportunities and dilemmas of the Liberal Democrats, some of which are continuing and not particular to the 1992 general election.

One issue was specific to 1992: the difficulty of adjusting our attack from one of a Margaret Thatcher-led Conservative government to one led by John Major. Labour must have shared the same fundamental problem of how to get an amiable, pragmatic, rather grey Prime Minister in the sights with the same clarity as we had his predecessor, the restless radical and, by the end, highly unpopular figure, Mrs Thatcher. In a sense Mrs Thatcher made small-c conservatives of us all, as we tried desperately to hold onto old verities and institutions in the face of her strongly willed assault on them. John Major was a very different opponent to fight, combining low-key affability and genuine classlessness with no clear policy thrust. His personality lowered the political temperature, calmed the young working C2DE wives, the universal target, with his ordinary next-doorness while his policies did not present an easy target. I believe that the change in the Conservative leadership from Margaret Thatcher to John Major, with the demise of the poll tax and the sense of a new start, represented for many people, who do not pay the same attention to politics as readers of this volume do, the new government that elections are supposed to bring about.

Des Wilson said how we planned, originally when Mrs Thatcher was still Prime Minister, to run a campaign of youth and vigour; yet paradoxically by the time the election came Paddy Ashdown was the oldest, albeit indisputably the fittest, of the three party leaders.

John Major's policies really only presented one significant target, economic failure. At the time this was a question on which the jury was out, although subsequently it was proved beyond doubt. The Conservatives were skilful enough to switch the issue to taxation and use the fear that higher taxes engendered to cast a halo of fearfulness over Labour's economic competence as a whole. Our own spirited attempt at a synthesis of Keynesianism and competitive market economics, billed as public investment *plus* private enterprise,

9

although amply vindicated subsequently (for instance, by the Japanese government's recent economic package), did not get much of a look in.

This brings us to the question of policy presentation as a whole by the Liberal Democrats. People are fond of saying that nobody knows what we as a third party stand for. It was our determination at the 1992 general election, and something to which Paddy Ashdown and I, as the coordinating 'author' of the manifesto, *Changing Britain for Good*, were particularly dedicated, to be crystal clear and sharp in putting forward our policies.

Of course, when people say that they do not know what we stand for they are not necessarily referring to policies. They may be thinking about our position between the perceived poles of the Conservative Party and Labour Party, or our lack – to my mind a strength in itself – of any clear class or sectional basis in society. But to the extent that their confusion sprang from a muddled perception of our policies, we were determined to focus and clarify our stance.

Having being involved in the Alliance manifesto of 1987, an exercise in tortuous negotiation under the brooding eye of the then Doctor Owen, which resulted in excessive blandness, and also recalling those often very senior figures in the SDP in the early 1980s who favoured a rose-tinted blank screen on which electors could project their favourite policy images, I can assure you that this search for sharp definition marked a significant culture change.

We also sought some coherence around main themes, dubbed the '5 E's' – Enterprise Economy, Education, Environment, Europe and Electoral and Constitutional Reform – to give a shape to our offering rather than merely presenting the conventional shopping list or catalogue, organised by government departmental headings.

I believe this approach was worthwhile. It certainly helped with our own members and workers so that, in Cromwellian terms they could 'know what they love and love what they know'. Questionnaires to candidates and constituencies after the election showed a high level of confidence and enthusiasm in the policy area and in the manifesto. We also got a good reception from the serious press. *The Independent* said of the manifesto that the Liberal Democrats were 'more in sympathy with the spirit of the times than either of the two big Parties', and that we were 'the party which most nearly reflects the instincts and hopes of the nation'. *The Guardian* found that 'here, ranged at the radical end of the spectrum were many of the answers beyond Labour's mumbles'.

On the other hand, as I have already implied about John Major, it is easier to attack clarity than vagueness, and we were certainly subject to sharp specific attack by leaflet and telephone from the Conservatives in seats where we threatened them, on such issues as the abolition of mortgage tax relief and the introduction of petrol tax, as the forerunner of a gradual shift to resource taxation. On the whole, at the national level we evaded the main Conservative counter-attack on taxation both because it was aimed at Labour and because although our policy was as redistributive as Labour's, our top rate was 10 per cent lower than theirs.

Let me move onto another matter to which Des Wilson has referred, the decision to focus our campaign in a quasi-Presidential way on Paddy Ashdown. There was nothing new in this. As readers of the Nuffield Studies know, party leaders get 75 per cent or so of television coverage, and certainly in previous elections Owen and Steel, Steel and Jenkins, Steel on his own, Thorpe and Grimond had all been the centre of third-party campaigns.

In 1992 we had the additional incentive of research which demonstrated that, unlike Neil Kinnock who lost votes for Labour and John Major whose effect was neutral, Paddy Ashdown's appearance on television made voters significantly more inclined to vote for us.

He had emerged with credit from the difficult revelation about his private life and he had over the course of the parliament, particularly during the Gulf War, become an increasingly popular and well-respected national figure.

The strategy was amply justified. Paddy Ashdown had an outstandingly energetic and well-received campaign. Its very success, however, opened us up to another hardy perennial criticism: we were a 'one-man band'. The one hasty attempt to rectify this misfired with the coalition government story in *The Times*, in which incidentally I had the private misfortune to be tipped as Minister of State for Northern Ireland. However, we could probably have made more use of popular figures such as David Steel and Shirley Williams who had proven media skills and high public recognition, as well as Alan Beith and our younger spokesmen, who were well used.

Finally, let me address the issue of the balance of power. Just as the polls misled us all about the likelihood of the Conservatives losing their overall majority, so they misled Liberal Democrats, and indeed most of the media and John Major himself, about the likelihood of our holding an influential and possibly even a pivotal position in a hung parliament. I must emphasise, in case *ex post facto* rationalisation has set in, that a balanced outcome with us playing a key role looked likely for months and even years beforehand and certainly seemed the best single bet of an outcome in the last week of the campaign.

This posed both a problem and an opportunity to us. As Des Wilson has said, we wanted a chance to put forward our own agenda, obscured as far as possible by the need to respond to endless questions as to what we would do in the event of balance. We defined and promulgated in the autumn of 1991 a position with three elements: equidistance between the other two with no preference between them; a readiness to treat in a responsible way with whichever party got most seats; and a determination to achieve PR and as much of the rest of our policy priorities as we could in any negotiation post election.

Armed with this we tried to fend off further inquisition, often incidentally appearing rather brusque and even mysterious in the process.

However, as election day approached, with us showing well and no clear water between Conservative and Labour in the polls, it was obvious that the dam would break. Moreover, as I believe we could have anticipated since it has been a feature of every election I can remember, the Conservatives attacked us as being a back-door vote for Labour, a particularly economic way of lining up two bodies and shooting one bullet through both of them.

The effectiveness of this attack was paradoxically confirmed and enlarged by Neil Kinnock's half-hearted flirtation with proportional representation which, far from widening Labour's appeal to 'moderate' voters made John Major's assault on our shared and muddled alternative even sharper.

At this point, despite some efforts on our part at the daily press conferences to re-establish our political equidistance, we were rowing against the stream.

Moreover, given the likelihood of a hung parliament, it should also be admitted that to some extent, although very gingerly, we had begun to position ourselves for post-election negotiations, using PR and to a lesser extent education as virile demands to demonstrate our muscularity in this event.

The continuing dilemma for Liberal Democrats is that if elections are about government we must have something to say which is relevant about ourselves to that prospect. If a vote were simply an expression of values life would be a lot easier.

3 The Labour campaign

Robin Cook

I crave your indulgence and forgiveness if I do not present you with a prepared text but as an economic spokesman I do have to admit to you that this conference has not been in the forefront of my mind. I also have to say after the dramatic events of the last forty-eight hours [Britain's departure from the ERM] studying closely how the Conservatives came home to win the last general election would be almost as relevant as studying how Cromwell won the battle of Marston Moor. But for what it is worth, one can encapsulate what I am about to say as that at the last general election the Conservatives were successful in persuading a sufficient number of people, not a majority (something that as a committed supporter of PR I am bound to slip in) that the election of a Labour government would lead to higher taxes, higher interest rates and a falling pound and that the election of a Conservative government would lead to economic recovery, would boost business confidence and would be the return of the party of economic confidence.

I would very much like to have a re-run of the Spring general election to see if any of that would wash with the same people now. John Wakeham said that they won and that they were always certain that we were going to lose. Indeed, a large part of my problem in explaining the result is that we did fight a good campaign. It would be much easier for me if I was able to say that a really rotten campaign contributed to the result, in the way that we could console ourselves after the 1983 defeat by the fact that we did run one of the most inept general election campaigns in the history of democracy. We did, though, lose. We are therefore obliged to look more searchingly at that campaign than we would have done in other circumstances and I would agree with points of John Wakeham's analysis of why we lost and they won. Let me begin with one area of agreement which I think is of a technical character, but one where I think he is quite right and quite shrewd in his criticism.

My first criticism of our campaign is that I do think we failed in our preparations for a last-week initiative which were ostensibly and reportedly in place before the campaign began. In the grid that we prepared for the general election there always was firmly fixed in there last-week initiatives to be led by last-week task teams. And, even though by the time we came to the last week we were exhausted both physically and also in terms of having used all our best shots in the previous weeks. I myself was rather startled on the Monday of the following week to be rung up to be asked if I could do the press conference the next morning on health. At that point I had no health stories – I had used all my health stories – and there was nothing in particular we could pull out of the locker and then fire. Even if there had been it would have been sensible to have had more than the twenty-four hours notice that we were required to produce it and aim it at the other side. In the event we found that by that stage the press were not at all interested in new stories. The press at that stage were only interested in doing a reprise on the general election campaign, and on that particular day's press conference I was successful in raising the question of 'where is William Waldegrave and why has nobody seen him for the last fortnight?' – which actually ran much better than many of the previous stories we had been putting out on the damage to the Health Service.

My second criticism – again I have some sympathy with one of the points John Wakeham made – is that I think we were unwise to raise in the way we did the question of electoral reform. I do not say that as somebody who is critical of electoral reform or who believes it is unpopular. On the contrary, electoral reform is one of my own King Charles' heads. But I do think it was unwise of us to raise the question of electoral reform when we ourselves had not worked out what our answer would be to the question when it was played back to us. The result was that it became an issue in the election but not on the merits or otherwise of electoral reform. It became a damaging issue for us in the election because Labour appeared to be prevaricating when it was asked the pointed question about the very issue on which we had chosen to fight for those two or three days.

This problem was compounded for us when at the end of that week Paddy Ashdown, in what I think was the most extraordinary mistake of any of the three parties in the course of the general election, chose to express doubt and anxiety about the problems that would arise from a hung parliament. Since a hung parliament was the very best outcome that the Liberal Democrats could have been hoping for, it is still a mystery to me why the leader chose, in high-profile terms, to demonstrate that there would be severe problems from a hung parliament. The backwash of that did not simply damage the Liberal Democrats but also damaged the Labour Party, which was seen as the other party that was likely to be participating in any hung parliament scenario.

Those would be my two principal criticisms of the campaign which otherwise I thought was fought well. But you would all be rather surprised if I sat down without addressing my mind at some point to the 'War of Jennifer's Ear', in which I was a principal participant. Let me say that the 'Jennifer's Ear' broadcast was designed for one clear, simple purpose. It had absolute clarity of position in our campaign. That party political broadcast was designed to be played on the Monday of that week in order to raise the profile of the health issue throughout the week. I have to report to you that in *that* objective it was 125 per cent absolutely successful! It was an extraordinary week which followed. In retrospect, what is quite clear is that we walked into an ambush of a Conservative Party which was already prepared with material from the

Bennett family to criticise the broadcast. On the subsequent lunchtime I went around four or five studios with William Waldegrave debating the ethics of our party political broadcasts. William was armed with a folder of some six or seven letters from the Bennett family to each other about the participation in this broadcast and was plainly under instructions to get them on air, so I talked at even greater length than I would normally have done. After four or five broadcasts he had failed to get them on air and at the last one in sheer frustration he proceeded to read them to me. (Laughter.) I have to report it did not change my vote (more laughter) but it did send me scurrying upstairs from the Millbank Studios to our own party offices to ask the very obvious question that, given we had somebody who had spent a fortnight researching this programme, how in the name of God did they miss the fact that the mother was a Tory candidate and the father-in-law was a previous Tory mayor? To which I received the really alarming reply that of course we knew that, but we did not think it mattered. I tell this tale because I think the one clear lesson out of that episode was not that the Labour Party had too much glitz and glamour but that the glitz and the glamour was not under sufficient political control and political judgement. I speak as somebody who through the previous five years had used individual cases repeatedly and not one of those individual cases had been successfully discredited despite many attempts to do so. Had I or any of the people around me who had run that health campaign for those five years with relative success been involved, we would have told those preparing it to run a mile rather than draw on that particular family. Having said which I am bound to report that we did win the war. The object was to raise the salience of the health issue. At the start of the campaign it was 32 per cent, at the end of the campaign it was 50 per cent. We won the war also because William Waldegrave cracked first and the Conservatives had to shelve their plans for a major anniversary of the Conservative health reforms on the first day of the subsequent week and William Waldegrave was only subsequently taken for an outing on Yeovil hospital radio. And lastly we won because the broadcast did touch a nerve of truth with a large number of people who use and experience the National Health Service. Although this point was missed by the national commentators, on regional television bulletins, on local radio stations, and local newspapers throughout every corner of Britain, there was high profile given to the 'Jennifer Bennett' who was in a similar position to the girl portrayed in that broadcast.

This brings me to one very obvious qualification on anything one says about the campaign. We are playing back our view of how successful those campaigns were in the light of the knowledge of the subsequent results. In the knowledge that Labour lost, the 'Jennifer's Ear' broadcast and the Sheffield rally may be seen as negatives. I rather suspect that had Labour won on 9 April the 'Jennifer's Ear' broadcast would be becoming a set text in future politics examinations and the Sheffield rally would be seen as the way forward for future campaigning in Britain. These are not, in my judgement, the stuff on which the election was lost. If anything that occurred during the campaign helped to determine the outcome of the general election that issue was taxation. And I say taxation rather than the Shadow Budget because it is very important to disaggregate the impact of what was thought of as taxation by the electorate during the campaign from what Labour was actually trying to say in the course of the Shadow Budget.

The Shadow Budget took place at the *start* of the general election campaign. Moreover, at the time it took place it was seen and was generally recognised as a success. Indeed, if anything, the biggest problem the Shadow Budget caused for us was that it gave us the impression that we had successfully neutralised the tax issue and tax did not appear as a salient issue in our soundings throughout the next two or three weeks. When tax did come back it came back as part of that late surge in the last seven days, and it did not come back because we had chosen to do a re-launch of a highly successful Shadow Budget. It came back, and took off, because the public had been terrified by a succession of Conservative posters and was obviously, by the repetition of the theme of those posters in Conservative tabloids, terrified of the Tory version of our tax plans. I am bound to say here that I think it was very magnanimous of John Wakeham to say he was not going to complain about the media bias. I also think it is no joke that so many papers support the Conservative Party. It is certainly obvious, and it is very serious, and it did deeply damage us in that last week. There was a blissfully ironic moment when Philip Gould was doing a presentation to the NEC on our post-election soundings among waverers. When interviewing a Conservative waverer who had contemplated voting Labour she expressed in the course of the discussion group the moment at which she decided to vote Conservative rather than Labour was when Labour published its tax plans in *The Daily Mail*!

For the record, Labour never published its tax plans in *The Daily Mail* nor did *The Daily Mail* undertake to do so. What *The Daily Mail* did publish was a version of Labour's tax plans, prepared by Conservative Central Office. It is perfectly legitimate for *The Daily Mail* to publish the Conservative version of Labour's tax plans; it is not legitimate for *The Daily Mail* to publish that tax table without attribution to the Conservative Central Office, leaving the reader with the impression that it was Labour's tax plans. And those 'tax plans' turned on a very simple, crude and dishonest calculation, which was to aggregate total spending commitments in Labour's documents over the previous four years, bring it out as £38 billion, which itself is heavily disputed, assume it is spent either in one year or over five years in which there is zero economic growth, divide it by the head of every tax payer in Britain, assume that it is all put on income tax (which is an odd assumption since income tax makes up only a quarter of the tax revenue to the Treasury under the Conservatives) and come up with the figure of £1,250. This gave rise to the bizarre discussions that many of us had up and down the country during that last week in which we would meet pensioners living in old people's homes with a weekly income of £9 from their benefit after their payments for the home had been deducted, who told us they could not vote Labour because they could not find £1,250 to pay under Labour.

I think that this distinction between how tax hit us, and hurt us in the last election, and the Shadow Budget, explains the paradox that in fact Labour did best among the very people who would have been hit hard by the Shadow Budget, namely social classes As and Bs, and did comparatively badly among the DEs and the C2s who would have benefited from that Shadow Budget but who believed on the contrary that they were going to have to pay much higher tax under Labour. In so far as the campaign made a difference, the single most effective element was that the Conservatives invented a dishonest tax price tag and were successful in frightening enough people into voting against Labour because of it.

My depressing conclusion from that is that whatever John Wakeham may have said about their campaign having a positive side, I have not the slightest doubt that the Conservative Party is now concluding that negative campaigning worked and is preparing to campaign in a negative way at the next general election, even more strongly than it did at the last one, which I find regrettable, not simply as the politician who is going to be on the receiving end of it, but also as a participant in the democratic process.

Let me finally address my mind to the other strategic lessons that emerged for Labour from the last election, looking beyond the way we fought that election to the changes we might make to our campaigns in the future. There are various lessons. The first is actually a point on which I do agree with John Wakeham. The clearest and most powerful lesson for Labour to absorb is that we wrote the details of our policy far too soon and that in retrospect it was a mistake to get involved in an extremely long and detailed exercise in writing policy over 1988/9. The result was that we wrote policies that were prepared in a boom but were presented in a general election fought in the middle of a very long recession. We wrote policies at a time when Thatcher was in the ascendent and there was no sign that she would depart before the general election. As a result our policies were more expensive than we might have written had we prepared them for a recession, were relatively lacking in punch or relevance to recovery from that recession and were essentially concerned with defending the services from Thatcherite attacks, rather than being aggressive about John Major and his own record.

The second lesson may be more controversial. Although I myself note the arguments of those who argue that we need to appeal to the new emerging classes, I do think that the results of the exit polls prompt the question of how Labour can recover ground among its own core voters, many of whom did not support us in the way that some of those new emerging classes did on polling day. Our swing was weakest among some of our traditional supporters; there was absolutely no swing to Labour among unemployed people. And the truth remains that had Labour polled among the DEs and C2s as powerfully as it did in the 1960s Labour would now be in power and would almost certainly represent Basildon. There is an issue there that Labour has to address while modernising its message. It has to work out why it has lost support and how it can regain support in those core areas.

The third strategic area which Labour must address is the very substantial gender gap in support for Labour as opposed to Conservatives. In 1987 there was only a 1 per cent difference between the support of men and women for Labour and the Conservatives. In 1992 it was 9 per cent and that was because we failed among women, particularly women aged about thirty-five, to register the same support for Labour that we registered among men.

Support for Labour among women below thirty-five was actually quite impressive, which is odd because some of the discussion of how we should now appeal to women has addressed itself to policy issues which, of course, are targeted to women under thirty-five, such as child care, child benefit and training for employment. I think the reason why we have done worse among women who are over thirty-five is not to do with specific women's issues but to do with questions of style, tone and presentation, with the fact that we are perceived as male-dominated and too often blamed for using aggressive rhetoric rather than a conciliatory style. Curiously, our polling suggests that the Conservatives can be negative and get away with it because people think they are gentlemen. Labour cannot be negative and get away with it because people know we are not gentlemen.

The final paradox – and it is a most depressing conclusion – is that we did actually succeed in persuading people we would win and then we failed to win. This flies in the face of received wisdom that when people decide which party will win they are more likely to vote for that party. Our problem is that we thought that we would win and that was the reason why some of them refused to vote for us.

That is a measure of success in that we did convince people that we were going to win and we also convinced them that we ought to win because we did represent a fairer, decent, community and society. But it is also a measure of the task ahead of us because although people were convinced that we would win, although they appear also to have been convinced that we ought to win, they decided they did not want us to win. It is a bit like going to church. It is not something you do because you wildly want to do it, it is something you do because you believe you should do it and you will feel better afterwards. The task for Labour over the next four years is to persuade people that voting Labour is not just something that will make them *feel* better, but is something that will also make them better off. I am bound to report that in the third week of September 1992 that task looks a lot easier than it did in the third week of April.

Part II
The strategists

Part II
The strategists

4   The Conservative Party's strategy

Shaun Woodward

> All men can see these tactics whereby I conquer, but what none can see is
> the strategy out of which victory evolved.
> (Sun Tzu, *The Art of War*, *c*. 500 BC)

Eighteen months before the 1992 general election, many were sceptical that a
fourth Conservative victory was possible. Yet on 9 April 1992 John Major led
the Conservative Party to its historic result; historic not just as a fourth
successive victory but in securing the highest vote by any political party in a
general election.

It was an extraordinary achievement for both John Major and the Conservative Party; it was all the more considerable because the election took place
against a background of very deep recession, high interest rates, profound
economic uncertainty and rising unemployment. The implications of John
Major's achievement go far beyond the Conservative Party, posing critical
questions for Labour; not least, if under these conditions Labour could not
win, under just what circumstances could Labour hope to win ever again?

Every election is unique; arguably, some are more unique than others. The
opportunities created by the advent of television as well as the input of
advertising and marketing techniques have radically altered not only the way
elections are reported by the media but also how they are waged by the political
parties. 1959 has been described as the first television election and 1979 noted
for the impact of marketing techniques and the advertising input of Saatchi and
Saatchi. 1992 will be remembered for the role played by John Major, trans-
forming the party's political prospects, and for its near-term campaign
strategy, the 'tax' row which intensified in the early months of 1992.

The personal role of John Major is crucial in understanding how both the
result and the conditions for victory could be created. The appointment of
Chris Patten as chairman of the party was central in masterminding the
election campaign and the strategy to transform our electoral prospects. It was
none the less a strategy which came under considerable scrutiny and in the four
weeks of the election campaign, very great pressure for revision, even a
dramatic change of course. The pressure to change strategy was resisted and
despite the prophets of doom, John Major confounded his critics.

The Conservative election campaign was not the darling of the media. Their
love affair, particularly television, was by and large with Labour's campaign,

occasionally indulging in a flirtation with the Liberal Democrats or specifically Paddy Ashdown's own brand projection.

Disaffection with a Conservative election campaign is not exceptional; for those involved it has become more a way of life. In recent elections, only the 1983 campaign received vaguely heroic reviews; others have afforded, even by the most considered political journalists, opportunity for the kind of blood sports rarely seen out of the arena of the Coloseum in Rome.

None the less, in 1992 there was a striking difference in the starting positions of the 1979 and 1987 campaigns. Then the jousting was conducted with the knowledge the Conservatives were always pretty certain to win, however 'badly' they campaigned. But in April 1992 these parameters were expunged. A curious restraint, almost nervousness, initially hung over certain doomsday predictions, but when coupled with the polling evidence during the campaign itself, the much discussed style ('negative', 'lacklustre') of the campaign became evidence for predictions of certain defeat; the engine was out of steam, the organisation bankrupt and, so the journalists felt, Mr Kinnock was heading for Downing Street.

This is not the place for a detailed consideration of the merits of the media's conclusion that Labour ran – as in previous elections – the best campaign. But in the context of an election there is a curious irony in a prevailing view that despite defeat, the campaign which led up to that defeat can subsequently be judged to have been 'the best'.

Whilst such a reflection may cheer up those who must live through defeat, it is wholly unrealistic for a Labour Party which wishes eventually to form a government. Although many remain bemused why a campaign of such glitz and glamour could possibly fail, the former deputy leader of the Labour Party succinctly described the malaise shortly after the election. He wrote:

We needed to modernise the penny farthing image. But the only purpose of the roses and the celebrities, the background music and the photo opportunities is to attract attention to our ideas. They must never again be allowed to punch the ideas out of the headlines. We must not be so obsessed with the glitz and glamour that the medium becomes the message in the provision of communications strategies.

It is possible to argue that the obsession with glitz and glamour was not a neurosis confined to Labour. It also preoccupied large sections of the media who seemed only interested in writing about presentation and style, judging the respective parties' campaigns by their glitz and glamour quotients. Supported by the apparent evidence of the opinion polls it seemed safe to conclude that not only did the Conservatives lack glitz and glamour, but that this was symptomatic of a deeper malaise within the campaign itself, that it was failing. The outcome could safely be forecast as a write-off for John Major.

To some extent, we were all misled by or paid too much attention to opinion polls. To what extent they reflected or determined public opinion (and in turn voting behaviour) is an interesting question. They undoubtedly coloured and in some cases determined a view taken by some that John Major would not be Prime Minister after 9 April. Discussion over the veracity of the figures, the methods of sampling, the nature of the questions asked and so on have provided enormous scope for the polling industry to examine their own practices; the attempt to define the precise moment at which the election campaign 'turned' will doubtless continue.

There are those in the industry, such as Bob Worcester, who have argued that people were 'turned at the very last minute by the argument – as the Labour Party has put it – of fear'; there are others, such as Peter Kellner, who now doubt whether '. . . Labour was ever in the lead in the election campaign. I think throughout the campaign the Conservatives were probably narrowly in the lead.'

But what difference would it have made if the polls had shown the Conservatives in the lead? Undoubtedly it would have discouraged either in substance or at least in tone the pack mentality which wrote off John Major's electoral chances. Some commentators became aware of the fatal attraction in using slender poll leads to support this kind of conclusion: Matthew Parris writing in *The Times* on 9 April:

Imagine the morning after John Smith's Shadow Budget. The word was that this was the false move which was to doom Labour's campaign. Now imagine the tide of opinion polls began to turn, not in favour of Labour . . . but against. Imagine it continued so that, by now, it was clear the Tories were winning . . . Imagine that, apart from this difference, both campaigns had continued just as, in the event, they did . . . Are you confident that Mr Kinnock's cellophane wrapped insulation from unscripted encounters with real people would be earning the media's applause?

Think back to the TV interviews you saw the Labour leader handle; suppose them accompanied by worsening polls, and ask yourself whether the vocabulary of 'statesmanship', 'Prime Ministerial qualities' and 'diplomacy' would be flowing as freely from our pens. Of course not.

Whilst greater caution should have been given to the use of voting intention polls in the 1992 election campaign, other polling evidence gathered in the election and the preceding eighteen months could have provided at least cause for greater restraint in predicting a Conservative defeat, and more probably a case for predicting a Conservative victory.

The rest of this paper sets out some of that evidence and examines the broad aspects of the Conservative strategy in the election campaign.

Transformation of political fortune

In the three months preceding John Major's election as leader of the Conservative Party, Labour's lead averaged twelve points over Conservative. As a consequence of the change of leadership, Labour's lead disappeared and an average of nine polls during December 1990 gave the Conservatives a 3.5 per cent lead. This was maintained during January and February, falling to a smaller 1 per cent lead in April.

The change in leadership also improved the standing of the image of Prime Minister. Where 71 per cent had expressed dissatisfaction with Mrs Thatcher as Prime Minister (MORI November 1990), only 22 per cent expressed being dissatisfied with John Major in December 1990; by January 61 per cent were satisfied, 24 per cent didn't know and a marginal 15 per cent expressed dissatisfaction.

In a February Gallup poll on the new leader's qualities John Major was felt to be a clear winner (78 per cent), a good team player (76 per cent), firmly in charge (65 per cent), decisive (78 per cent), likeable as a person (89 per cent), and someone who listens to reason (88 per cent), is able to unite the nation (70 per cent), is concerned for the country as a whole and not just his party (77 per cent), caring (86 per cent), cautious (68 per cent), competent (87 per cent) and trustworthy (78 per cent).

John Major was perceived to be not only a popular leader but also a new leader. His succession led not only to a transformation of our political fortunes – expressed in voting intention – but also as a specific consequence of making the change, created a feeling that an election (albeit not a general election) had already taken place. People were prepared (and although their support would waver over the following sixteen months the potential was indicated) to return to the Conservative fold in December 1990 even without any substantial and expressed changes of policy. So when Labour would inevitably campaign under the banner 'time for a change', the strength of their case had been considerably diluted by a feeling amongst many people in Britain that 'change' had already taken place.

Election preparations

Chris Patten, newly appointed party chairman, was anxious that any complacency which arose as a consequence of the change of leader should not disguise the need for a number of changes at Central Office. The problems within the party organisation were considerable, not least an inherited budget deficit of nearly £10 million. The appointment of John Cope as party treasurer did much to control expenditure costs which were fast running out of control; however, a debt of such large proportions meant that to a greater extent the horse had already bolted.

Any election campaign would have to be planned in the light of the deficit. Calculations estimated that in 1987 we had outspent Labour by 228 per cent, with a Conservative poll lead of 13 per cent on the day the election was called. For the forthcoming election we could count on no significant poll lead and we knew Labour had increased their budget, planning a sustained newspaper advertising campaign, amplified by a co-ordinated advertising campaign by Union allies. Patten knew that for the first time we would have to plan an election campaign which in real terms meant spending less money than Labour. Given the closeness of our respective positions in the opinion polls this was a sobering prospect. At most we could only spend £5 million during the election campaign itself (nearly 3 million was spent just on newspaper advertising in the last week of the 1987 campaign).

A determined and confident hand from party leader and chairman allowed embarrassing divisions with constituencies following the leadership election to be contained, although Cheltenham remained a problem for the early months of 1991. But if there were enormous difficulties in some divisions of the party, other preparations would be invaluable. The marginal seats campaign, put in hand the day after the 1987 general election in the 100 most marginal seats, was well advanced. The benefits of this very considerable exercise were incalculable, not only in allowing us to focus our efforts on likely 'switchers', but also in giving us better predictions of voting intention and increasing support during the election campaign itself. Significantly the Conservatives won back every single seat lost in by-elections during the general election.

In the Research Department considerable work had been in progress to prepare vital background material. This research would be invaluable in the months preceding the general election and during the campaign. The Labour Party had nothing to match the service of the Department.

A preliminary assessment of our political prospects in January 1991 defined three periods when an election would be possible: from early May to late June 1991; October and November 1991; or from early April to late June 1992. In practice, there were probably a maximum of twelve Thursdays between January 1991 and July 1992 on which an election could take place. Disentangling the October dates because of party conferences, the number of suitable options was reduced to single figures. The position could be stated very simply; we had to be ready to fight an election in May of 1991 but in fact it would probably not be fought until the Spring of 1992. Although it was inevitable and a necessary precaution, the amount of time which would be spent planning for dates which were never likely to be realised was a heavy burden. It was to the credit of Chris Patten and senior Central Office staff that the effects of this never impinged on the final campaign.

The merits of going early were considerable. As a new Prime Minister, securing his own mandate and therefore legitimacy for governing was highly attractive for John Major. Britain would have the certainty of a government with an assured life with clearly set out plans for the next five years. On the other hand, delaying the election (and it would have to wait until the conclusion of hostilities in the Gulf) would allow the Prime Minister to establish the foundations of his own record before going to the country. John Major had a solid majority in the House, he commanded widespread support and was very popular in the country. As a new leader he was able to emasculate the argument that the government was tired. He could argue that until the economic difficulties had been resolved, the problems of local government finance (the poll tax) addressed, the Gulf War hostilities safely concluded, and the potential problems of Europe as set out in the forthcoming inter-government conferences resolved, that this gave him a programme for governing without the need to call an election and secure his own mandate. Once he had addressed this 'in tray', an election would be a logical next step.

The decision for an early or late election was not easy. In comparison with 1983 and 1987 when the Conservative Party had substantial poll leads in the immediate months preceding the elections, the problems of early 1991 demonstrate just how much more complicated it would be to decide the right moment to call the election.

Polling of economic optimism was also central in determining the party chairman's advice to the Prime Minister. In 1983 and 1987 the election had been called with optimism reaching into double figures (MORI recorded figures of + 14 per cent). But in August 1990 the figures showed − 43 per cent as a balance of pessimists over optimists; in September this figure worsened to − 46 per cent. Although the figures improved when John Major became leader, the first time a net surplus was recorded by MORI came in April 1991.

For the next three months the figures were negative and only moved into positive ratings in the early autumn. In as much as these polling statistics influence judgement, it was clear that the mood of the country did not believe that the recovery lay around the corner in 1991. That mood was certainly reflected in voting intention figures.

In early January 1991, Chris Patten had called together a small group of individuals at Hever to begin discussions for a communications strategy for the general election. The party had no appointed advertising agency at the time; Saatchi and Saatchi had publicly resigned the account following difficulties during the 1987 campaign. One of the first priorities identified would be the appointment of an advertising agency.

The appointment of Saatchi and Saatchi in 1991 was always going to be controversial and some felt unwise. Strained former relationships, the high profile nature of Saatchi's and a feeling that a new leader should have a new agency lent considerable weight to the case against their appointment. Their eventual re-appointment followed considerable internal discussion, not least because of uncertainty about their own financial security. Without the persuasiveness and commitment of Bill Muirhead, the agency's managing director, and Jeremy Sinclair, the creative director who had worked on the previous three election campaigns, the agency would never have been short-listed. Saatchi's won the account for two reasons. First, they emphasised the need for a dual thrust strategy: it was essential to parallel positive campaign selling our identity as the brand leader with a campaign to undermine and expose the weaknesses of the Opposition (reminding all of us how it had been crucial in 1979 with 'Labour isn't Working'; in 1983 with 'Like Your Manifesto Comrade'; and in 1987 with the poster depicting the soldier with his arms in the air and the caption 'Labour's Policy on Arms'). Secondly they had experience of fighting elections and as well as proving they would cope with the pressure, if the Prime Minister wanted an early rather than later election, their experience would be crucial; we could not afford to be all learning on the job.

The advantages of incumbency in politics are readily assembled. As the incumbent you can control, at least more effectively than anyone else in Britain, the timing of key governmental actions, policies and announcements. In a time of rapidly changing world affairs (as would be the case in the summer of 1991), the incumbent can take a leading role in improving the world state. A Prime Minister leading his party for re-election gets double media coverage, both as Prime Minister and as leader of a contending political party.

The disadvantages, however, are less often recognised. The records of the incumbent and the government provide considerable ammunition for attack by the Opposition (Labour spent much effort in 1991 trying to link John Major with a slogan 'twelve wasted years'). While a Prime Minister can control some events he is unable to control all events, especially global issues (such as the Gulf War). A Prime Minister finds every action under scrutiny from the press, a media more likely to focus on failure than success. The problems of incumbency are further exacerbated after twelve years in government and a feeling of having run out of steam. A lot might have been achieved, but what was left to conquer? Where were the dragons left to slay?

In 1979 Mrs Thatcher was able to muster a veritable array of dragons, offering both political strengths of the Conservatives and ineluctable liabilities for Labour as each target was picked off. Communism abroad brought the threat of war and the need for strong defence. The trade unions needed to be controlled and offered a cornucopia for restrictive legislation. Nationalised industries were a drain on public resources and offered a mine for privatisation and the growth of market policies. Punitive taxes for individuals and companies needed to be drastically cut.

By 1991 however these dragons had been vanquished. Communists abroad were in retreat; defence was seen as increasingly a question of how to spend the peace dividend; union militancy had been superseded by lowest levels of industrial action in fifty years; tax cuts were seen as largely completed and privatisation virtually accomplished in all industries where it was practical.

At the end of the eighties the Conservatives agenda had shifted to public services. Although spending in real terms had increased in all major public service areas since 1979, it was felt right now to highlight these issues. More, it was felt that market forces, particularly in the health service, could bring new benefits and raise standards. Effectively we had put a strong Labour issue – public services – at the forefront of the political debate. In raising the saliency of health and education some believed that we were virtually conceding a large section of Labour's argument, that these services were neglected and required urgent government attention. Whilst Conservative policy for treatment of public services would be radically different from Labour, the consequence of raising the profile of public services was to be helpful to Labour's political profile.

The Conservatives had presented this task as a final frontier. If market economics could be effective in areas of the economy, why not for public services? Ironically, good intentions by Conservatives would provide Labour with an opportunity. By addressing the need to improve public services, we might be seen as moving to Labour's strategic ground (as the economy is identified as Conservative high ground). Refusing to tackle an issue because it may not be to your immediate political advantage is of course not a reason to avoid the issue. Nonetheless, the consequences of opening up the debate on public services would inevitably play to Labour strengths.

Monmouth by-election

The first clear demonstration of how the health issue would be exploited by Labour came during the Monmouth by-election in May 1991. A combination of opportunism and deceit led Labour to campaign on the allegation that the Conservatives would privatise the NHS, forcing the local Monmouth hospital to 'opt out' of the health service. Whatever the local candidate and national party figures said to dispute the allegation, it served only to weaken our position in the polls.

For the first time since John Major became leader, at the end of May 1991, Labour had opened up a significant lead in opinion polls. The strategic advantage which Labour gained every time the agenda became dominated by health became increasingly clear as the year wore on. During both the Conservative Party Conference and at the time of the Langbaurgh by-election, sustained discussion of the alleged Conservative intention to privatise opt-out hospitals led to a worsening of our poll position and an improvement for Labour.

Whilst the case for putting forward our rebuttal of Labour's unfounded claims was inviolable, the consequences of the response was harmful (certainly in our short-term poll position). It was clear that if the election were fought on public services we could expect little strategic advantage.

The situation was further complicated because the traditional area of Conservative strength in an election – the economy – continued to offer little comfort as a campaign issue. There was still little or no sign of the economy improving, and although inflation was falling rapidly, unemployment continued to rise. Every day seemed to bring fresh rounds of bad news from closing businesses, loss of confidence and declining order books. Waiting for the economy to improve was a dangerous strategy and not to be relied on for the election campaign. The economy would still be the central issue in the election, but it would have to be defined in terms of Conservative strength, not weakness.

Attention therefore focused on an advertising strategy which would play to our strategic strengths. Crudely these could be identified as taxation, cost of living, management of the economy, and defence, with law and order. John

Major's own position continued to ride high in all polls, particularly on issues of trust and leadership. The strategic goal would therefore be an election campaign focused and co-ordinated around our high rating issues, with John Major at centre stage.

Our ability to define and determine this battleground was another question. John Major's initial honeymoon with the media was long over and although he retained the public's trust, his leadership came under relentless scrutiny from the press. This split between support by the public but attack from the media would be a hallmark of the coming months. From time to time the attack was revived with new vigour, not least in the wake of the party's defeat in Monmouth. One editorial from *The Financial Times* in June 1991 will serve to illustrate the vehemence of their criticism:

The complacency of 1987–1989 has been replaced by a nervous anxiety, a sense of fevered amateurishness, that is all the more striking for the political professionalism of Labour ... the Tories, bruised and perhaps exhausted by the events of the past two years appear to be adrift, without an overall strategy, with not a clue as to how to bring these policies into a coherent form and convince the public that they are right ... What is required is proper generalship. In short, Labour gives the impression that it knows exactly what it is doing. Mr Major and his team look lost.

Whether justified or not, the inception of the Number 12 Committee, co-ordinating political activity, was the first in a series of steps to rectify problems of management. At Central Office, organisational changes followed. Chris Patten was determined to reproduce the small disciplined internal organisation of 1979. His own close rapport with the party leader was important in achieving this end. He was equally anxious to avoid the divisions during the campaign which had taken place during the 1987 election; he ensured that those key political staff attached to the leader were tied in to the planning and strategy meetings at Central Office.

Although opinion polls of voting intention were disappointing, other poll findings were encouraging. On all the key questions about management of the economy (handling inflation, reducing interest rates and so on) the Conservatives continued to maintain a clear lead over Labour. Labour were demonstrably not trusted on these key issues. John Major's personal popularity also remained high. Expressions of satisfaction against dissatisfaction by Gallup found a consistent lead for John Major over Neil Kinnock. For example, following the Monmouth by-election, Major enjoyed a rating of + 13 against Kinnock at − 16, a 29 per cent lead over the Opposition leader.

Through this period and into 1992, John Major continued to record high poll ratings on 'trust'. The combination of 'trust' in the party leader and 'trust' in our ability to deliver on the economy was vital in the formulation of the election strategy. Conversely, despite the recession, Labour were not trusted to get the economy out of recession and Mr Kinnock's personal low standing remained a very damaging negative.

The near-term campaign

Although formal recognition of the strategy as the near-term campaign would wait until late autumn, the first wave was launched in mid-June with 'Labour's Going For Broke Again'. Spearheaded by David Mellor and Chris Patten, a co-ordinated assault was made on the impact of Labour's spending promises and pledges. These had been costed as an additional £35 billion of public spending. Our question, posed in a series of co-ordinated party political broadcasts, press conferences, poster launches and speeches by key political figures all over the country, was how are Labour going to pay for their promises and pledges? Would there be increased borrowing or high taxation? Nearly twelve months later we would pose the same question in a PEB, 'where's the money coming from?'

The initial response from the media was scepticism about the figure of £35 billion. Yet prolonged media coverage of our costing of Labour's spending proposals, ensured that the agenda was transformed from health to public spending and the economy. It was Monmouth in reverse. Our decline in the opinion polls was halted and Labour lost their momentum.

The lesson of this exercise was clear. Our strategy should in part hold Labour to a defensive posture, dealing with their spending pledges and therefore the impact on taxation. In so doing we would move the battleground to the economy, revealing both Labour's Achilles' heel and our strength.

The difficulty for Labour was clear. Numerous policy documents such as 'Opportunity Britain' had been written and agreed at a time of boom; they now served as spending commitments in a time of recession. Labour were inextricably bound by these commitments.

Gradually scepticism by the media about the figures we cited turned into a relentless pursuit of both Labour's key spending and taxing spokesmen. It was a debate which raged not just in tabloids but also broadsheets and television media. Throughout the autumn, John Smith and Margaret Beckett would find themselves answering questions on *Frost* or *On The Record* in which the vital question was pressed; how will you pay for your promises? A climate of deep mistrust was growing around Labour's promises and the consequences for public spending and taxation. The more Labour ducked the questions, the greater the suspicion grew about their economic plans.

However, the full attack came at the beginning of 1992 and the commencement of the 'Near-Term Campaign', the cornerstone of which would be converting Labour's spending proposals into a specific figure of increased tax for the average taxpayer.

The likely effectiveness of this campaign could be identified from polling evidence taken in late 1991. Three times in 1991 we had faced the onslaught of Labour's allegation that the Conservatives would privatise the NHS. There was still no evidence for the charge, but each time it was made, it scored dramatically in Labour's favour. Polls showed that on average 60 per cent of the country believed this to be our intention. Private polls showed that very high numbers of our own supporters believed it was our intention. We were being damaged by a prejudice held by 60 per cent of people. So long as Labour could stimulate the argument, any refutation only served to sustain further damage to our position in the polls.

In October 1991 we therefore commissioned extensive polling of people's attitudes, including covering issues such as law and order, crime, and cost of living, interest rates and taxation. We found that nearly 80 per cent of people believed that Labour would raise taxes. This was crucial material and evidence. If it were possible to sustain a row over Labour's spending plans and focus the attack in the consequences for taxation, we would further undermine Labour's economic credibility. The evidence of this polling was that we had an angle on the economic agenda which was very damaging for Labour and which, if we could raise the salience of the issue in the run-up to an election, would give us a great advantage.

This then became the brief for Saatchi and Saatchi and the crux of the near-term campaign which began in the first week of January 1992. We began with a co-ordinated campaign using posters, a PPB, press conferences and newspaper advertising, under the slogan 'Labour's Tax Bombshell'. The poster (launched 6 January) used an image of a bomb and alongside a caption which warned the average tax payer of the £1,000 increase they faced. A PPB was used on 9 January on the theme how much worse off the average voter would be under Labour. On 21 January a press conference was used to launch a national newspaper advertising campaign, using the image of the bomb, but stating the average extra tax payable by readers of specific newspapers (for a *Daily Mail* reader the figure was £1,350, for *The Daily Star* £1,025 and so on).

The campaign had an immediate effect. We began the year with a MORI poll on 29 December giving Labour a six-point lead. By the end of the month we were ahead in most polls. Surprisingly, Labour did little to move the agenda away from our battleground issues and compounded their own poll slide when Neil Kinnock appeared to be rewriting Labour policy on National Insurance to a group of journalists in Luigi's Restaurant. The ensuing breakdown of communication within Walworth Road, and particularly John Smith's office, gave the media further cause to continue coverage.

The tax campaign continued through later January and into February. Labour continued to respond to the agenda we were now setting. When media attention waned we launched the 'Double Whammy' poster. The press had virtually stopped running the poster photo-opportunities; however, the 'Double Whammy' gave us front-page coverage in many papers and others carried it inside. The papers asked, 'What was a 'Double Whammy'? Had Patten taken leave of his senses? As the media mocked, the public read again and again about the 'Double Whammy' – more taxes, higher prices. The message was repeated and expanded in a PPB three days later. Double whammy has, of course, now firmly entered the language.

The pending Budget statement now presented both an advantage and a problem. Media speculation on the contents of the Budget would inevitably put the economy at the top of the political agenda. However, the need to avoid being cornered on budgetary issues meant that it became increasingly difficult for the Chancellor and treasury minister to continue their high profile attack on Labour's economic policies. The consequence was that, as we were compelled to ease up on the tax strategy, Labour's decline was arrested and the parties moved back to neck and neck in the polls. Whilst it meant we would not enter the election with the poll advantage of 1983 and 1987, we had managed to significantly improve our position from being six or seven points behind at the beginning of the year.

Tax was not the only issue we intended to run during the near-term campaign. The objective was to control the battleground, the issues covered by the media, in the run-up to the election. Each week had a theme and although many weeks would revolve around tax and the economy we tried to push defence, law and order, crime and issues on which we held commanding leads over Labour. The strategic aim was to dominate and keep Labour from pushing their high rating issues. Surprisingly, Labour produced neither the onslaught nor guerrilla warfare tactics we anticipated on the big public service issues.

The campaign was described as negative. Yet how much more negative this election was than any other post-war campaign is a dubious debate. From Macmillan's 'Don't Let Labour Ruin It' to Margaret Thatcher's 'Labour Isn't Working', the hallmarks of these successful campaigns have been their ability to expose the weakness of the Opposition. This campaign was no different.

The strategy for the weeks of the election campaign changed very little from the planning meetings, chaired by Chris Patten from mid-1991 to March 1992. The campaign focused on the economy, highlighting two central issues; which party could most be trusted to get the economy out of recession and what would be the tax impact of Labour's spending pledges and promises? Central to the campaign was the standing of John Major; decent, honest and a leader you could trust. Conversely we would present the alternative, focused on the proposition, 'You Can't Trust Labour'.

This theme and slogan would be the first poster of the campaign; it had also been the subject of exhaustive research long before the election took place. Concern had been expressed that to put up posters all over Britain containing the word Labour, would be free advertising to the Opposition. We therefore tested the poster in focus groups up and down the country. The proposition was widely recognised in all the groups in which it was tested. Ironically, we now know from David Butler and Dennis Kavanagh's election study that as far back as 18 December 1990, Philip Gould wrote in a Labour strategy paper his prediction for our central message: 'You can't trust Labour. You can trust Major'. Labour's own internal polling had revealed the power of this message, playing to concerns which were held even amongst their own supporters.

Although the media derided our use of the slogan, 'You Can't Trust Labour', in March 1992, both Labour and Conservative strategists knew its potency, long before the election was called. In the exit polls, voters' distrust of Labour would feature as a crucial reason why they felt unable to support Labour.

The tax strategy thus became supporting evidence for this proposition. Continued television and press interviews probing how Labour would fund their spending programmes only highlighted the party's twists and turns. Changes in policy by the Labour leader added not only to a sense of distrust in Labour but also in Neil Kinnock. The Shadow Budget launched by John Smith in the first week of the election kept the economy as the main battleground issue. In dealing specifically with issues of taxation and national insurance, after the initial media adulation of Labour's tactics, it served to rekindle public concern about just who would be paying Labour's extra taxes.

The media's praise for John Smith's Shadow Budget had a sapping effect on Conservative Party morale. Coupled with the series of appalling economic statistics and the inevitable surge which the Opposition enjoys in the first week of an election campaign, Chris Patten recognised the need to keep up morale and avoid the campaign being deflected. The kind of panic which the party had witnessed in 1987 would have been catastrophic under the assault of the first week's media coverage. Patten's decision to structure the operation in the style of 1979 paid dividends when the party came under greatest pressure and allowed the strategy to continue as planned.

The poster 'You Can't Trust Labour' was replaced in the second week with a poster depicting the Labour Manifesto, over which were the words, 'Oh No, It's a Tax Demand'. This in turn was replaced with '5 Years Hard Labour' showing a victim pulling three balls and chains with the words 'Taxes Up', 'Mortgages Up' and 'Prices Up' stamped on each ball. A revived 'Labour's Tax Bombshell' poster carrying the new figure of £1,250 extra tax (based on calculations of the cost of Labour's manifesto) ran in the penultimate week. The final five days of the campaign saw every one of the 5,000 posters (the largest ever poster campaign in Britain) replaced by a photograph of John Major, surrounded by children with the words, 'The Best Future for Britain' emblazoned below.

At the press conferences every day we used reproductions of the posters behind the main desk, so ensuring that the visual poster image was carried into everyone's home for every television news bulletin whenever the report used pictures from the day's press conference. It did not matter if the television view of the story being told was unrelated to the subject of the press conference, what mattered was getting the image of the poster message into people's homes. To some extent we were appealing over the heads of the media, directly to the voters.

The party election broadcasts were planned to echo the themes of the posters (with the exception of PEB 3 which covered defence). Often the broadcast would include stills of the poster itself, reinforcing for the viewer images they would be certain to see when walking or driving in their constituency or on television news programmes every day.

If the strategy remained on course, the tactics constantly changed. At times they appeared chaotic; they sometimes were. Labour on the other hand stuck rigidly to their tactics (rarely changing press conferences). More than half of our press conferences touched on tax, the economy and recovery. As the campaign drew on we learnt to take advantage of opportunities as they arose, abandoning material which would have been distracting or irrelevant. Dennis Kavanagh and Brian Gosschalk's analysis of the press conferences is instructive for both parties.

Having failed to raise the health issue in the months before the election, Labour brought the issue into focus in the campaign itself. The first time, using a 'real' case, was on the afternoon the election was called. This strategy fell into wild confusion when nearly two weeks later they imploded their own campaign with the screening of the PEB which became known as 'Jennifer's Ear'.

Originally commissioned as a broadcast in which a child would be used to represent a broad range of similar cases, the PEB quickly slid into a debate first about whether the case used was a specific instance (Mr Kinnock said it was) or based on a series of cases and not a specific instance (as argued by the Shadow Communications Agency). The argument then degenerated into a row over which party had allegedly leaked the name of Jennifer Bennett to the newspapers. For three days the agenda was dominated by the question of who had leaked what and to whom. If at Monmouth and on the other two occasions when Labour had raised the health issue in 1991, they had been victors in the polls, this time there was no immediate movement in the polls in their favour. The row muddied the issue for Labour.

However, one week after the broadcast was shown a series of polls gave Labour (albeit for just twenty-four hours) the first clear lead in the election. ITN actually led bulletins on the breakthrough (an edict from John Birt in the BBC banned news programmes from leading on poll data). Some strategists claimed that this was proof the row over health had paid off for Labour; some wanted another PEB on health to be screened in the belief this would secure Labour's position in the polls as it now appeared.

John Major now launched into a clear warning that a vote for the Liberal Democrats would put Labour in by the back door. The message was stark and powerful. His direct attack caught the attention of the media and, based on our own canvassing evidence, caused many 'switchers' who thought it might be safe to make a protest vote against the government to think again.

If the consequence of John Major's direct appeal was to pull voters back, Labour's mass rally in Sheffield alienated the electorate. Lip service to proportional representation at the beginning of Labour's final campaign week seemed almost irrelevant to the campaign at this stage (an example of where rigid tactics are a mistake) and gave John Major further opportunity to demonstrate the strength of both principles and commitment to the Union and to the British constitution.

Clear messages and a disciplined strategy throughout the campaign allowed the Conservatives to take maximum tactical advantage of the election battle-ground. John Major's personal strengths shone throughout the campaign. Before the election campaign had begun, he had been dismissed by many as unlikely to campaign well. Yet his campaigning skills proved formidable. He was seen as a man of the people and in touch with people. His use of the soap box was further evidence of the figure he had always presented himself to be and which had been apparent in all his personal poll ratings from the time he became party leader.

So did we win on the back of a late swing, a sudden conversion on the road to the voting booth? On polling day Harris asked in their exit poll how may voters had made up their minds in the last week. Of the 21 per cent who said yes, 9 per cent decided on polling day. Evidence of a late swing? The same question asked in 1987 produced virtually identical figures: 18 per cent in the final week and 8 per cent on polling day. The same figures apply for 1983 and 1979. It would be dangerous to extrapolate on these figures that a dramatic late swing had taken place.

The Conservative victory of 1992 was indeed remarkable. The central role played by the Prime Minister has already been acknowledged. It would not have been possible without his leadership and the transformation of the political fortunes of the party in late November 1990. The near-term campaign helped create the conditions for victory and during the election ensured that Labour's momentum was arrested and their share of the vote squeezed. But ultimately I believe the role taken by John Major in the campaign was crucial; his determination to win, and belief that we would win, made certain that the Conservative Party secured its fourth successive victory.

5 The Labour Party's strategy

David Hill

My predecessor, Peter Mandelson, addressed this same event some five years ago. And his message, in many ways, was very much the same. By and large, commentators concluded that Labour had run a better campaign than the Conservatives; nonetheless, the general public had voted for the return of the Conservative government. Then, in 1987, the Conservative vote was roughly 43 per cent; and it was roughly 43 per cent again in 1992. The principal difference between the two campaigns, was that the major task for Peter Mandelson and his colleagues at the time was to ensure that Labour finished as the second largest party, and saw off the threat from the Liberal/SDP Alliance. In 1992 we went into the campaign with people generally believing Labour were going to win. And, recalling what Neil Kinnock said after the election about the success of fear over hope, I think it is fair that we look at some of the developments both before and during the campaign which relate to this.

I should, however, emphasise that for us, in opposition, the campaign was an immensely long one. I became Director of Communications in July 1991 and was, from that moment, effectively in an election campaign. None of us knew when the election was going to be called. Indeed, in August of that year, there was a slippage in our support in the polls. The Prime Minister undertook a semi-world tour and as a result, as is often in the case under these circumstances, he saw a boost in his ratings almost immediately. Labour therefore had the urgent task of knocking the government off a November election which we felt they might have a reasonable chance of winning, especially on the back of the immediate popularity of the Prime Minister. Thanks to our anti-privatisation campaign, including the skeleton poster, we successfully forced the government off the November election date that they may well have had in mind.

From then on it was clear that there would be an election in the early spring of the following year. Our plan was to launch a campaign focusing on the government's failure in its economic strategy and its management of the economy at the beginning of 1992. We launched an attack essentially on their lack of any industrial strategy, arguing the need for economic recovery, and the methods by which it might be obtained. This was part of our twin-track approach, whereby we attacked the government over privatisation and economic failure, while running in parallel the need for there to be changes in social policy, highlighting in particular the prospect of privatisation of the National Health Service and at least part of the education service.

The next two months were spent in trench warfare over taxation, over the state of the British economy, and over health. Then we moved into the period of the Budget. The decision we had made long before was that, when the Budget was published, John Smith would publish his Shadow Budget. We felt that producing our alternative was absolutely vital and, with hindsight, I still think that it was vital. You can argue about whether or not Labour could succeed by addressing taxation direct, but I believe that it was vital that John Smith should set out the fact that Labour had a rational alternative view to that set out in Norman Lamont's Budget.

Looking back, we all recall the phases of the campaign, including the last week, and the media's infatuation with the issue of a hung parliament. I consider the pivotal moment in the campaign was not the Sheffield rally, which the Conservative Party talked up as being a key problem within hours of their victory, but the period in the previous 24–48 hours. The important thing to remember is that throughout the campaign many believed that Labour was doing better than the Conservatives, that the Conservative campaign was essentially in a shambles; there was no doubt that, time and again, there were announcements about changes of strategy and changes of course. The commentators and the journalists were looking for a sign – a sign which said, 'suddenly the dam has burst'. The night before the Sheffield rally, three opinion polls put us 7, 6 and 4 points in front; that was the moment when everyone believed that the dam had burst.

On the night of the rally itself the polls changed back to roughly where they had been previously. But I think that night was pivotal, because it created a sense of fear amongst certain people in the City who did not want Labour to win. It concentrated the minds, not only of journalists and commentators, but of the wider electorate, which began to concentrate not on the nebulous prospect of a Labour victory, but, for the first time, on the reality of a Labour victory. For some twelve to eighteen months it was culturally part of political thinking that Labour was likely to win, or, at least, that the government was likely to lose. But suddenly, with eight days to go, everyone's mind was concentrated on the reality of Labour being 7, 6, 4 per cent in front. From then on, but not beforehand, it became apparent that people who were not sure how they were going to vote, including those who felt very angry with the Conservative government but who were natural Conservatives, began slowly, but steadily, to decide that they were going to vote Conservative on 9 April and not run the risk of a Labour government.

There is no doubt that the concentration on a hung parliament in the last week was, to some extent, of assistance to the government. It gave a sense of firmness to John Major and the Conservative Party and slight uncertainty about what sort of government you would get if you did not get a Conservative government. That was essentially because, having made their minds up that there was going to be a victory for someone other than the Conservatives, commentators, particularly on television, decided that they had to spend their time discussing what that alternative would look like and how that alternative would operate. And so, in the last seven days, we suffered most, in my opinion, from the strengthened perception on that previous Tuesday that we were going to win.

One important point that I would make about those last few days is the way in which the newspapers behaved. For much of the campaign, the Conservative supporting newspapers had behaved with a certain degree of restraint, partly because there was a tacit understanding that some of the more unpleasant character assassination that we had seen in previous elections was not going to take place; but also, because there was concern amongst Conservative-supporting newspapers about the apparent inadequacy of the way in which the Conservative campaign was being run. Unlike the Conservatives, the Labour Party had a game-plan and stuck to it. We said what we were going to do day by day, week by week, and day by day, week by week the commentators and the broadcasters were able to follow the pattern and to see that we stuck almost exactly to it. There was only one major press conference that we held that had not been planned at the beginning of the campaign.

The situation that we faced in the last week was of trying to get the agenda back to the issues of health, and of the state of the economy and the recession.

I tend to share the Peter Kellner view that, because so many people were declaring that they did not know which way they were going to vote, that in reality there was never really much change during the campaign. By and large, people who said they did not know in answer to the voting intention question turned out to vote Conservative on election day. Once people felt that there was a clear prospect of the Conservative government losing, and particularly of Labour becoming the victors, then disgruntled Conservatives decided they were going to put aside their anger and frustration at the government's behaviour and actually turn out and vote Conservative.

The question is, why did they feel they had to do that? After the general election, there was a word that I used which has been used in a number of newspapers and which has occasionally been misinterpreted by various people within the Labour movement. That word is 'baggage'. Immediately after the election I said that the main reason why, when it came to the crunch, people felt that they could not vote Labour, was because they were concerned about Labour's history. They were not just concerned about their perception of Labour's links with the trade union movement, which were built up by some as the major obstacle. The party's links with the trade union movement certainly were exploited. But basically, the problem that Labour had was that people had very long memories. Our canvassers discovered, especially over the last few days when people were finally concentrating their minds after the phoney war had been going on for months, that people on the doorstep were remembering 1979. They were also remembering the arguments that took place inside the Labour Party in the early 1980s. These memories were fostered by the newspapers in particular. And people recalled, or thought they recalled, that

Labour had a history of internal conflict and a history of chaotic government. As people saw it, they could not be confident that they could trust Labour, that Labour was a party which, when it got into power, would behave in a way with which they felt sympathetic. By trust I do not mean it in the way that Shaun Woodward was talking about earlier. I do not think people felt that we were a party which was desperate to take their money off them, or desperate to tax them; but I do believe that they felt that Labour was a party which was no longer in tune with them. The great difficulty that Labour faced, and a task that we now face, is that the section of the general public which we ought to win, but do not win, was concerned that the Labour Party's approach to life was not consistent with their own perception of their aspirations, their outlook and their wish for success, for themselves and their families.

I believe that the lesson is learnt and it is the task of the Labour Party over the next years to ensure that the way in which we conduct ourselves, the policies that we adopt, and the way in which we project them, are such that we can win back the confidence of a key section of the electorate.

During the campaign itself, we succeeded in creating the sense that the slogan 'It's time for change' was in tune with the way people were thinking. It caught on in the country, and it caught on among commentators and journalists. However, the great problem we faced was that not only were we fighting this election against a background of this lack of public trust, but we were also fighting this election against the background of a recession. We were therefore faced with the problem that there was a basic underlying uncertainty about whether Labour's aspirations were my aspirations and your aspirations, and at the same time, we were asking people to take a risk at a time of recession. And so, although time for a change was something which we rightly fought on, the fact is that people were wary of change, both because of the recession and because of their lack of trust in Labour. They also sensed that the replacement of Margaret Thatcher by John Major had produced the change.

I am convinced that this was the basic problem that we faced with regard to opinion polling. The culture of Labour being the party that was likely to win the election meant that, when people were questioned against that background, they were unwilling to declare themselves because they were surrounded by people who were saying that they thought Labour would, and should, win. Therefore, the polls misled us all, because they did not pick up this underlying lack of trust in Labour.

There are three other points I would like to make. Firstly, negative campaigning. Shaun Woodward makes the fascinating claim that the Prime Minister led a positive campaign. We have to remember that it was actually the Prime Minister who, in a speech just before the election, devoted a significant period of time in his speech to the nightmare of Kinnock Street. If that isn't negative campaigning, I don't know what is. We knew that the decision would be made by the Conservatives at the very outset to pursue a policy of almost totally negative campaigning. Of course there is no need to spend a great deal of money on newspaper advertising when the press is going to do the job for you. In fact, I am amazed the Conservatives actually sat around and bothered to discuss whether or not they need advertise in a series of newspapers which could devote fourteen pages for free to Neil Kinnock being the nearest thing we have ever seen to Judas Iscariot! They could rely upon having the newspapers on their side. Just after the election I said quite a lot of things publicly about the role played by newspapers, because we do feel that there ought to be an element of scrutiny of political coverage in newspapers which is, at the moment, lacking.

But I also feel that the Labour Party needs to take seriously what actually happened during those last few days. It is not in any sense our thesis that all *Sun* readers suddenly turned Conservative because of the way in which *The Sun* behaved and because of the headlines about the last one out of the country turning the light out. In what turned out to be a close election in terms of seats won and the number of votes that might have made the difference in a simple arithmetic sense – the twelve or fourteen hundred votes that would have made the difference between a Conservative Government and a hung parliament – it is perfectly legitimate to say that you only need 1 or 2 per cent of *Sun* readers to be affected by what happened and 1 or 2 per cent of *Mail* readers, and 1 or 2 per cent of *Star* readers to be affected, for that to have had a significant effect in key marginal seats which Labour lost. So I do not in any sense pull back from the criticisms that I have made of the influence of popular newspapers. They may, at the very least, have caused an additional few people to go out and vote Conservative who might not have done so otherwise. And an additional few is very significant given the results in some of the marginal seats.

There are two ways of looking at the election result. There was a 7 to 8 per cent difference between the two parties' share of vote; the difference between the two in terms of seats won and the size of the Conservative majority, suggests a much more close-run affair. This vindicates one of the key decisions that we made early on, to have an organisational system which concentrated on key marginals over years and not just months. If one examines the actual return on polling day, and the forty-one seats that we won, it is clear that we were right to adopt that approach. This is one of the very positive messages that we draw from the election: that our own organisational capacity was much improved from 1983 and 1987. From one perspective you can say, if only a few of those marginal seats had not been lost because of the extra few votes we needed. From the other you can of course say, 'well, we were very lucky to win one or two of those seats – we just got an extra few votes which brought them to us'. But the fact is that the organisational strategy that Labour adopted was very effective.

In the end, however, organisation alone cannot defeat an underlying mistrust amongst key sections of the British electorate. It was this factor that lost us the election on 9 April, a factor which had actually lost us the election well before the campaign even began.

6 The Liberal Democrats' strategy

Des Wilson

Those of you who attended the 1987 version of this event will recall John Pardoe's particularly bitter account of his experience as the Alliance campaign director. Perhaps because I didn't have to contend with the leadership he endured, and because, as I'll make clear, I'm content that we got close to achieving all that was possible, my account of the 1992 Liberal Democrat campaign will be much more positive.

In February 1990 when I undertook, unpaid, the post as the party's general election campaign director, I said my aim was the best result possible in the circumstances of the time. I was not being disingenuous. My task was to build a campaign from where we were in 1990 and fight it in 1991/2 conditions and to achieve what was realistically possible on polling day. It was not to strive for a result comparable with that achieved by the Alliance in the entirely different circumstances of 1987 (I can, of course, understand why academics will compare results, but in my view it will be to no worthwhile effect, for the circumstances *were* worlds apart).

So let us begin by looking at the circumstances of the time. In June 1987, the then Alliance achieved 23 per cent of the popular vote – nearly one in four voters . . . a respectable result considering it was, as John Pardoe made all too clear, a flawed campaign. Thanks to the bungling of the general election aftermath – not by the ordinary members of either party but, as in the case of so many of the Liberal Party–SDP–Alliance–Liberal Democrat blunders of the late 1980s, by the arrogance, incompetence, and, in some cases, self-service of a few at the centre – by the time Paddy Ashdown finally emerged as leader (incidentally, not really from the ranks of the Westminster 'elite' but from the grassroots of the party) we had already thrown away that 1987 base. The Liberal Democrat Party was almost stillborn. On the day Ashdown became leader, the Inland Revenue were at the door, threatening to close down Cowley Street because, with a huge deficit and weak membership, the party was technically bankrupt. Memories of the merger shambles remained all too alive, the process being aided by sniping from the fringes of British politics by David Owen and the kind of poor initial party management that allowed the party's name to be one of the main items on its agenda.

By the following summer, 1989, two years out from a possible 1991 general election, the party was at 4 per cent in three consecutive MORI polls. In the same year's European elections, the party won 6 per cent of the vote; even the

Greens won 15 per cent. It was shortly after this that Paddy Ashdown asked me to take responsibility for the general election campaign. In my planning document, I stated: Our campaign will be, at worst, about survival; at best, about building a stronger base for the years ahead. That was the initial objective: survival. And, if all went well, a party hammered into shape and fit to make a stronger challenge later in the decade. That is why Paddy Ashdown began talking publicly about a staging-post election; he was seeking to condition the party, the press and the public to that kind of result.

We knew that at least 20 per cent of voters – one in five – had for some time been voting for an alternative to the Conservatives and Labour at general elections. We set out, therefore, to see off the Greens and what was left of the SDP and get as close to that 20 per cent as we could.

We knew we would enter the election at a lower point in the polls than for many years. We did. We knew we would have a fraction of the resources of the other parties. We did. Our expenditure was in the region of one pound for every thirty of the combined Conservative–Labour budget (a problem aggravated by the phoney war). We knew we would get a raw deal from the media. We did. The broadcasters allocated us only 80 per cent of the other parties' PEBs and, by implication, 80 per cent of coverage generally. This compares with parity in 1987. As for the mass circulation newspapers, they more or less ignored our existence, our manifesto getting two paragraphs in one tabloid with a huge readership. To a whole section of Britain's newspaper readership our involvement in the election was all but kept a secret! And we knew Labour would enter the election with more credibility than in 1987, and fight their most professional campaign ever. On the whole, they did.

Those were the circumstances we faced, and why my (ambitious) objective throughout the last eighteen months to polling day was 20 per cent of the popular vote, and twenty seats. We got the twenty seats. We got just under one in five voters – 18 per cent of the popular vote – and I believe we lost between three and five per cent over the last few days as many 'soft' Conservatives returned to the fold, fearing that a vote for the Liberal Democrats would put Labour in. I do not present that as a triumph; but I do think it was a considerable achievement given the daunting and difficult context I have described.

Our objectives, as finally spelled out in our campaign plan, developed in Spring 1990, were as follows:

(a) to win as many seats as possible in the circumstances. This was about survival.
How did we do? We know now that my (published-internally) target was twenty and we won twenty. I am satisfied that is 'objective achieved'.
(b) to be externally judged to have run a good campaign and to have done well in the circumstances. This was about respect and self-respect – about the future.

How did we do? Answers to specific opinion poll questions during the campaign and our experience from talking to the public since, indicate that the public thinks we ran a good campaign. Undoubtedly the public liked out positive approach.

(c) to ensure the leader was judged to have had a good election. This, too, was about respect and related to the future.

How did we do? Judging by the polls, Paddy Ashdown rose steadily in popularity during the campaign. All the evidence suggests this objective was achieved.

(d) to establish a clearly recognisable identity and stance.

How did we do? We aimed for a bright image, using the 'My Vote' symbol, the party colour, and the action-man nature of the leader's tour, and on the whole I believe we did establish our identity as a positive and likeable party – one that, in my view, was right for the longer term. We did particularly well in establishing education as our priority by stressing that we would raise income tax to pay for it. We also established constitutional reform as our issue – whether this was wise I will return to later.

(e) to out-strip the other minority parties and thus re-establish our position as the alternative to Labour and the Conservatives.

This was crucial to achieving the overall objective of building a base for the future and was achieved before the actual campaign began. The Greens and Owenites were wiped out.

(f) to leave the party united, well organised, and in good heart.

How did we do? The campaign team was united. The grassroots were happy with the service they got and, on the whole, with the campaign, as our subsequent questionnaires have established. We had no major blunders. And we left the party with no financial hangover whatsoever. The party was, however, disappointed with the result. This is understandable at one level, for everyone worked so hard, the polls a few days out suggested better, and expectations had risen unrealistically. It is not so understandable at another; the party should have been only too aware just how deep was the hole it had dug its way out of. On the whole, however, this final objective was also achieved.

That is what I hoped for. That is what Paddy Ashdown hoped for. That is what we did. It is my case, therefore, that we achieved our objectives in the 1992 general election. Could we have done better? Possibly a little, but I do not think we could have done much better. One final point about the result – if we had a fair electoral system, we would have won more than 100 seats.

Let me turn to a number of the key issues in our campaign.

A positive strategy

From the start we decided on a positive approach. Expecting a heavy confront-ation between the main two parties, we wanted to look positive where they were negative, young and forward-looking where they would appear old and obsessed with political infighting. This decision to fight a positive campaign was a crucial one. We were determined from the start to try to link the two old parties as both having failed when they had their chances, as both being responsible for a steady course of decline and neglect, of both propping up the system, of both being unwilling to do what needed to be done. But we would do this more in sorrow than in anger. We wanted to be the voice of principle in the election, and if there were any signs of public disgust at the nature of the campaign, we wanted to be its voice, not one of its targets. In 1990 I wrote in our plan: 'We must use the nature of the two party confrontation to contrast with our own positive, likeable, above-the-fight approach'. Two years later that was put to the test in the war over 'Jennifer's Ear'. We kept out of it, despite the temptation (and the pressure from some) not to miss out on the media opportunities of engaging in the fight. And it paid huge dividends, for we went up in all the opinion polls as the only beneficiary from that particular episode.

Fighting every seat

There was some considerable debate about whether we should fight every seat or concentrate our manpower on target seats and only some others. We had decided this would be a developmental election. Because of that, we took the view that we should fight every seat. We felt it was vital to achieve as big a share of the national vote as possible, and that we should pick up every vote we could. We felt that to establish ourselves as the only third party of consequence we must be there, on the ground, in every constituency.

Target seats

Just the same, we analysed every seat in the country, and ranked them in a number of categories, giving them all objectives. At the top, the objective was to win. At the bottom, the objective was to at least field a candidate, circulate an election address, and establish our presence. Between these two categories there was a wide variety of objectives, all aimed at leaving the constituency stronger than before.

I want to stress that because a seat was a target seat, it did not mean that we believed we would win it. The target seats incorporated our existing MPs, one or two of whom we expected to lose, and also a number of other seats that were targets because there was a chance of winning them, and − whatever else happened − we did not want on polling day to discover that we could have won them with a little bit more effort. There were probably in all about forty target seats. But, as I have stressed before, the ones we expected to win never exceeded twenty (in my case) or twenty-three or twenty-four (in the case of my closest advisers).

My advisers concluded after the campaign that we scored 7 per cent (i.e. 3,000 to 4,000 votes) better in our targeted seats than in non-targeted but socially similar constituencies nearby.

The leader

There has been considerable debate as to whether we over-exploited Paddy Ashdown's personality. Some have said we looked too much like a one-man band.

From the start we decided we would build our campaign around the leader in the way that we subsequently did, and I have to say that, given the chance, I would not alter that aspect of the campaign in any way. Not for this election; things may have to change for the next when Ashdown will not be such a fresh face and when I believe it will be necessary to promote a team.

Not that this is entirely in our hands. The fact is that general elections have become more Presidential-style and the emphasis on the leader is dictated as much by the media as by the parties. For instance, we had a variety of speakers at every press conference in the morning, but the television news bulletins invariably extracted from Paddy Ashdown. A crew was assigned to Paddy Ashdown by both BBC television news and ITN and fed segments into every major news bulletin; that was their decision, not ours. We simply created the kind of campaign tour that would cater to and benefit from the way it was going to be covered anyway.

Apart from that, Ashdown represented an attractive face for the party – the ideal projector of the message we wished to convey. Throughout the campaign his popularity rose, as did the ratings for our campaign, and as that campaign was largely based on him, the policy of deploying him as our main weapon was in my view fully justified by results. The fact is that, for the purposes of campaigning nationally, we treated the country as a global constituency and the leader as a global candidate who incorporated within his own philosophy and personality what the party had to offer. It worked extremely well.

There was a lot of nonsense talked at the beginning of the campaign about whether he could stand the pace. He keeps extremely fit, thrives on campaigning, and, while he was working eighteen hours a day, he always works hard. He was doing the thing he likes doing most – campaigning.

It is a nonsense to suggest, however, that we fielded him as a 'one-man band'. Alan Beith made innumerable appearances as our 'Shadow Chancellor' and in a general election dominated by the economy, played a crucial role on radio and television (and, incidentally, participated in the general election operation with great generosity and good humour; when it was over I felt considerably in his debt). We did, in fact, have what we called the

A-Team who were directed to as many television appearances as they could cope with.

But it was extremely difficult; our MPs come from far-flung corners of the country, with huge constituencies to cover and a tradition of the MP being highly visible in the constituency. Many of them were fighting marginal seats. The Scottish ones felt a particular responsibility to spend time resisting the Scottish Nationalists' challenge and getting a good result up there. Thus the availability of our better-known figures was strictly limited and my press officers will confirm that having enough able people to satisfy the appetite of the broadcasters was, throughout the campaign, our biggest headache. Finally, the media had its own view of who we should be fielding on TV, but appeared to base its views on factors that had little to do with a credible election campaign.

One younger MP was said to be particularly good on TV. My concern was that he was a lightweight on policy and this was proved by a bad viewer reaction to his appearances on one or two phone-in-style programmes. Another MP, I was told by the media, was a proven TV performer and should have been used more. Setting aside the fact that he was extremely unco-operative when it came to making himself available, he got an emphatic thumbs-down from viewer panels who judged him a man of the past. I had to take the decisions on a variety of factors that could not be shared with my critics – and I did so. I am afraid if you are going to run a Liberal Democrat campaign – and I suspect it is the same with the other parties – you just have to be tough and if they don't like it . . . well, too bad.

At this point I must make a reference to myself. I do so because one of the criticisms of our campaign is that I appeared in the media too much. I was appointed to not only direct the campaign but speak for it. In that respect, my brief can have been little different from that of Chris Patten, Conservative party chairman responsible for overall decisions about his campaign and for speaking for that campaign, and Jack Cunningham, Labour's campaign co-ordinator, responsible for co-ordinating that campaign and speaking for it. Of course I made a considerable number of television appearances in that role; so did they. That is what I was there for, and that is what they were there for. I had extra problems: the non-availability of star performers. Often in the daytime, I was the only one in London with sufficient experience to appear on television programmes; as our press officers will confirm, I had often to respond to their begging me to participate in programmes when I would have been far happier to nominate someone else.

I believe that if I had been an MP, no comment would have been made about the number of my appearances, just as no critical comment was made about the number made by Patten or Cunningham, or at the previous general election by people like Bryan Gould and Cecil Parkinson.

Part of the problem was straightforward jealousy by three or four members of our parliamentary party, who for over eighteen months never missed an opportunity to complain on 'lobby terms' to journalists that my prominence was getting out of hand. Fortunately, I knew that I had the whole-hearted support of the party leader in this and all else I was doing, and I treated this sniping with the disdain it deserved, never once acknowledging it publicly, although I do so now for the record.

I also had to put up with a rather strange form of political snobbery; this was reflected in constant battles with BBC Television as to whether or not I was qualified to appear in by-election results programmes. What it came down to was this: was I or was I not a politician? Incidentally, I looked up politician in a dictionary. Surprisingly, it does not say 'member of the House of Commons'; it says 'one engaged in political life – one skilled in the way of party politics'. Is there anyone who would seriously suggest that the campaign director of one of the main three parties in the general election campaign is not 'engaged in political life'? Yet several times TV people, trying to get someone else on the programme, actually told our people: 'We want a politician'.

I had the full weight of responsibility of running our campaign, and the responsibility of speaking for it, and I must stress that if I were to have the chance to start afresh, I would conduct myself in exactly the same way. And the practical need to do so would remain the same.

The media

When it comes to the media, I must comment on an extraordinary report by the International Press Institute (IPI). In it Peter Preston, the editor of *The Guardian*, writes of 'bullying' of the media and says 'interestingly, the Liberal Democrats seem to emerge with the least credit'. Bullying? The media? By the Liberal Democrats? Oh dear!

When I think of how the tabloids treated Paddy Ashdown; when I think of how publicly unknown, undemocratically appointed officials at the BBC were able to arbitrarily impose their will that we should receive only 80 per cent of the PEBs and of the coverage of the other parties; when I think of the huge resources available to the media and its power to affect what the voter sees and hears, compared with our own meagre resources, I would find the charge of 'bullying' laughable and pathetic were it not that I take considerable pride in the fact that it reflects the success of the legitimate fight we put up for some justice in this area.

The account in the IPI document by Richard Tait of *Channel 4 News* of Paddy Ashdown's non-appearance on that programme on the day our manifesto was published is a complete misrepresentation of what occurred. As this affair created considerable comment and became a kind of 'cause célèbre', and seems to represent the bulk of the case that we were 'bullying', let me give you the facts.

Mr Tait says *Channel 4 News* had asked Paddy Ashdown 'in principle' to appear on that day. This is untrue. In fact, the words 'in principle' were never used. Ashdown was booked for a specific time – at the top of the programme.

Mr Tait then says: 'On the day the Liberal Democrats wanted, as a new condition of Paddy Ashdown appearing, an assurance that we would lead on the manifesto rather than on the [Labour Party's] Shadow Budget'. This is also untrue. What happened is that the terms of the invitation were changed. We did not contact *Channel 4 News* to impose a condition; we were contacted by them and told that Ashdown was required for a later time. It is indeed the case that I protested vehemently, both about the running order and the change of time, and I still believe their decision was mistaken. But a condition was never imposed. The fact is that on manifesto day Ashdown's programme was under enormous pressure and had been determined to the last second. I had to decide whether the programme's importance justified making changes that would cause inconvenience. I decided it was not of sufficient importance – and that it would do Mr Tait and his colleagues no harm to be told that. This may not be good for his programme's collective ego but, frankly, one non-appearance in the context of the general election as a whole worried me not one iota.

But then Mr Tait goes on to say: 'But the fact that his withdrawal and the circumstances received wide publicity may have helped the broadcasters by deterring party managers from trying to impose unfair conditions upon them.' I am sorry, Mr Tait, but rather than deter us it made me all the more determined to fight for fair coverage and this I did, including holding a press conference on the nature of the coverage we were getting and having high-level meetings with both the BBC and ITN; and I am satisfied – indeed, from our monitoring I can prove it statistically – that we were given fairer treatment from the moment of that protest on.

A brief word about 'stop-watch' coverage: of course I accept that the stop watch is not the ideal way of establishing fair coverage of a campaign. Of course quality of coverage is also an issue. But the balance that a healthy democracy has the right to demand has to be imposed by more than journalists' interpretations of what is news value. If news values were an exact science presumably the front page of *The Guardian* and *The Sun* would be the same! News values are a matter of opinion – not a science. The monitoring of quantity of coverage is at least one precise way of assessing whether parties, and in particular a third party, are being given a fair deal. When I met the BBC and ITN they, to be fair, acknowledged that, and said the stop-watch monitoring would continue, but that it would be one factor and not the only factor. On the whole I was reassured by the promise that quality of coverage would continue to be monitored and satisfied with what they said, and on the whole I was satisfied with the coverage with the exception of Channel 4. Its news programme came out by far the worst in our monitoring of coverage of the Liberal Democrats and below what the crude 80 per cent figure would have justified.

Channel 4 also treated the party election broadcasts with contempt, showing them after midnight. Given that we do not allow TV advertising by parties in

Britain and that these broadcasts are the only chance for the parties to talk directly to the public in their own terms, I think this decision of Channel 4 was a disgrace and I am amazed the other parties did not protest as strongly as I did.

Finally, we did experience one other problem: as the third party we did not get the more experienced political journalists assigned to our campaign and, in particular, to the Ashdown tour. As a result, we had from time to time to put up with some bizarre reporting, sometimes unfairly to our detriment. The BBC's Carol Walker, for instance, assigned to the Ashdown tour, said in the IPI report, 'His aides were not particularly pleased when I reported the repetitive nature of parts of Mr Ashdown's speech'. What Ms Walker did not seem to understand, but more experienced reporters may have done, is that while the speech seemed repetitive to her because she was hearing it several times, it was not repetitive to an audience hearing it only once. The fact is that Ashdown was saying what he wanted to say on the once chance he had to speak to a particular audience; did Ms Walker really think he should have devised a special speech every night just for her?

Ms Andrews and a similarly inexperienced reporter (when it comes to political campaigns) from ITN made a ludicrous fuss, not in private, but on air, about a note issued to them by a relatively junior aide on our bus asking for co-operation in the way they door-stepped Ashdown every second of his tour. When I heard about it I called them in and we sorted it out amicably. Yet that night ITN's reporter raised it on air once more, this time more-or-less claiming the outcome as a triumph for her. Their complaint, incidentally, was that we were trying to stop them asking questions at every conceivable opportunity. Their more experienced colleagues, travelling with Major and Kinnock, would have rolled in the aisles had they heard the complaints and had the chance to compare them with the generous access we provided.

A final word about the media and politicians. Of course the parties and the media have widely varying objectives. Inevitably campaign managers are going to fight for every bit of coverage and complain at every bit of perceived injustice. Is this so surprising? I find the media alarm and indignation at all this to be a bit wimpish. And let there be no doubt: when it comes to power to really hurt, we cannot touch the media compared with what they can do to us.

Overall strategy

For nearly twenty years I have tried to advocate, first in the Liberal Party, then in the Alliance, and then with the Liberal Democrats, that with limited resources, we should concentrate on a relatively small number of issues, offering a distinctive position on each, but each relating to the other so that there is a distinctive feel about the party as a whole.

Two years back we decided to do that, building our campaign around the five Es: education, the environment, electoral and constitutional reform, the economy and Europe. Under each of these headings, we stressed investment: investment in education; environmental protection as an investment in the future; Europe as an investment for economic co-operation and peace; the economy and the need to invest in building a strong economy for the future; and electoral and constitutional reform as an investment in the kind of democracy we will need in the twenty-first century.

Just how much we succeeded in getting this across to the public I do not know, but it did serve to unite and even to educate the party and undoubtedly paid its way in terms of a sharper and more effective campaigning message.

The wasted vote

At the end of the day, however, there was never any question about the biggest problem we had: how to overcome the problem of the 'wasted vote'. I decided that whereas in past elections we had simply suffered the effects of it without really fighting it directly, we simply could not afford to do that this time. I decided we should take it head on, in a number of ways.

First, we stressed in how many seats one of the other parties was a wasted vote – stressing that, on the basis of the 1987 result, we were the main challenger ... having been second then in more than 250 seats. And by encouraging candidates at local level to repeat over and over the result of the last election in order to show that the only wasted vote in that constituency was for either the Conservatives or Labour. We took the unprecedented step of listing every seat where we were the main challenger in a party election broadcast. Above all, the work on this was done at local level – especially in the target seats. Second, we tried to exploit the polls that suggested a balance of power, and to present this as a positive thing. The more Liberal Democrats were elected, the more we could avoid the extremes of the other parties – the more we would get a commonsense, moderate government. Finally, we developed the line that the only wasted vote was for those two old parties that had had their chances and failed.

It is not clear to me whether this positive approach to a negative actually helped or hindered. But the wasted vote problem will be there for us next time as well. It is a problem that remains unsolved.

The missing factor

Frankly, what I had not anticipated was the emphasis that the Conservatives would put on the theme that a vote for the Liberal Democrats was a vote for Labour. I anticipated neither the ferocity of the attack nor its potency. I also failed to anticipate the extent to which people would be convinced by the combined Conservative and tabloid attacks on Labour. I had no strategy to deal with this particular line and this meant we ineffectively defended ourselves over the closing days of the campaign. This was perhaps the biggest flaw in our campaign; and one I feel some responsibility for.

Balance of power

Finally, I come to the subject of the balance of power. From the start I never felt as confident as some that the idea of coalition or shared power would be attractive to the public.

From the start I argued strongly, and indeed insisted, that we should do all in our power to avoid balance of power questions dominating our press conferences and other interview programmes. The strategy we deployed was to raise the issue ourselves well in advance of the election and make our position so clear that there really was little else to be said – other than to repeat what we had already said – over and over.

This actually worked. By the time the election was under way we had answered the questions. They continued to be raised, particularly in the main setpiece interviews with the leader, but the constant repetition of our position only served to make them sound reasonably comfortable and familiar to listeners and viewers. Until the last week of the campaign we largely avoided the balance of power becoming a central issue.

With the newspapers over the final weekend suggesting, however, that the election was very close, and with balance of power being the issue, whether we liked it or not, we did put our own emphasis on it over the last few days. Now I believe this, too, was possibly a mistake.

This is very much a retrospective judgement, for the arguments for the way we handled it were strong at the time. However, there was a case for devoting our last PEB much more to our distinctive message. Instead, we used it largely to address the nation on the balance of power.

The result

What happened in the end? To put it bluntly, the Conservatives pulled it off. They convinced people that having got the economy into a mess, they were best placed to get the country out of it. They scared the hell out of people about tax and they used fear of the very problems they were creating to scare people away from change. In this they were helped massively by the tabloids. Only recently I was at a social occasion with a number of Conservative voters who were furiously criticising the Conservative administration's performance, but when challenged as to why they elected it, repeated tabloid headlines almost word for word.

We felt over the last few days an erosion in our vote. From the doorstep the message came loud and clear – the people who had moved to us from the Conservatives were slipping back, not because they particularly wanted to, not because of disenchantment with us, but because they had accepted the argument that we could put Labour in. Further, Neil Kinnock's apparent movement in our direction on electoral reform helped to give that impression. Our own emphasis on balance of power, and the assumption by many people that in a balance of power we were most likely to forge a partnership with Labour, probably contributed to this. It was just enough to knock us back between 3 and 5 per cent from our position in the early 20s to 18 per cent, and to put the Conservatives over the top.

Summary

To summarise, I believe we ran a bright, likeable campaign and achieved most of our objectives. We could possibly have done better if we had anticipated and planned for the 'Liberal Democrats will put Labour in' scare tactic of the last few days. I believe this general election will prove to be all that Paddy Ashdown hoped for – the builder of a base, and the forger of a more effective campaigning party for the next general election. I look back on it with pride – as an experience of happy teamwork, an exercise in professional campaigning and the practice of the politics of integrity.

Appendix   Selected posters of the 1992 British general election campaign

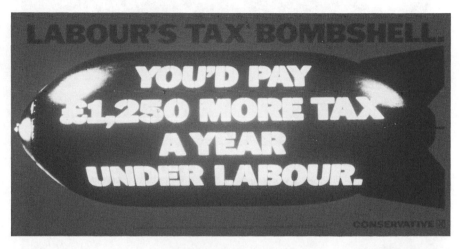

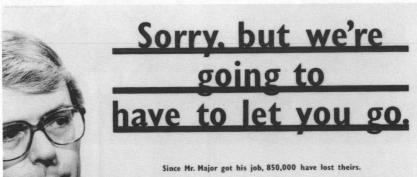

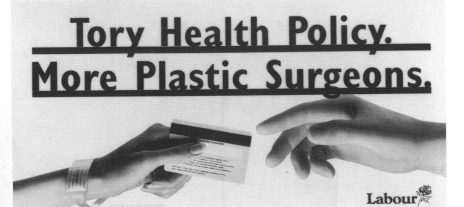

This is a Major recession.

Every country in the EC experienced economic growth last year, with one exception. Britain.

Our economy shrank by 2.5%.

In fact, this country has been in recession for the past 20 months, the longest recession since the war.

John Major says the British recession is the result of a world recession.

Sorry, John, but that's a major distortion of the truth.

Labour

Part III
The campaign on television

7   The parties and television

Richard Tait

The broadcasters and the parties may not have agreed on much during the 1992 general election, but they had no doubts about the central role of television in the campaign. In February 1992, NOP polled 1,400 potential voters, asking the question, 'How much do you trust each of the following to tell the truth in the coming election campaign?' In the category 'a great deal/a fair amount', 67 per cent said ITN, 66 per cent BBC News, the political parties polled between 31 per cent and 36 per cent, and 'your daily newspaper' polled just 29 per cent.[1] 1992, like 1987, was for good reason a television election.

I would like to look at three aspects of the relationship between the parties and television. First, I would like to examine the changes in approach by broadcasters and politicians and how before and during the campaign they dealt with one another; second, whether changes in the structure of British broadcasting affected the way television covered the election; and finally, I shall look ahead to see whether in a rapidly changing broadcasting environment the conditions of 1992 are likely to hold good for the next election.

Broadcasters and politicians

Both the broadcasters and the parties were determined to improve on their 1987 performance. No one responsible for television news was complacent about the way news programmes had covered the previous election – believing there had been overall too little analysis, and probably too much coverage of photo-opportunities. The 1991 Edinburgh Television Festival even staged a mock trial in which the BBC and ITN were charged with collusion with the political parties, and some cynical observers thought, a little unfairly, that the broadcasters were found not guilty only because the jury was entirely composed of other broadcasters.

One area where both the BBC and ITN tried to learn from the past was in putting more resources into analysis. The BBC invested in creating pools of specialist reporters and developing a more analytical approach to news bulletins, particularly on the *Nine O'Clock News*.

ITN too put greater emphasis on analysis and explanation, but also abandoned one of the main restrictions under which broadcasters had traditionally operated – the so-called 'stop watch rule'. This was the convention, observed by the BBC, ITV and Channel 4, that the amount of time devoted to each party in news bulletins should be determined by the ratio of electoral broadcasts allocated to each party, which was 5-5-5 in 1987 and 5-5-4 in 1992.

ITN felt that 'stop watching' was a fraud on the public – in the past it had led to meaningless photo-opportunities being passed off as news because they filled the required time. It created an editorial environment in which normal news values were suspended and stories which did not justify inclusion in news terms were put into bulletins to ensure that the preordained balance of time was observed. So ITN informed the parties that it would not use the stop watch rule during the 1992 general election campaign and allocated time in news bulletins during the campaign on the basis of news values alone.

Overall, the actual time that was spent by ITN's programmes on each of the three main parties over its total of 43 hours of news coverage on ITV and Channel 4 during the campaign only differed by a few percentage points from the 5-5-4 formula which would otherwise have applied. The important difference was that all the coverage was driven by editorial judgement. Abandoning the stop watch made for coverage which ebbed and flowed with the development of the campaign rather than rigidly allocating a predetermined amount of time to each party.

The Liberal Democrats, to their great alarm, found that at the start of the election they were receiving less coverage than they had hoped for, partly because they had decided to concentrate on education and stand back from the economic and health issues on which the Conservative and Labour campaigns initially concentrated. They then found themselves getting proportionately more coverage later in the campaign as the news agenda moved towards strong Liberal Democrat issues such as constitutional reform and the balance of power in a 'hung parliament'.

If the opinion polls are to be believed, however, the Liberal Democrats gained in support in the early part of the campaign when the amount, if not the quality, of their television coverage was at its low point, and lost some of that support over the last few days, when the amount of their coverage was at its height, but on subjects like constitutional reform which were perhaps not as attractive to the electorate as their earlier emphasis on education.

The BBC decided to continue with the stop watch as one of their criteria for deciding coverage. I know many of their editors regarded, and still regard, the stop watch with as little affection as their ITN counterparts, so perhaps the BBC too may abandon it altogether in the next election.

While the broadcasters were trying in different ways to make their coverage less formulaic and predictable, the main parties were gearing up to try and exercise more influence over the content and style of news bulletins.

In parties' campaign teams there was greater emphasis on, and faith in, television expertise. In the eighteen months before the election a number of television producers and reporters with network news and current affairs experience joined the parties' public relations machines. They became known in the trade with suitable irreverence as the 'spin doctors'. They supplemented and in some cases replaced existing press and publicity officers who had tended to come from print journalism. This may explain why it was, that as well as the general complaints about balance and fairness, the parties embarked on detailed critiques of how the programmes were being made, how discussions were being organised, and even how individual items were being structured.

The 1992 campaign began early with a period of 'phoney war' which ran from the 1991 party conferences to the actual announcement of polling day. It was accompanied by an unprecedented campaign of pressure on the broadcasters which was remarkable both for the weight of criticism and for its technical detail. For example, ITN's political editor was taken to task by the Labour Party over the length and pace of a panning shot which had travelled from Neil Kinnock to Roy Hattersley in the course of an item. A reporter in her edit booth finishing a report got a call from a Labour politician – just checking that she had fully understood the Labour Party line in the story she was writing for transmission in a few minutes time. A BBC news editor received a complaint from a government press officer who objected strongly to the way in which a particular graphic had been used in an item on the economy and the length of time it had been on the screen. A reporter whose health story included a doctor who was a Labour Party member took a series of calls from government press officers arguing that the interview should not be shown as the doctor was clearly politically biased. When ITN transmitted the item, Conservative Central Office told the press they were going to complain, but in the event no complaint was received.

There were also more conventional, one might even say traditional, attacks on the balance of the coverage. The Conservatives had a spectacular row with the BBC over one item of health coverage in the autumn of 1991, and in the immediate run up to the election, Kenneth Baker, the then Home Secretary, warned more generally 'the BBC has got to be very careful indeed over the next eight to ten weeks. The country expects the BBC to be absolutely impartial as it is the state funded body.'[2]

The Labour Party complained that the BBC was devoting too much time to Conservative attacks on Labour's tax proposals, and tried to persuade both BBC and ITN to spend more time challenging the government about what Labour saw as Conservative policy failures. The pressure of calls and complaints eased somewhat once the election got underway – at least partly because the 'spin doctors' and their political masters had other demands on their time.

During the campaign itself the television experience of some public relations managers in the party teams showed again in their tactics. When the Conservatives discovered that the BBC had failed to film a confrontation between Neil Kinnock and a *Daily Express* journalist which they thought reflected badly on the Labour leader they asked ITN if it could make the material available to the BBC. ITN said no.

The parties used their own video units and tried to persuade the broadcasters to use their pictures of events such as rallies. Again, the broadcasters declined, preferring to use their own cameras and retaining editorial control over what was shot as well as what was transmitted.

The parties also worked hard to provide pre-researched stories as well as photo-opportunities for the broadcasters. In the aftermath of the 'Jennifer's Ear' broadcast a Labour Party unit run by a former television news producer tried with some success to interest the popular early evening regional news programmes in stories which Labour had researched of sick children on waiting lists. Some Labour campaign managers believe that the extensive local coverage of health service problems which followed contributed to Labour's lead in the polls in the days immediately after the row over the party election broadcast.

There were also arguments about interviews and discussions on news and current affairs programmes. The parties tried to negotiate the basis on which interviews were given, who would appear with whom, who would have the last word. The broadcasters tried to resist what they saw as unreasonable conditions, as when the Liberal Democrats objected to *Channel 4 News* planning to run a proposed interview with Paddy Ashdown about the Liberal Democrat manifesto after its coverage of Labour's Shadow Budget. That difference of opinion on what was the right running order of the bulletin ended with the Liberal Democrats withdrawing Mr Ashdown from the programme.

That incident, like a number of the other examples already given, became public knowledge. Arguably, one of the most important differences between the 1987 and 1992 elections was that in 1992 there was much more known about the relationships between the broadcasters and the parties, and the disagreements which occurred between them.

The media campaigns themselves became part of the election coverage to the point where they seemed at times to attract a disproportionate amount of attention. And on at least one occasion – the claims and counter claims of the 'War of Jennifer's Ear' – it seemed for a moment that the conduct of the election campaign had spiralled out of the control of Labour and Conservative leaders, whose judgement and indeed integrity were apparently hostage to what their public relations teams had or had not done in their name, and had or had not told them. The impression after that episode was that as far as the Labour and Conservative parties were concerned, the politicians seem to have taken a tighter grip on the campaign. There were fewer stunts and more orthodox election politics.

It is important not to be too fastidious about all this pressure. Political public relations men and women are employed to bend the ears of journalists and win whatever advantage they can, fair or unfair, over their opponents. The lobby, the foundation of political reporting outside of elections, is based on a relationship of give and take. Overall, I think little damage was done: the editors and journalists of both the BBC and ITN resisted unfair pressure, although Jay Blumler and his co-authors did find some BBC journalists prepared to admit that complaints from the Conservative Party resulted in some effect of 'intimidatory self-censorship'.[3]

Changes in the structure of broadcasting

However, in this election there was another potential source of pressure on broadcasters, aimed more at the management of the television industry rather than its journalists and editors. The 1992 election was being fought at a time when British television was going through unprecedented change. The BBC was facing the prospect of negotiating its future after the election with the winners, with the debate about the Charter renewal and the licence fee.

Commercial television was also facing fundamental change. It had had to lobby hard – and not always successfully – against the most worrying clauses of the Broadcasting Bill throughout 1989 and 1990. By the time the election arrived, however, commercial television knew its fate. Although the Broadcasting Act was law, the changes in the system had not yet taken place. For example, Thames knew that it had lost its licence, but Carlton had not yet replaced it. ITN knew that its shareholding structure would have to change in the future, but it was still in the hands of its existing management and ownership.

There is little evidence that this uncertainty had much effect on the way the broadcasters dealt with the politicians. It appears to have had no significant effect on commercial television's news and current affairs coverage, although in their comparative study of BBC and ITN coverage of the 1992 campaign, Dr Holli Semetko and her co-authors suggest that it might have been a factor in what they perceived as the more cautious approach of BBC News compared with ITN, and also suggest that the commercial channels may have been less anxious than the public service channel about political pressure because there was little left to worry about in their relations with the government.[4]

Broadcasting and elections in the mid 1990s

For the terrestrial broadcasters, both commercial and public sector, the real test is still to come. In this area there are no answers, only questions. It is not yet certain that the BBC will still have both its television channels and the resources to continue high quality news and current affairs after the Charter renewal. The new ITV network has already signalled a lack of enthusiasm for current affairs in peak time. It is far from clear that it will want to run extensive election coverage beyond the news bulletins which it is obliged to carry by the terms of its licences. The combination of recession and falling audiences confronts both ITV and Channel 4 with the prospect of falling revenues. It remains to be seen whether they will both have the income and the will to fund a news service which would continue to be wholly competitive with the resources of the BBC and provide the viewer with an immediate means of comparison of how well the different news programmes are withstanding party pressure.

Even if the answers to all or most of these questions are yes, an even more important question is whether the BBC, ITV and Channel 4 will be able or indeed willing to reach virtually the whole of the electorate with extended political coverage by the time of the next general election. The forecasts of audience share for cable and satellite television – either offering no news at all or news which will escape the strict obligations of quality and impartiality imposed by the regulators on BBC, ITV and Channel 4 – suggest that by 1997 cable and satellite may be in two fifths of homes and will have perhaps 12 per cent of the total television audience. By the year 2002 that figure could be 14 per cent, with another 5 or 6 per cent for a Channel 5 service.[5]

Audience research figures reveal there is already a marked lack of enthusiasm for some television election coverage. The election editions of *This Week* and *Panorama*, for example, lost between one and two million viewers on their pre-election figures, although news audiences did not suffer so badly. It is therefore quite likely that a significant number of viewers will be tempted in future elections to escape from wall-to-wall political coverage to the films, sport and entertainment offered by the new channels and stations.

It may be that over the next decade the politicians will find it harder to address the public via television at election times and that individual incidents and items, whose importance is already grossly exaggerated in the hot-house atmosphere in which television producers and politicians operate at election times, will have even less power to influence the outcome of the campaign. The broadcasters may find themselves under less political pressure at least partly because with so many channels and fragmented audiences they will not matter so much.

Notes

1 NOP, *The Independent*, 27 February 1992.
2 *The Observer*, 16 February 1992.
3 Jay G. Blumler, Michael Gurevitch and T. J. Nossiter, 'Struggles for meaningful election communication: television journalism at the BBC, 1992', this volume.
4 T. J. Nossiter, Margaret Scammell and Holli A. Semetko, 'Old values versus news values: the British 1992 general election campaign on television', this volume.
5 ITN forecast, first quarter 1992.

8 Struggles for meaningful election communication: television journalism at the BBC, 1992

Jay G. Blumler, Michael Gurevitch and T. J. Nossiter

In many competitive democracies, election campaign communication is increasingly tension-laden. Three sectors of heightened conflict may be identified.

Firstly, *inter-communicator struggle* – politicians vs. journalists – for control over news agendas has intensified. A cross-national analysis of agenda formation in elections comments:

> Once a campaign is announced ... a common element in both the United States and Britain is the unleashing in earnest of an implacably competitive struggle to control the mass media agenda, a struggle that pits not only candidates and parties in contention for agenda domination, but also political campaign managements against news organization teams.[1]

Before and during the British general election of 1992, the increased professionalisation (some termed it 'Americanisation') of the major parties' approaches to campaign publicity had put a special spin on this tussle.

Secondly, *intra-journalistic dilemmas* have been sharpened. During the 1992 campaign these took on a distinctive flavour at Britain's 'cornerstone' public broadcaster, the BBC – between being serious (focusing on the issues, informing electors, performing a democratic civic role) and responding to conventionally journalistic impulses (pursuit of the horse race, campaigners' gaffes and anything humanly dramatic); between recognising campaigners' rights to set the terms of electoral choice and asserting journalists' autonomy to contribute to the debate; and between core journalistic norms of objectivity and impartiality and helping viewers to make sense of the issues and conflicting party claims. Moreover, the onset of structural changes in British broadcasting, shattering the BBC–ITV duopoly and raising questions about the future of the BBC after renewal of its Charter, had brought to the fore a competitive dilemma, between providing more substantial coverage than ITN but risking falling behind it in audience appeal, as well as an identity dilemma, between serving a principled purpose and looking pragmatically to organisational survival.

Thirdly, a chorus of doubts over the relationship between media-dominated election campaigning and democratic values has been approaching a crescendo in many ostensibly democratic societies.[2] On this matter, Doris Graber, shedding the scholarly judiciousness for which she is noted, concludes categorically:

Although the canons of news reporting have remained unchanged for many decades, the news product has deteriorated when judged as a resource for public opinion formation. The information needs of citizens have skyrocketed in the age of the global society and the guardian state intrudes ever more deeply into personal and collective behaviors. The news media have not kept pace. That is why the paths of democracy and news have been diverging.[3]

Much food for thought on all these tensions stems from our observation attachment for eight days of the 1992 campaign to BBC Television News, focused mainly on the Corporation's flagship bulletin, the *Nine O'Clock News*. We approached this occasion (the fifth in a series, stretching back to the 1966 election)[4] with two primary questions in mind. Firstly, how have changes since 1987 in the British communication system (especially developments in parties' publicity methods and in the commercialisation of ITN within ITV) affected the production of election news at the BBC? Secondly, what implications for public service coverage of election campaigns flow from the philosophy of John Birt (then the Corporation's Deputy Director General and Director General designate), whose influence was known to run strongly throughout BBC News and Current Affairs?[5] Access for our research was exceptionally open and generous, including not only attendance at policy and editorial meetings, newsroom observation, and interviews with executives, editors, correspondents and producers, but also, for the first time, presence at a post-mortem meeting, where a dozen principals candidly reviewed their campaign performance a week after polling day.[6]

In fact, when invited to voice our own assessment at the conclusion of that meeting, one of us summed up as follows: 'You did the best job of election coverage possible within the limits in which you had to operate.' Both the compliment and the qualification of it were sincere.

On the one hand, the public service spirit was vigorously alive in BBC News and Current Affairs and drove many of the impressively conceived endeavours to provide meaningful campaign coverage. Advance planning and personnel dispositions were set in train from spring 1991. An extra sum of £9.25 million was allocated for election tasks throughout News and Current Affairs. For the daily output, a division of roles between News and *Newsnight*, more clear and satisfactory to all concerned than in 1987, was agreed: News, much fortified and deepened in its editorial resources and experience since the last election, was considered able to cover the campaign without the heavy current affairs imports thought necessary in 1983 and 1987; while *Newsnight* was expected to provide an arena of debate and more free-wheeling commentary than would be appropriate for News. In addition, newsroom and studio geography had been rationalised. Overall, a strong and purposive team had been assembled, working on closely collegial terms, even when discussing contested options (in marked contrast to the fierce splits that disrupted their 1983 counterparts).[7]

On the other hand, the limits circumscribing such an effort, some externally imposed, some internally generated, were also formidable. In certain respects they appeared more constraining than at any previous election reporting operation we have observed.

The public-service approach

Changes afoot in British broadcasting may have had a unifying influence on BBC journalists. They shared a public-service perspective on their election mission and presumed that they primarily bore its attendant obligations. Such a mission has been defined in terms of 'a sense of some responsibility for the health of the political process and for the quality of public discourse generated within it'.[8] Three propositions reflect BBC applications of this idea to the 1992 election:

(1) *Public service implies giving extensive, prominent and well-resourced coverage to the campaign.* As a producer explained, 'We've tried to reshape the *'Nine'* according to an understanding of the role of public service broadcasting in a mature democracy. Plenty of contributions will be vulgarising the argument in this campaign; the task is how to raise it.' Consequently, the *Nine O'Clock News*, normally thirty minutes long, was extended to forty-five to fifty minutes and given a three-part structure: part I to report the day's campaign news; part II to report the day's *non*-election news; and part III to present a range of more reflective approaches to the campaign, including pre-prepared films, often a report on the latest opinion poll results, and a two-way exchange on the overall politics of the current situation between the newsreader and the BBC's authoritative political editor, John Cole. As another producer put it, 'To do less than that would mean that either important election news or non-election news would get squeezed.'

(2) *Public service implies that the coverage should be predominantly serious and substantial.* The more conventionally journalistic assumption, that politics is essentially boring and therefore must be spiced with jolting news-value angles, was conspicuously absent. As a producer put it, 'The old newsroom attitude of knowing in your gut that something demands a certain kind of attention no longer prevails.' Or as a senior member of the *Nine O'Clock News* team explained, 'Our task is to get the right balance between a WEA-like feel to the presentation and something more attractive and popular.' One producer told us that the aim of certain campaign reports was to make concepts with which *Financial Times* readers would be familiar accessible to *Daily Mail* readers! Another confessed that they were prepared to test 'viewers' boredom thresholds' to do justice to the campaign.

There was one major exception to all this in the devotion of a regular slot in part III to a jazzy, unashamedly horse-racist, graphics-animated coverage of opinion poll findings. The most costly element in the programme (because of the graphics and the back-up research), it was justified on the grounds that 'In part this election *is* a horse race, and I'm sure that's how many viewers regard it' and 'It's something that leading politicians themselves now give tremendous weight to'. In other words, it was considered a significant campaign factor, on which viewers should be kept informed.

Nevertheless, even this feature was surrounded by reservations, laid out in a printed set of guidelines, that were unique to the BBC. The BBC was not to sponsor any voting intention polls of its own.[9] Undue weight should never be given to the results of a single poll, however spectacular, since they might not reflect a trend. And poll coverage should be confined to part III.

(3) *Public service implies that the coverage should be rationalistic – based, that is, on much prior thought and considered planning.* This proposition particularly reflected the influence on BBC journalism of John Birt. As a newsreader put it, 'This is the first election we have covered under Birtian rules of engagement'.

What did this imply? A Current Affairs executive described it in terms of a paramount 'mission to explain'. This should apply not only to weekly public affairs programmes but also to daily journalism for the mass audience so that its need for information would not be shortchanged by the mere packaging of daily events and party statements. This required prior consideration at editorial level of the implications of the most significant current developments to which the audience should be alerted, drawing on strong resources of 'in-house expertise'; Birtianism involved a certain 'mistrust of generalist journalists'. Another feature of this philosophy was its stress on *responsible* journalism. As one informant put it, people should have 'opportunities to check the suitability of what they are providing' and guidelines for gauging what might count as 'suitable' in problematic situations.

The Birtian approach, then, values philosophic clarity, managerial leadership and the creation of a team aware of shared purposes and standards. In line with this, since 1987 a merger of the BBC's formerly separate News and Current Affairs Divisions had been completed; many individuals with Current Affairs backgrounds were appointed to leading positions in News programmes; journalists unable to work with the prevailing outlook were weeded or eased out; four large and well-funded specialist units – for Westminster politics, foreign affairs, business and economic affairs, and social policy, respectively – were set up to serve all factual programmes; and steps were taken to fashion and induce acceptance of what some termed a 'new journalistic culture' at the BBC (e.g., the occasional convening of seminars to review programming and the handling of critical situations as well as to anticipate upcoming ones). As a senior executive told us, 'I think you'll find we've got an exceptionally confident team here, particularly sure of their values'.

It is not that an unquestioning acceptance of the Birtian outlook prevailed throughout News and Current Affairs. One individual unrepentantly termed himself a 'Cavalier in a Roundhead machine'. Others voiced doubts in the following terms:

With so much emphasis on pre-scripting, we may have lost the knack of good story telling.

The analytical approach can become very hard to watch and ignore where the audience is at.

We should be looking for ways of creating events on television and be more imaginative.

There is more of the hairshirt attitude to news than I would adopt. I don't see why we should be saying to the audience that in effect you have to work your way through this.

Such reservations, however, were usually tempered with much appreciation of what had been achieved in the recent past. In the words of an executive from another department, 'The election is being covered by people who have now worked together for such a long time that they practically approach their tasks and problems as if of one mind.'

Given this 'upmarket' drift and certain contrary developments at ITN,[10] it was perhaps natural that the way ITN covered the election often seemed on BBC journalists' minds. Transcripts of *News at Ten* were available to editors for perusal the next morning. A newsreader, noting that *News at Ten* had not been extended for the campaign, commented that:

The gap between the BBC with its public service orientation and ITN with its commercial one is undeniably widening. We are entering a situation where we will be the sole repository of public service values in news and current affairs.

ITN's performance, day-by-day and overall, was accordingly a frequent source of comment – some positive, some critical and almost always comparative. Thus, it was variously said, ITN:

Have an ability to go for the jugular.

Are sometimes more intelligible when dealing with economic affairs.

Have had better press conference camera angles than us.

Lack our more analytical approach and seem to do more channelling of party propaganda on to the audience.

Lack the specialism that is our strong advantage.

Seem to have a more relaxed attitude to internal balance.

Have not really been trying.

Have gone tabloid; I sense their heart's not in it.

Findings from the Broadcasting Research Department, showing that the *Nine O'Clock News* audience had not fallen disastrously and that the BBC was rated more highly than ITN on a number of campaign coverage attributes (for fairness, accuracy, informativeness, trustworthiness, etc.) were therefore welcome to all.[11]

The constraints

In practice, the BBC's public service approach to the 1992 campaign seemed to be circumscribed by five major sources of limitation.

Party publicity management

The most pivotal of these was the thorough-going professionalisation of the parties' strategic approaches to their media campaigns. In a brief encounter with John Birt in the newsroom one day, the first author defined this as the intensification of publicity competition, concerted efforts to dominate the news agenda, increased reliance on specialist political consultants and campaign managers, and a ceaseless determination to cover all publicity-relevant bases, leaving nothing to chance.[12] BBC executives and journalists were certainly keenly aware of being surrounded by highly professionalised party teams, immersed daily in the message environment they were creating largely for television news. In the words of one:

There has never before been the same degree of self-consciousness about this complex of phenomena. Everyone is now walking into this, knowing to an agonizing, navel-scrutinising extent how the two pieces of the process are relating to each other.

Much was said in this connection about the parties' morning press conferences. Noting, for example, that they were kicking off at 7.30 am (considerably earlier than ever before), a newsman commented that, 'each party is determined to try to dominate the day's agenda from the morning through the rest of the day', starting with breakfast news. An editor perceived the conferences as closely controlled affairs through 'rules preventing anything happening because no supplementaries are allowed, attempts to control questions through phoney politeness supposedly aiming to give everyone a chance, an exercise in damage limitation all round'. An executive saw them as theme-setters, controlling politicians' other comments on the day concerned:

It seemed the debate during the day had been set off more by press conference statements than by interviews. It was as if the party strategists had laid down what would be said in interviews by virtue of their preceding [press conference] presentations.

Moreover, as the campaign progressed, the newspeople found the parties concentrating on a limited set of issues, only those that each calculated would best advance their cause with voters. There were also signs that the Conservatives had adopted a 'hardball' campaign ethic, based on the assumption, accepted by many US campaign consultants, that the quickest and most effective way to act on the balance of public opinion is to mount a strongly negative attack on one's opponent.

Such single-minded party professionalisation posed three main problems for the broadcasters. Probably the most vexing and subtle was how to make a significantly independent contribution of their own to the campaign, without intruding improperly into what should be a choice for voters between whatever the political parties were offering in their own terms. Key figures in News and Current Affairs keenly resented the fact that a rash of analyses had appeared in the serious press, mounting what one executive termed 'a fashionable attack' on TV journalists as little more than the parties' tame poodles, passively relaying to viewers whatever soundbites politicians chose to craft and whatever photo-opportunities party managers chose to stage.[13] In fact, BBC journalists had engaged since 1987 in a 'great debate' (a participant's term) over how much coverage should be given to photo-opportunities and reports from correspondents with party leaders on the campaign trail. Some downplaying of such materials without rejecting them altogether seemed to be the 1992 compromise over this. An editor summed up the dilemma: 'There is a real limit to how far packages from the campaign trail can take the campaign argument, since so much is laid on for the cameras.'

The BBC's core response to this problem was a two-sided formula. Its campaign role should be '*reactive but with value added*'. It was to be reactive in the sense of being obliged to report the parties' main campaign initiatives day by day. This duty derived from the BBC's long-standing sense of itself as a creature and servant of British parliamentary democracy, which is organised as a confrontation between government and opposition in the House of Commons. The BBC's role was also to 'add value', however, by putting party statements in a context helpful to viewers. As the editor of Television News expressed it, 'The parties are entitled to campaign in their way, and we are not entitled to ignore it. But we are entitled to put it in perspective.' The coverage's 'bread and butter', he went on, was what the parties were saying and doing on a given day. 'It would be a negation of our role to refuse politicians that kind of direct access', but 'we are not to be used simply as the politicians' news-agents' windows without their claims and arguments being tested in some way'.

But what more specifically did the value-added element amount to? For the news team it included two main kinds of contributions: one unmasking, the other informing. The first was to open viewers' eyes to what the parties were up to tactically – to expose their publicity intentions and why they were saying and doing what was coming across on the screen. In the words of a current affairs executive:

One thing the news people have done more of in this campaign is not only to report what the parties are doing but also to give an assessment of their reasons for doing it. They have been looking at the parties' campaign strategies and testing whether they are working.

Of course, such a response to candidate electioneering has long been prominent in American campaign coverage.[14] Terming items of this kind 'meta-campaign stories', a recently published comparative study of the 1988 Presidential elections in France and the United States found them uniquely recurrent in US television coverage of the campaigns, present in 15 per cent of the reports.[15] BBC producers, however, considered they should indulge in such a vein of comment only in moderation, stopping somewhere short of a full-throated 'disdaining' of party-fashioned election news. 'One shouldn't be so sceptical and derisive of the process', one said, 'that you undermine it – for you're part of the process itself.'[16]

The other value-added contribution was to call as often as possible on the BBC's large cadre of specialist correspondents 'to provide' (as one explained) 'information on the basis of which one can come back to the hustings argument with some perspective for judging it'. Whenever possible, then, the specialist voice would either be interwoven with what the parties were saying on some issue or would be incorporated into an informative follow-up package after a report on what the parties had said. In addition, the notion of a so-called 'Election Briefing' item was conceived 'to create' (as one put it) 'enough space so that, depending on the agenda of campaign news that day, we can take a half-step back, saying they have been going on about such and such and then asking what is the most important information which this fits'. Another producer elaborated:

[we are] creating a bit between what the camera is pointed at and the viewers' grasp of what is at stake. If we are supposed to have a role in an informed democracy, we have to ask how we can take up that responsibility. That means trying to present the arguments as politicians would choose to do (and giving them the right to do that) but to pull things together in a context laced by the information you have to share with the audience.

A second problem arising from party professionalisation was the 'narrowness of the party debate' (in an editor's phrase) or the limited agenda of issues on which the 1992 campaign pivoted, comprising mainly: (a) economic management issues, especially the recession and how it might be overcome, (b) the parties' taxation and spending policies, (c) the future of two social policy areas, health and education and (in the last week) (d) constitutional reform. As a producer summed up, 'The parties rarely stepped out of the circle of the economy and social affairs'.[17]

Although the parties were concentrating thereby on central issues vital to electors, many others of some significance (one editor seemed to have a checklist in his mind) were almost entirely ignored – for example, the environment, relations with Europe, defence and security, the rising crime rate and local government finance. Admittedly, some of the dozen films prepared for presentation in part III were designed to deal with less emphasised issues. There was a film on the environment early in the campaign, for example, plus others, later, on transport and on ethnic relations, as well as an Election Briefing on Europe and a short package on defence policy. But when asked whether any of these contributions had entered into the public debate, the responsible executive producer unhesitatingly replied: 'No. If you want to do that, you get famous people to say provocative things. The decision not to have politicians in these items ensured they were low-key.'

Although the third problem for BBC newscasters – advanced party professionalisation – is more difficult to define than the others, something characteristic of the 1992 campaign would be missed if one failed to identify it. A highly organised and controlled campaign can seem to lack some of the essential ingredients of attractive and meaningful communication: spontaneity, a bit of unpredictability, a sense of adventure that could lead to discovery, a sense of wrestling with reality instead of always trading smoothly in appearances and perceptions. As an editor told us, 'the parties are so effectively buttoned up, there ain't no surprises'. As an executive concurred, 'with so much planning on their part and ours, there was almost no room for the unexpected. It sometimes threatened to denude the campaign, taking the juice out of it.'

This diagnosis seemed validated by the glaring obviousness of those very few moments when the 1992 campaign *did* seem suddenly to spring to life at Television Centre:

(1) During the appearance of a clutch of dramatically unexpected opinion poll results twice in the campaign, described by a reporter on the first occasion as 'the first green shoots of a real election story, not fabricated for our benefit by the politicians'.

(2) The positive impression made on the BBC journalists by the freshness of an ITV programme, in which ordinary voters quizzed the three main party leaders in a studio in turn, occasionally putting them on the spot, wriggling for a convincing reply. That was 'terrific television', a producer said the next day, in contrast to many of our professional interviews, which are just 'repetitive and go on and on without getting anywhere'.

(3) The disproportionate three-day wonder of 'Jennifer's Ear', provoking comments like, 'This is the first time we have had a Grade A moving story' and 'This is the kind of day that lights our journalistic fires'.

Institutionalisation of complaining

A second potentially limiting influence in the newscasters' environment was the frequency with which party representatives telephoned programme editors directly, commenting on or complaining about how a bulletin had presented the election news. This was already almost a built-in systemic feature of British campaign communication in 1987;[18] by 1992 it had developed yet further.

A reason why this can happen in the British system is that senior BBC executives regard it as legitimate. As one told us, 'We don't want to convey the impression that if people complain, it's pressure and shouldn't happen.' Some new wrinkles introduced into the process in 1992 included, for example: making a complaint after the 6 pm news in the hope of inducing some change in the 9 pm bulletin; drawing attention to some weakness in something just advanced by another party and offering to provide a high-level speaker for an item on it; and sending a round-robin letter to all programme editors, warning them to be careful about being taken in by some tactic that a rival party was expected to try out. Some of the party comments we were told about were so detailed that the phrase, 'backstop editing', occurred to us to characterise the role being assumed, as if politicians were casting themselves as makers of superior new judgements.[19]

Complaints from the Conservative Party in particular might have had an intimidating ring, because the Home Secretary had said shortly before the campaign opened that the future of the BBC could depend on how properly it behaved during it. It is impossible to determine whether such threats had any influence, particularly since, in contrast to the aggrieved and depressed response of the 1987 team to party complaining, the typical reaction in 1992 seemed more one of resigned acceptance of it as an entrenched part of the election game. As a recent recruit to BBC journalism explained:

You go through a process of brutalisation in arguments with the Conservatives and with Labour. At first you lost sleep over it. But when it happened again, and again, and again, you realised that this is politics and not the end of the world.

Nevertheless, two individuals with whom we raised the prospect of intimidatory self-censorship were *not* prepared to deny any such effect. In the words of one:

Such a veiled threat is in the back of your mind. You hope it won't influence you. But you can't put your hand on your heart and say that it has never influenced you. You know how closely they are watching. You know how much pressure there is on you to be fair. So you think four times: should we lead on Labour tonight?

Taking objectivity to an extreme?

At times we were inclined to apply this label to the third type of limitation we noticed, internally imposed of course. This is the principle that nothing the BBC does should be construable as having tended to influence a significant partisan outcome. For example:

> A specialist correspondent said that if she unearthed a 'shock-horror scandal' in a public service, she would hold the story until it had appeared somewhere else;
> An executive criticised a news bulletin for having presented a heated press conference exchange as 'a disaster for the government', adding

'We have got to take a low-spin approach for preference to an event like that';

An executive cautioned that, when controversy erupts over economic statistics, editors should 'check with the Business Unit, think three times and don't go unattributed', but instead say 'one party is using the figures this way and the other that way';

Care was sometimes counselled over the language of stories so they did not appear to support one side's perception of a controversy.

But two sets of dramatic opinion poll results – earlier in the campaign and again in the penultimate week – suggesting that Labour was opening up a sizeable voting intention lead, provoked exceptional tumult on this objectivity front. Whereas many members of the team wished to give them full attention in part I of the programme (not to do so would make the BBC seem as if it had 'its head in the sand', one commented), this would have flouted the Corporation's guidelines (which were known to the parties). The 1987 election night poll debacle was still etched in some minds, and there was much querying (some of it flippant) over when a clutch of results could be regarded as forming a trend. After references up a long chain of executive command, it was eventually decided that the poll news should not be mentioned in the bulletin's opening headlines, could be mentioned briefly in the newsreader's follow-up intro-duction to part I but would otherwise be relegated as a formed story to part III. A justification for drawing such a fine line was that a headlined mention 'would put the whole weight of the BBC behind it'.

Fairness run wild?

This is a possible label for the fourth constraint on BBC election newsmakers. The point is that, in addition to its statutory obligations, the BBC has always prided itself on its voluntary fidelity to the principle of fairness when covering party affairs, particularly during election campaigns. By 1992, however, the scope of this principle had seemingly been extended to a remarkably broad range of news treatment of the opposing parties. According to our notes, this now covered a daunting list:

The amount of time given in bulletins to recorded extracts of politicians' campaign statements (though not necessarily so closely stopwatched as in previous elections);

Place in the running order, especially frequency of leading the bulletin;

Balancing occasions when much more time is given to one party leader than another;

Week-by week scheduling of leader interviews in programmes;

Reporting of second-string politician speeches;

Live reporting from press conferences;

'Equivalence of tone' in leader trail reports;

Similarity of placement of favourable opinion poll results in the bulletin (i.e., reporting a restored Conservative lead in the same headlines–introduction–part III pattern as previously for Labour, on the ground that 'We must be sensitive to a legitimate charge that we're not giving the same prominence to some possible Tory fightback as we did to Labour's lead last night');

Coverage of particularly newsworthy constituency candidates;

Complementarity in the framing by specialist correspondents of concluding assessments on some contested issue.

As one reporter put this last point, 'The need for balance in the specialist packages ... is very different at election time and sometimes very frustrating. You always have to end up your piece with an anodyne thought.' All this explains why one of us remarked to a senior executive during the campaign that BBC election coverage seemed to have become ever more rule-related in recent years – to which he agreed, only quibbling over 'rule-related', preferring 'guideline-related' instead.

Taking account of the combined impact of the last three limiting factors – non-stop party complaining, objectivity to an extreme, and fairness run wild – it seemed to us that BBC news producers were continually being encouraged to err on the side of caution. 'It's important not to put a foot wrong', an executive advised editors on the morning of the row over 'Jennifer's Ear'. Many on the receiving end of such guidance seemed to agree both that prudence was a 1992 watchword in the Corporation and that this was an advisable policy: 'I suppose we're a bit too safe, but it's as well to play it that way.' 'Of course we're likely to be regarded as rather cool in approach and style; but that's no bad thing.' 'If this policy leads to accusations of being not daring and adventurous enough, so be it.' Or, as a senior executive summed up, 'The thing I say to all our people is that you are the most powerful source of information for most people, and you must expect this sort of thing. *But don't make mistakes that could give the critics ammunition.*'

Role of the audience

A final limitation on the 1992 coverage concerns the shadowy role that the audience seemed to play in it. Normatively, it was supposedly paramount, the ultimate source and beneficiary of public service, several of our informants said. 'It all comes down to what we do for the viewer and listener', John Birt himself told one of us: 'If that is not our object and approach, it all loses point.' But the audience's needs and likely reactions tended to be assumed and taken for granted, reflecting perhaps the ease with which a rather Platonic (i.e., idealised) notion of the audience can be incorporated into the ethos of public service provision. In other words, the audience was more of a concept than a real force. For one thing, it rarely entered into the editorial discussion we observed and overheard. Admittedly, it sometimes entered for reassurance – as on the occasions when tolerably favourable viewing figures and broad-gauge comparative assessments with ITV coverage were received and circulated throughout the team. But comprehension, received meanings and potentials for involvement were relatively neglected criteria of audience reception of the coverage.

In mitigation, it may be said that a shadowy role for the audience is a common feature of many of the mass media production situations that scholars have studied (including our own past observations at the BBC).[20] Bringing the audience in as a real force is also inherently difficult, because of its multiplicity of needs and diverse ways of tuning into political affairs. In 1992, however, the problem at the BBC may have been exacerbated by two more specific features of the campaign coverage, noticed by some informants themselves. One was a technological factor mentioned by a more critically minded producer – the insulating influence of editors' and journalists' dependence on newsroom computers:

We're all linked nowadays to computers, and we can tell the story without moving out of the room – just by logging on. If something doesn't exist in our computers, it hasn't happened. The outside world has to come to us through the computer ... The issues we decide are important from day to day may well be isolated [therefore] from the issues that are important 'out there' ... There is so much on the computer that you can't keep track of it all, so you try to fit it into your agenda. [But] we could well be insulated from groundswells centring on different agendas of concern.

Another factor, rooted in the inter-institutional web of mutual dependencies among politicians and journalists, was mentioned by a producer after the election, when discussing the failure to detect the late-campaign opinion shift to the Conservatives. Relating this to 'the lack of an authentic ears-to-the-ground dimension to our coverage', he added:

We were in no position with our dispositions to understand what was moving voters. We were almost entirely focused on the press conferences, the leaders on the trail, reporting how the campaign was going, as if it were primarily a media-party based affair.

The producers take stock

We were impressed with the post-mortem review meeting we attended, which showed the team in a somewhat different light from how they had appeared during the campaign. Although pride in certain achievements occasionally came to the fore, a note of professional self-satisfaction (often ascribed to television journalists by outsiders, including ourselves) rarely surfaced. Instead, a range of important coverage issues was aired in terms that demonstrated how much the participants had thought and cared about them. Some of the points of concern were more fundamental than we had expected in advance, and speakers did not hesitate to propose different ways of conceiving and implementing their roles 'next time'. Debate was lively, and divergent views were expressed, although without heat, reflecting individual differences of emphasis rather than factional positions. If there was a hint of underlying structure to the differences, it may have been between *utopians* and *realists* – with the former presuming that coverage another time could be significantly different in certain respects from 1992, especially the assertion that broadcasters could make a more independent contribution, and the latter occasionally drawing attention to reasons why certain features were likely to abide.

Since the main object of the meeting was 'to identify some of the problems that we might like to address later more systematically' (Director of News and Current Affairs, chairing), no conclusions were reached. To convey something of the character of the occasion, we set out below the main issues addressed under five headings, illustrated with a few things that were said about each of them:

Commitments to campaign trail assignments and reports
Did we get full value out of the leader teams?

Correspondents assigned to the leaders are not really in a position to question searchingly what is happening there. Do we need our 'big hitters' to be there all the time?

We are still too soft with photo–opportunities, which can mislead viewers.

We should get away from a coverage pattern of a fifteenth shot of John Major saying nothing and a fifteenth shot of Neil Kinnock saying nothing.

We should think of using people like Polly Toynbee and John Simpson more as free thinkers and as correspondents who can look at whatever part of the campaign seems significant to them.

We should consider carrying the morning press conferences live, showing the press reacting to the country's main politicians, from which a different quality of information can emerge.

Lack of attention to popular reactions (relative to coverage of other voices)
That's the number one question: how can we plan next time so as to stand a better chance to gauge the popular verdict?

Absent from the coverage was a feeling for what was happening in the field. We must get away from programming based entirely on politicians.

There was too much of us at press conferences – almost interviewing each other.

The final-night leader interviews were wrong in news terms. Too many had already been aired.

Getting closer to the ground is the key for news.

Agenda-setting
We should swing more solidly behind the issues and do more of our own agenda-setting.

We should interpose ourselves more rather than less.

We have the strength to set the parties' agenda. If we say we are going to focus on health, they will follow suit.

Range of coverage

We hardly covered anything other than the two issues each that Labour and the Conservatives believed were theirs. We strayed out of this a bit with the Election Briefings but not enough.

On the range of issues, by the end of the campaign we had got there in the sense of having dealt with most of the important ones. Nevertheless, something on Europe at the tail end of the campaign is not enough, and one package on the environment is not enough for a four-week campaign.

We didn't get into the spread of personalities nearly enough. Was it right to treat the Liberal Democrats as a one-man band or not?

Many Liberal Democrat policies escaped our scrutiny.

Other matters

Perhaps we should aim for a marginally shorter coverage next time.

Though the *Nine* was terrific, it was sometimes very predictable. I missed the occasional showing of an incisive single interview, something that would take an issue or an event and mount a killer interview with somebody crucially involved in it.

The constructed balance in some of the reports seemed artificial.

The 5:5:4 balance was particularly difficult this time. I had to drop two or three good sequences due to that. The weight of obligations on us are a bar to adventure and to doing more interesting things.

Various explanations for the searching spirit of this occasion may be suggested.

For one thing, since the daily pressures and constraints of the campaign period no longer applied, members of the team could think more freely about their election roles. For another, the journalists' professional ideology, often suppressed during the election, had reasserted itself – as if 'disdaining' their own campaign-period behaviour. Thirdly, it was an organisationally useful safety-value occasion. And finally, the exercise was a genuine attempt to consider and find ways of providing a more significantly independent and worthwhile pattern of coverage at the next general election in circumstances that would, as always, be full of difficulties and dilemmas.

However applicable the first three interpretations, the last function of the meeting should not be cynically dismissed. Even from the United States there are signs that media organisations, reacting to external and internal criticisms of their reporting in the 1988 Presidential election, have become 'self-conscious about [their] past performance' and determined to 'do something about it'.[21] In Britain too, thoughtful journalists, committed to public service, aware of threats to the integrity of civic communication, and dissatisfied with disparities between their professional identities and their election roles, could become significant elements in the 'constituency for the reform of democratic political communication that seems to be [gradually] emerging'.[22]

The observers take stock

Electoral competition waged by highly professionalised political parties can have a deadening effect on the process of campaign communication – coming close to delegitimating it if American experience of the 1980s is any guide. If so, only journalistic enterprise stands some chance of retrieving or improving the situation, from which standpoint the more buttoned-up and prudential side of the BBC's approach to the last election is troubling.

In 1992 its journalists managed to be serious, dedicated, conscientious, responsible *and* cautious. There is much to admire in this model – and to build on (in the spirit of the post-mortem review described above). The election contest is not just reduced to a horse race or an elaborate game: seeds of trivialisation cannot germinate in its soil. Whatever the imperfections, it resists cynicism about the democratic ideal of an informed electorate served by responsible political communication. Public-service traditions and the determination of the BBC to be a serious public-service broadcaster may have helped to ensure that the 1992 campaign was still a relatively substantive one – even 'a remarkably numerical one' (as one informant pointed out, thinking of its recurrent focus on financial and social statistics). But in the long run such a combination of qualities may not be sustainable: without a stronger pulse of satisfying vigour and freedom in support, dedication may eventually wither. In any case, if public-service broadcasting is to flourish in the more taxing and competitive period that is imminent, it must above all be enterprising and sufficiently confident of its own place in the civic order to *be* enterprising.

Or should the terms of electoral choice be left entirely with the competing parties? Do enterprising journalists have a responsibility to go beyond what W. Lance Bennett terms 'indexing official voices' on the issues of the day if this yields a severely narrowed agenda of debate? Bennett considers that journalistic intervention is warranted only when the official debate excludes or marginalizes stable majority opinion in a society.[23] But, as a BBC editor pointed out when discussing this question with the first author, 'if there had been a burning but neglected issue out there in the electorate, one way or another it would probably have forced its way onto the agenda'. It nevertheless seems to us that there are three other valid justifications for independent contributions to civic agendas by journalists.

One stems from the original agenda-setting concept in the literature, namely the assumption that media agendas tend to shape the public's priorities, with some members of the electorate treating them as signs of which issues are most important for government attention, assessment of leaders and their own political awareness.[24] The concept thus implies that, since the media are necessarily involved in the campaign and cannot claim an outsider's position, they might as well assume a more considered contributory role. It follows that if journalists realise that certain important issues facing the future of the country are not being ventilated, they have some responsibility to draw attention to them. Another ground for such action is the fact that at the outset of a campaign the parties do advance a wide range of policy commitments in their manifestos, which they will feel entitled to carry out if elected. Those among them that are controversial should not escape attention, therefore, even if, for their own reasons, none of the parties is pushing them to the fore. The fate of the Community Charge – inscribed in the Conservatives' 1987 manifesto, rarely discussed in the campaign of that year, but fiercely controversial after its introduction – is an object lesson.[25] And a third justification for journalistic efforts to broaden campaign agendas springs from whatever value one places on diversity in civic affairs – in the range of issues drawn to people's notice as in other things.

The legitimacy of enterprising journalism, like the legitimacy of public-service broadcasting, ultimately must depend, however, on its relationship to the audience, the shadowy character of which in the 1992 campaign is another worrying sign for the future. An interviewed executive seemed to sense this when concluding from the spate of party complaints directed at the BBC, 'That is why we need to measure the audience's response to our coverage throughout, for otherwise almost all the response we get is partisan.' But in the new phase that public-service broadcasting is entering, such 'measurement' needs to move much closer to what viewers and listeners are striving to get out of programming, how they receive its informing efforts, and especially what it does and does not add to their understanding, than has yet been ventured by any major television service in the world. Followers of the 'Birtian model' in particular need to check how far the 'value added' to election stories has been successfully communicated to news audiences.[26]

Most serious for the future civic role of public-service broadcasting, however, is our impression that applications of the norms of fairness and objectivity were unduly restrictive. That judgement was challenged by leading members of the BBC team in exchanges over a previous draft of this report. They maintained that their independence had not been subjugated (said one, 'Through thick and thin, BBC journalists ... set out neither to appease nor to provoke, but to do their very best to broadcast what was journalistically right'). Their stance reflected considered principles of election journalism, they claimed – as in the following view:

It is in the nature of democracy that it is the voters (and only the voters) who should decide who's right and who's wrong in a political argument ... The BBC must at all times avoid making subjective political judgements, directly or by implication, *not* because of constraints imposed externally or internally, but because it is journalistically proper so to do.

The curbs on opinion poll reporting had been vindicated by the final election result, they pointed out, and in a 'many-headed monster like the BBC', central control was justifiable (according to one informant) because 'it was essential . . . that the BBC spoke with one voice'.

Although much of this response is understandable (except perhaps for the rejection of pluralism implicit in the last comment), it fails to address our central concern. It was not cravenness that troubled us so much as the one-sided inculcation of a culture of responsible carefulness, little leavened by corresponding supports for boldness. Of course a commitment to impartiality is critical for television and must remain so in a society with a partisan national press that often blatantly violates it. But in 1992 at the BBC, it was impossible to escape the impression of valid standards being pursued in an unbalanced way at the expense of other valid norms, notably freedom of expression itself. When broadcasters feel so closely bound to the terms of party debate, their scope to advance it will inevitably be severely limited. That conflicts with viewers' concerns, often elicited in research, for a fair but vigorous televised source of political news that will stand up for their interests without pulling punches.[27] Even broadcasters' credibility may be at risk, the more plausibly their coverage can be depicted as predominantly collusive.

Although this is not the place to propose solutions to these issues, we suspect that they may have to be sought in fresh approaches to broadcasting regulation. A nub of the present problem may be the excessively detailed burden of self-regulation, even self-censorship, that has fallen on broadcasters to toe the line of fairness and objectivity on even the minutiae of political coverage. Perhaps the debate over renewal of the BBC Charter should focus on how best to achieve two conditions in the multi-channel future: more scope for broad-caster freedom and enterprise within a continuing overall commitment to political impartiality; and conferral of the prime responsibility for policing impartiality on some external body, charged both with adjudicating complaints of serious violations of fairness and with monitoring its realisation.

Notes

1 Holli A. Semetko, Jay G. Blumler, Michael Gurevitch and David H. Weaver, *The Formation of Campaign Agendas: A Comparative Analysis of Party and Media Roles in Recent American and British Elections* (Hillsdale, NJ: Lawrence Erlbaum Associates, 1991), p. 176.

2 Typical specimens of recently expressed concern may be found in: Jeffrey Abramson, 'The new media and the new politics', *Annual Review of Communications and Society* (1990), 1–31; Jay G. Blumler, 'Elections, the media and the modern publicity process', in Marjorie Ferguson (ed.), *Public Communication: The New Imperatives* (London, Newbury Park and New Delhi: Sage, 1990), pp. 104–25; Bruce Buchanan, *Electing a President: The Markle Commission Research on Campaign '88* (Austin: University of Texas Press, 1991); Robert M. Entman, *Democracy*

without Citizens: The Decay of American Politics (New York and Oxford: Oxford University Press, 1989); L. L. Kaid, J. Gerstle and K. R. Sanders, *Mediated Politics in Two Cultures: Presidential Campaigning in the United States and France* (New York: Praeger, 1992); Douglas Kellner, *Television and the Crisis of Democracy* (Boulder, CO: Westview Press, 1990); Semetko *et al.*, *The Formation of Campaign Agendas*; and David L. Swanson, 'The political media complex', *Communication Monographs*, 59 (1992), 397–400.

3 Doris A. Graber, *News and Democracy: Are Their Paths Diverging?* (Bloomington, IN: School of Journalism, Indiana University, 1992), p. 25.

4 Reports of our previous election attachments at the BBC appeared in: Jay G. Blumler, 'Producers' attitudes towards television coverage of an election campaign: a case study', in Paul Halmos (ed.), *The Sociology of Mass-Media Communicators* (Keele: The University of Keele, 1969), pp. 85–115; Michael Gurevitch and Jay G. Blumler, 'The construction of election news: an observation study at the BBC', in James S. Ettema and D. Charles Whitney (eds.), *Individuals in Mass Media Organizations: Creativity and Constraint* (Beverly Hills and London: Sage, 1982), pp. 179–204; Jay G. Blumler, Michael Gurevitch and T. J. Nossiter, 'Setting the television news agenda: campaign observation at the BBC', in Ivor Crewe and Martin Harrop (eds.), *Political Communications: The General Election Campaign of 1983* (Cambridge: Cambridge University Press, 1986), pp. 104–24; and Jay G. Blumler, Michael Gurevitch and T. J. Nossiter, 'The earnest versus the determined: election newsmaking at the BBC, 1987', in Ivor Crewe and Martin Harrop (eds.), *Political Communications: The General Election Campaign of 1987* (Cambridge: Cambridge University Press, 1989), pp. 157–74.

5 Readers should bear in mind the precise scope of our study – news-and-elections – when considering what we have to say about this; we are in no position to evaluate Mr Birt's views on the organisation and social role of the BBC more broadly.

6 We are most grateful to all concerned for their informative and thoughtful responses to our numerous questions and for admission to their counsels in the strenuous and demanding circumstances of an election campaign. We are also indebted to four leading members of the team for their reactions, in writing and personal discussions, to a previous draft of this report.

7 Blumler, Gurevitch and Nossiter, 'Setting the television news agenda', pp. 108–10.

8 Jay G. Blumler, 'Television and politics; the British public service model', paper prepared for an Aspen Institute Conference on Television Coverage and Campaigns, Wye Woods, Maryland, November 1990, p. 11.

9 *Newsnight*, however, was allowed to take voting intention readings in connection with polls commissioned to track the electorate's responses to campaign issues.

10 See the chapter by Holli A. Semetko, T. J. Nossiter and Margaret Scammell in this volume, pp. 85–103.

11 For details of the findings, see BBC Broadcasting Research, *Reactions to 1992 General Election Coverage* (London, 1992), SP 92/33/230.

12 Discussion of more concerted party efforts to orchestrate and manage the 1992 campaign may be found in David Butler and Dennis Kavanagh, *The British General Election of 1992* (Basingstoke and London: Macmillan, 1992), p. 77; Dennis Kavanagh, 'Private opinion polls and campaign strategy', *Parliamentary Affairs*, 45 (1992), 518–27: p. 518; and Sebastian Barry, 'Party strategy and the media: Labour's 1992 election campaign', *Parliamentary Affairs*, 45 (1992), 564–81: p. 565.

13 The theme was developed in a Channel 4 special during the campaign as well.
14 See Jay G. Blumler and Michael Gurevitch, 'The election agenda-setting roles of television journalists: comparative observation at the BBC and NBC', in Semetko *et al.*, *The Formation of Campaign Agendas*, pp. 33–61.
15 Jacques Gerstle, Dennis K. Davis and Olivier Duhamel, 'Television news and the construction of political reality in France and the United States', in Kaid *et al.*, *Mediated Politics in Two Cultures*, pp. 119–43: p. 139.
16 A searching critique of 'unmasking' forms of commentary in the 1992 election reports of both ITN and BBC News may be found in Michael Billig, David Deacon, Peter Golding and Sue Middleton, 'In the hands of the spin-doctors: television politics and the 1992 general election', in Nod Miller (ed.), *It's Live . . . But Is It Real?* (Sevenoaks: Edward Arnold, forthcoming).
17 See also the chapter by Dennis Kavanagh and Brian Gosschalk in this volume, pp. 160–74.
18 Blumler, Gurevitch and Nossiter, 'The earnest versus the determined', pp. 165–7.
19 See also the chapter by Richard Tait in this volume.
20 See, for example, Blumler, Gurevitch and Nossiter, 'The earnest versus the determined', pp. 172–3.
21 The Freedom Forum Media Studies Center, *Covering the Presidential Primaries* (New York: Columbia University, 1992), p. 11.
22 Semetko *et al.*, *The Formation of Campaign Agendas*, p. 186.
23 W. Lance Bennett, 'Towards a theory of press–state relations in the United States', *Journal of Communication*, 40 (1990), 103–25.
24 Maxwell E. McCombs and Donald L. Shaw, 'The agenda-setting function of the mass media', *Public Opinion Quarterly*, 36 (1972), 176–87.
25 Martin Harrison makes a similar point about the striking absence of the Maastricht treaty and the future of Britain's relationship to the European Community from broadcast news of the parties' 1992 campaigns. See 'Politics on the Air', in Butler and Kavanagh, *The British General Election of 1992*, pp. 155–79: p. 165.
26 For such insight, qualitative enquiry must supplement the traditional quantitative approaches of in-house broadcasting research. Discussion of recent relevant developments in audience reception analyses undertaken by academic scholars can be found in John Corner, 'Meaning, genre and context: the problematics of "public knowledge" in the new audience studies', in James Curran and Michael Gurevitch (eds.), *Mass Media and Society* (Sevenoaks: Edward Arnold, 1991), pp. 267–84 and in Sonia M. Livingstone, 'Audience reception: the role of the viewer in retelling romantic drama', in Curran and Gurevitch (eds.), *Mass Media and Society*, pp. 285–306.
27 See David E. Morrison, *Conversations with Voters: The 1992 General Election*, A Report to the BBC and ITC on the General Election 1992 (Leeds: Institute of Communications Studies, 1992), pp. 44–56.

9   Old values versus news values: the British 1992 general election campaign on television

T. J. Nossiter, Margaret Scammell, Holli A. Semetko

Introduction: public service broadcasting on trial

After the battering of the Thatcher years, the 1992 general election presented broadcasting's no-longer-comfortable duopoly with its most challenging campaign since commercial television made its electoral debut in 1959. The ITV network and the BBC have never prepared for an election less assured of the future and under such pressure to control costs.

The Thatcher era saw fundamental changes in the broadcasting system – with the Peacock Committee's inquiry into the future of BBC funding in 1986, the 1990 Broadcasting Act with its much-criticised 'blind auction' for Channel 3 licences, and the growth of satellite and cable TV. The BBC seemed more than usually vulnerable: its Royal Charter was up for renewal in 1996 and the future of its licence fee was not yet settled. The ITV network faced unprecedented pressures to prune costs and emphasise ratings amid the financial strains of the licence bids, the deepening recession and the additional squeeze on advertising revenue from the growth of satellite and cable.[1] Competition for viewers was intensified further by the late 1980s boom in video recorder ownership; 72 per cent of all television viewers had a VCR in 1991 compared with just 55 per cent in 1987.[2]

In the year before the election, ITN reduced its staff by more than 20 per cent in order to trim costs, and there have been further cuts since. The cuts were one of a number of signals which prompted concern that the new forces of deregulation and tougher competition might adversely affect the range and quality of political programming on the mainstream channels.[3]

At the heart of these concerns was the threat to the future of Britain's distinctive tradition of public-service broadcasting (PSB). The concept of PSB is rooted as much in culture and convention as statute and, until the 1990 Broadcasting Act, had been shared by the BBC and ITV alike. Its significance for general election coverage is put into sharpest relief by contrast to the totally free market situation of the United States. American network news is driven far more by ratings and less by abstract notions of public interest, a distinction which has clear effects in practice.[4] US election news focuses more on the 'horse race' and less on the substantive issues.[5] It is more dominated by personalities, partly because of the Presidential system, but also because broadcasters believe candidates' personal qualities are more digestible fare than

policy and issue analysis. Crucially, news values, rather than broader considerations of public interest, largely determine editorial selection.

In marked contrast, Britain's PSB rules demand fair and 'balanced' coverage
of the main parties. 'Balance' at election times has been interpreted in a
uniquely rigid way which has tempered the usual considerations of news-
worthiness. By convention, the stopwatch provided a vital statistic of balance;
newstime devoted to each of the major parties was rationed according to the
allocation of party election broadcasts (PEBs), which in 1992 was 5:5:4 (Con-
servatives:Labour:Liberal Democrats). Broadcasters and parties carefully
monitor the amount of airtime given to each party in each programme, a
process known as 'stopwatching' or the 'tot'.

Normal, non-election news values can be superseded as television news
prudently pursues second-for-second balance; party activities with limited
news value might well run in bulletins primarily to satisfy the stopwatch. The
tot, unloved by broadcasters and criticised by academics, is clearly an unwieldy
and rather artificial conception of balance. Equally clearly, if it were jettisoned
completely, parties would face a tougher battle to influence the media agenda.

This is no small matter for those who rely on television for fair coverage; in
April 1992 six of the eleven national daily papers supported the Conservatives
(with a combined circulation of 8.7 million), three backed Labour (3.6 million)
and none supported the Liberal Democrats.[6] The minor parties have most to
lose if 'stopwatch balance' were shoved aside by editorial selection driven
purely by news values. Not surprisingly, therefore, the Liberal Democrats have
been the most ardent advocates of the stopwatch.[7] An early indication that the
new competitive pressures might, indeed, be prodding Britain down the
American route came in mid-1991 when ITN announced that it would not
'stopwatch' its election news coverage; news-worthiness alone would determine its bulletins.

This chapter explores how television treated the 1992 election. What were
the main subjects of election news on the main news programmes? Did
coverage of the issues remain prominent or did opinion polls and the 'horse
race' predominate with reporters scarcely able to contain their excitement at
the closest race since 1974? How far did the party leaders dominate the news
screens? What factors in the production process help to explain the content of
election news on television?

Our primary source of data is content analysis of the flagship evening news
programmes on BBC1 and ITV, that is, the BBC *Nine O'Clock News*
(6.2 million viewers on average during the campaign) and ITN's *News at Ten*
(6.3 million). We use these data to identify the patterns in news coverage for
each week of the campaign.[8] The subjects of television news stories and the
main political actors are compared with similar studies of television coverage
of the 1987 and 1983 general election campaigns to determine whether the
campaign information environment has changed in any important ways.[9]

Our second data source comes from observation of and interviews with television newspeople at ITN and *Channel 4 News*.[10] We believe this to be the first election observation study of the flagship commercial news programmes, which is precisely where effects of media market changes and increased competition were most likely to show, if they were to show anywhere. Although ITN and *Channel 4 News* were formally separate with their own correspondents and production crews in 1992, the programme-makers were housed in the same building, consulting one another over the course of the news day and often sharing film. The ITN/Channel 4 observation and interviews had three aims: to identify the constraints under which broadcasters in these flagship commercial news organisations worked to produce election news; to identify the factors which helped to shape election news content; and to illuminate commercial broadcasters' understanding of their roles and overall programme goals at election time.

The more competitive battle for audiences did not result in a lessening of election 'overkill' on television. All told, there were more than 300 hours of political programming on the four main terrestrial channels, including news bulletins, political discussion and current affairs programmes, over the four-week period – much the same as 1983 and 1987. The BBC continued with its normal practice of extending the *Nine O'Clock News* by about fifteen minutes throughout the campaign. ITN was not free to bargain for such a lengthy addition, mainly due to its need to air commercials, but *News at Ten* was offered a two-minute extension on request and this was taken up more than 70 per cent of the time. In short, if someone visiting Britain turned on the television set during March and early April, it would have been almost impossible to have avoided the election campaign. Indeed, a MORI poll shows that most viewers (78 per cent) found the coverage 'too much', up from 71 per cent in 1987 and 50 per cent in 1983.[11] Audiences for both the ITN and BBC main evening news dipped over the course of the campaign.

Subjects in campaign news

Opinion polls and the horse race dominated the campaign, accounting for 23.9 per cent of news stories overall and fully 31.6 per cent of *News at Ten* stories. The emphasis on the polls and speculation about the result intensified on both channels as the campaign moved into weeks three and four. Again the trend shows spectacularly on ITN with 38.5 per cent and 46.2 per cent in weeks three and four respectively. Table 9.1 presents the main subjects of election news stories, for each week of the campaign, beginning on 16 March, the week in which the parties launched their manifestos.

The economy was the second most prominent subject and the main substantive issue of the campaign, taking 17.8 per cent of stories overall, and rather more on the BBC than on *News at Ten* (19.5 per cent compared to 15.4 per cent). The economy was the single most important issue during the first week of the campaign-proper, beginning with the launch of the Liberal Democrats'

Table 9.1. *Main subjects in BBC (9 pm) and ITN (10 pm) election news stories week-by-week: British 1992 general election campaign*

Subjects	Week 1 BBC %	Week 1 ITN %	Week 2 BBC %	Week 2 ITN %	Week 3 BBC %	Week 3 ITN %	Week 4* BBC %	Week 4* ITN %	Overall BBC %	Overall ITN %	Overall total %
Economy	24.6	29.7	18.0	14.7	18.6	10.3	13.9	3.8	19.5	15.4	17.8
Social welfare	6.6	0.0	30.0	32.3	16.3	5.1	5.6	3.8	14.7	10.3	12.5
'Jennifer's Ear'	–	–	(18.0)	(17.6)	–	–	–	–	(4.7)	(4.4)	(4.6)
Polls/horse race	13.1	24.3	16.0	20.6	20.9	38.5	27.8	46.2	18.4	31.6	23.9
Party leaders	11.5	8.1	10.0	5.9	4.7	0.0	2.8	0.0	7.9	3.7	6.1
Constitutional reform/PR	6.6	10.8	14.0	8.8	23.3	20.6	22.2	11.5	15.3	13.3	14.5
Conduct of campaign	4.9	13.5	8.0	14.7	9.3	20.5	11.1	11.5	7.9	15.4	11.0
Defence	0.0	0.0	2.0	0.0	2.3	0.0	0.0	3.8	1.1	0.7	0.9
Energy/environment	3.3	2.7	0.0	0.0	0.0	0.0	2.8	3.8	1.6	1.5	1.6
Other*	29.6	10.8	2.0	2.9	4.6	5.1	13.9	15.3	13.8	8.0	11.4
Total	100	100	100	100	100	100	100	100	100	100	100
N (stories)	(61)	(37)	(50)	(34)	(43)	(39)	(36)	(26)	(190)	(136)	(326)

* Other includes the manifestoes, foreign affairs and Europe.

manifesto on Monday, 16 March. This was also the day that Labour chose to present its Shadow Budget, an event unprecedented in previous elections. Labour's Budget dominated the coverage on Monday – it took the first nineteen minutes of the *Nine O'Clock News* – to the dismay of the Liberals whose manifesto played second fiddle – and the Shadow Budget remained prominent for the rest of the week.

During this week, a great number of stories concerned the details of the parties' manifestos. This was particularly marked in the BBC coverage, accounting for 26.2 per cent of first week stories, compared to 10.8 per cent on ITN.

The polls and the economy were topped during week two by social welfare issues, particularly health and the fate of the National Health Service (NHS), triggered by Labour's controversial 'Jennifer's Ear' party election broadcast PEB (Monday, 23 March). Over the course of this week, the ensuing 'War of Jennifer's Ear' accounted for about 18 per cent of stories on both main evening news programmes and helped push social welfare issues into the most prominent position for the only time during the campaign. However, the news focused heavily on the *ethics*, *style* and *sources* of Labour's PEB rather than the actual party policy differences on health. Table 9.1 shows the sizeable chunk of the social welfare coverage taken by 'Jennifer's Ear', close to half of all ITN's social welfare coverage and about a third of the BBC's.

During weeks three and four, the focus of debate shifted to questions about the possible consequences of the election outcome. The polls showed that the main parties were still running neck-and-neck and speculation about the result and the prospect of a hung parliament dominated the media agenda. Issues of constitutional reform and proportional representation were discussed in this context, and accounted for some 23 per cent of BBC stories during weeks three and four, and 20.6 per cent (week three) and 11.5 per cent (week four) on *News at Ten*.

There were some notable differences between the coverage of BBC and ITN in the main subjects of election news stories and these are presented in figure 9.1.

The polls and the horse race took a much higher proportion of ITN election news stories than on the BBC, partly perhaps of John Birt's (the BBC Director General-designate) strictures that *Nine O'Clock News* should avoid emphasis on polls at the top of news broadcasts. The *Nine O'Clock News* never once made polls its first headline. By contrast, *News at Ten* reported the poll results prominently, commissioned polls of its own, and headlined polls four times during the campaign.

In keeping with this, the conduct of the campaign – including campaign strategy, tactics, advertising and endorsements – was also featured far more prominently on ITN than the BBC (15.4 per cent compared to 7.9 per cent). Generally, ITN focused far more heavily on the polls and horse race and the dynamics of the campaign, while the BBC aired more stories about the substantive issues of the economy and health.

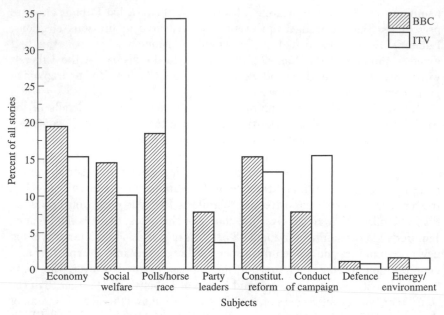

Figure 9.1   Subjects in election news stories. Overall total: BBC and ITN

The one exception to the general rule that ITN concentrated more on the electoral game is the focus on the party leaders, which accounted for more stories on the BBC (7.9 per cent) than on ITN (3.7 per cent). The relatively small ITN figure is surprising given ITN's election coverage strategy with its emphasis on the Target Teams who were to report nightly from the leaders' campaign trails (see below). However, many of the Target Team reports have been subsumed under the heading of 'conduct of the campaign'. Our category of 'party leaders' is narrowly defined as stories whose main subject was the personal and/or political qualities of a leader.

Focus on the leaders

A measure of the 'personalisation' of campaign news – the extent to which it focused on the party leaders – is obtained by looking at the political actors in campaign news stories. Table 9.2 presents the *main actors* in the news (up to four were counted for each story). Coverage of the campaign was highly leader-oriented, and the leaders themselves and their wives were the subjects of a number of stories on both channels. Of course, this partly reflects the parties' campaign strategies which were predicated on the promotion of their respective leaders; in the cases of the Conservatives and the Liberal particularly, their leaders were seen as the parties' strongest campaigning weapons.

Table 9.2. *Main political actors* over the whole campaign: BBC 'Nine O'Clock News' and ITN 'News at Ten'*

	BBC		ITN	
	Frequency	Percent	Frequency	Percent
Major	27	13.6	25	16.2
Kinnock	24	12.1	24	15.6
Ashdown	19	9.5	20	13.0
Other Conservative	28	14.0	21	13.6
Other Labour	33	16.6	14	9.1
Other Liberal Democrat	13	6.5	8	5.2
SNP	4	2.0	5	3.2
PLC	4	2.0	0	0.0
Other minor	12	6.0	8	5.2
Other**	35	17.6	29	18.8
Number of actors	199	100	154	100

Note: * Actors appearing in stories were logged and timed in order of appearance. This table is based on the first three actors in each story. Non-political actors (experts, media correspondents, public etc.) are not included.
** Other includes Mrs Thatcher, party supporters and activists, Mrs Major, Mrs Kinnock and Mrs Ashdown.

Judging by the appearances of the main political actors, ITN's stories were more leader-focused than the BBC; the leaders accounted for 24.5 per cent of the total on *News at Ten* compared to 18.6 on BBC.

Parties in the balance

Coverage of the leaders also offers an indication of the balance of the news. It can be seen from table 9.2 that the treatment of all three major party leaders was much the same on both *Nine O'Clock News* and *News at Ten*. Kinnock had slightly fewer appearances than Major or Ashdown on both channels, possibly reflecting Labour's strategy which, especially in the first week with the Shadow Budget, presented Kinnock as the leader of a team, rather than as an individual. Proportionately Ashdown fared rather better on ITN than the BBC, although he numbered fewer appearances. His apparently higher profile on ITN reflects *News at Ten*'s tendency to concentrate on the leaders rather more than the BBC, at the expense of less senior spokesmen.

A further measure of balance may be gleaned by examining the origin of the main subject of stories, to see which party generated more coverage (for

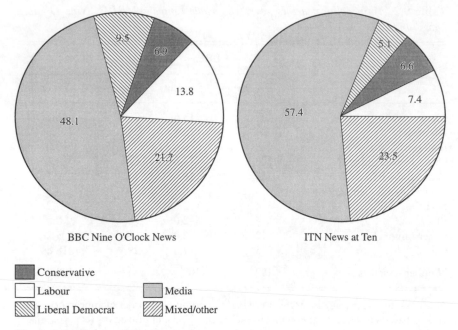

BBC Nine O'Clock News   ITN News at Ten

- ■ Conservative
- □ Labour   ▨ Media
- ▧ Liberal Democrat   ▨ Mixed/other

Figure 9.2   Origin of election stories

example, from press conferences, speeches, campaign trail).[12] By this standard ITN appears more balanced than the BBC, as figure 9.1 shows.

The BBC's story-initiation imbalance was striking, with the Conservatives initiating nearly twice as many stories as Labour. The BBC achieved a much closer balance when initiation of *all* subjects – as opposed to just the *main* subject – is taken into consideration. However, our findings reflect the BBC's tendency to lead on Conservative activities in nightly overview stories of the day's events. We can merely speculate on the reasons for this; possibly a manifestation of deference towards the party of government; possibly the Conservatives, on the brink of defeat, were inherently the better story. ITN, by contrast, tended to treat the parties' campaigns as three separate news items, and thus story-initiation balance was more easily assured.

A final point to note is the large chunk of the pie taken by media-generated stories (for example, opinion polls, interviews, expert analysis). Media-oriented stories took a bigger slice of *News at Ten* than the *Nine O'Clock News* (57.4 per cent compared to 48.1 per cent).

News content analysis: summing up

Figure 9.3 displays graphically the pattern of coverage over the course of the campaign. The key substantive issue – the economy – topped the news agenda

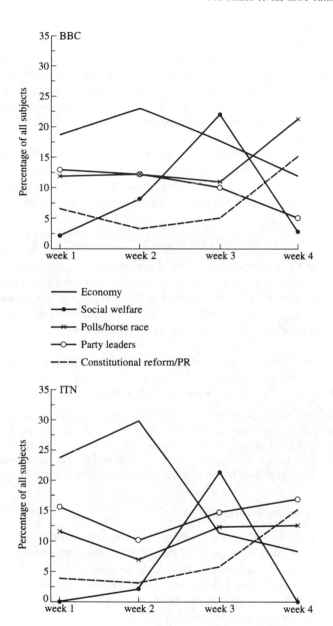

Figure 9.3   Subjects in election news stories week-by-week: BBC (9 pm) and ITN (10 pm) news

on both channels in the early part of the campaign, with social welfare displacing the economy for a time as the parties debated 'Jennifer's Ear'. On both news programmes, the issue of constitutional reform and proportional representation – often discussed in the context of the possibility of a hung parliament – increased as election day drew nearer, as did the coverage of the polls and the horse race, particularly on ITN. By the final part of the campaign then, the issues had become less important as the possibility of a hung parliament increased.

In sum, our content analysis of the main evening news on BBC and ITN shows that election coverage was largely dominated by the parties' positions in the horse race as depicted in the polls, by the economy and by the possibility of a hung parliament and the prospects for a deal on electoral reform.

Influences on campaign news content

Broadcasters at ITN approached the 1992 general election campaign troubled by financial difficulties and acutely aware of increasingly competitive pressures. One senior ITN management official expressed his concern that 'efforts to constrain costs could lead to the lowest common denominator in terms of programming and maybe (this is ITN's concern) news will also be affected'.

ITN did not, however, cut back on its coverage of the general election campaign and instead, reallocated internal resources to accommodate full coverage. One senior producer commented shortly after the election:

We had a separate campaign budget but much of it came from taking resources from elsewhere and putting them into the campaign. So, for example, we took our key foreign correspondents and put them on the campaign trail with the leaders ... We'd decided that the campaign was *the* story of the month and we put our resources into it ... Most of the time at least fifteen minutes of our broadcast was the campaign.

Maintaining audience interest

The need to hold the audience's attention was the key consideration for ITN news producers at the start of the 1992 campaign. Behind this was not only the fear of competition for audiences, but also an awareness that a 'phoney campaign' had been waged since January and had been the focus of a great deal of news coverage. Many viewers were likely to begin the intense 'campaign proper' period already somewhat tired of it all.

A senior editor expressed concern at maintaining viewer interest and described ITN's response to the problem: 'What we've set out to do, very determinedly, is to ensure that our coverage is comprehensive and infused with measured and relevant analysis and, on the other hand, to make sure our coverage is exciting and interesting.'

'Live' with the leaders

Specific efforts were made to inject fresh liveliness into election news. Technology provided one of the new approaches taken by ITN in 1992. At the start of the campaign, ITN went 'live' each evening to each of the Target Teams – the three correspondents assigned to follow the three main party leaders – for an assessment of the day's events. The process of going 'live' to the campaign trail was intended to provide a sense of excitement and anticipation. This also gave the reporters travelling with the party leaders a stronger personal presence in the news – they were charged with not only describing the key events of the day but also, and more importantly, assessing the state of each party leader's campaign.

Technology was not the only reason for the emphasis on the Target Team's field reports. Their focus – the party leaders – was especially important. The election was framed largely as a contest between three men, Major, Kinnock and Ashdown. Their personal lives with their wives and families were also the subjects of profile stories aired in the early part of the campaign. And their ability to lead their parties and the country featured in interview stories with each of the three leaders, broadcast later in the campaign. ITN, therefore, adopted a more 'personalised' view of the election campaign, giving more attention to the party leaders and their personal qualities than the BBC.[13]

The combination of live reporting and the nightly focus on the leaders' campaigns provoked some internal debate, however. By mid-campaign the decision was taken not to go live every evening. In the words of one senior producer:

I was not a fan of doing the live reports from the campaign trail with the party leaders. I thought our coverage was too presidential, but that was in part what the parties were planning and in part a function of where we'd decided to put our resources. Early on in the campaign we decided to rein back a bit on that and after that we didn't do many live reports with the reporters on the campaign trail.

The party leaders nevertheless featured more prominently in ITN's main evening news than the BBC's, as can be seen in table 9.1 above.

Channel 4 News also brought the party leaders in on more than one occasion for studio interviews. During the last three days of the campaign, each of the party leaders was interviewed by anchorman Jon Snow. Kinnock appeared on Monday, Ashdown on Tuesday and Major on Wednesday, the eve of the election.

The increasing emphasis on the party leaders in television news in 1992 cannot be reduced to the influence of party strategies and new production techniques. The 1992 campaign followed a decade in which leaders' personalities, especially that of Mrs Thatcher, dominated the political arena. It is also worth mentioning that the notion of presidentialism in British campaigns may not be entirely out of place. In comparison with the US President, the British prime minister, because of the parliamentary system, has considerably more power to put through his or her programme. It could be argued, therefore, that this is even more reason why the personalities of the British party leaders should be featured in the news.

How the voters (viewers) decide

ITN commissioned its own polls, conducted by Harris, during the campaign. The results were available on Tuesday evening and broadcast in the main evening news. The three cross-sectional nationally representative polls (each with $N = 2,000$) provided evidence of shifts in party support and the results featured as headline news each week, as did polls conducted by other media. But the main reason for commissioning the polls was to provide background on the different groups in the electorate and the factors influencing the voting decision. The polls were used in extended analytical reports during the campaign. One reporter who worked on ITN's polls commented in a post-election interview:

We commissioned the polls in order to answer the question *why* people were making up their minds in the way they did. During the first week of the campaign, we did a piece on the C2s and what the poll result meant for them. We focused on Cannock and Burntwood, a Tory marginal, which did go to Labour. The second week we looked at women's voting patterns using our poll and showed that they were not leaving the Tories as much as expected. And in the election result we saw the biggest gender gap in over 10 years. We'd used the polls during the campaign to provide information as to *why* people were voting the way they did or why the voting shifts were taking place and what factors were linked to it. We were not using the polls so much to show the horse race but to provide analysis.

The polls therefore provided another avenue for attracting and holding audience interest. They provided fresh evidence of shifts in support for the parties, which was reinforced by the many other polls published regularly by other media. But they also were central to reporting about the electorate – how voters (viewers) were reacting to the campaign and the party leaders. The question of who would make the best prime minister featured in ITN's reports on C2s and women voters, as well as in reporting on the election results programme.

Channel 4 News used a different approach to analyse voters' reactions. A group of one hundred undecided voters participated in a panel throughout the campaign to assess reactions to the parties' television PEBs. Focus groups of six to eight people later discussed what they liked and disliked about the broadcasts. These lengthy reports included clips from each of the three main parties' advertisements and were aired every Friday of the campaign. The focus groups were an innovative way of handling political advertisements in the news, without falling into the trap of providing a 'free puff' by replaying the ad just as it was aired. One *Channel 4 News* executive commented:

The focus groups are the single most exciting TV news development in this campaign. It is very graphic in television terms and it allows us to show how the key undecided voters, the floating voters, are responding to the media messages of the professional advertising of the party politicians themselves. *The Sunday Times* and most of the other newspapers have their own panels of floating voters and it shows how in 1987 only 37 per cent of the electorate went into the campaign undecided. This time around it was 42 per cent. But after the first week of the [1992] campaign it's down to 32 per cent, so that means that 10 per cent of voters have already made up their minds and they've actually made up their minds based on some of the things we've been talking about. So it's actually allowing the viewer to see the whole process of democracy in action, how it triggers people's responses.

BBC News, by contrast, not only did not commission any polls, but was under instructions not to report poll results prominently in the bulletins. (*Newsnight* escaped this stricture, however, and commissioned its own polls in collaboration with *The Independent*.) ITN's decision to commission polls for *News at Ten*, and the way in which they were used in the ITN and *Channel 4 News* broadcasts, thus represented one of the major differences between the public service and commercial news bulletins in the 1992 campaign.

The reality behind the scenes

Reporting on campaign tactics and strategies was another feature of ITN's and Channel 4's campaign coverage. ITN's award-winning reporter, Michael Nicholson, produced a lengthy report on campaign managers' assessments of the other parties' campaigns, using former Conservative, Liberal and Labour campaign managers to accompany another party's leader for a day on the campaign trail and comment on the successes and failures of their strategies and tactics.

Revealing the reality behind the scenes was also a feature in the *regular* daily reports from the campaign trail. According to one senior ITN editor: 'This election is not any more media-managed than the last time, but we now want our reporters to be more robust about saying that.'

Others disagreed, citing evidence that the 1992 campaign *was* more stage-managed than any other. Whereas the Conservatives were the first to hold invitation-only evening rallies in 1983, by 1992 all the parties were doing so. In one planning meeting, a senior ITN manager expressed this concern:

How should we cover the evening rallies? ... We are still telling ourselves things in meetings that we're not telling our viewers – do we need to say more? People are bitching like crazy now because its so stage-managed. Tony Bevins [*The Independent*] is breathing fire now because there is no time for questions at the press conferences. Please ram that message home to the *Target Teams*. We're giving our correspondents a chance to tell it as they see it ...

Normal coverage of the 1992 campaign went deeper into the issue of manipulative campaign techniques than in previous campaigns. By 1992, the staged photo-opportunity was old news. One *Channel 4 News* executive put it this way:

I think our viewers are now actually sophisticated enough to recognise that politicians do it and we tell them what's happening. So for instance we had a shot on the Neil Kinnock train on Tuesday, when he did his first campaign tour, when Julie Hall the press officer was briefing the Channel 3 [ITN] correspondent upstairs about the arrangements when Neil Kinnock got to the school, which was tightly controlled: 'Tim you've only got one question. Mr. Kinnock will be coming in from this direction. You ask your one question.' That was part of our script and part of our commentary in the story, whereas in 1987 we'd probably do a whole feature about stage management. Everyone accepts now that stage management is normality.

Both Channel 4 and ITN took precautions to ensure that their coverage would not be driven by the parties' photo-opportunities. The Target Teams, and the leading political editors, played an important part in this. According to one senior ITN news editor, the Target Teams offered an 'assessment', they did not merely follow photo-opportunities.

Dealing with the issues

'Elections are about the issues and the personalities of the people who want to lead the country.'
(Senior *Channel 4 News* executive)

We have already discussed the emphasis placed on the personalities of the party leaders in television news coverage, and particularly in the coverage on *News at Ten*. But as the above quote suggests, the issues were at least of equal importance to the broadcasters. And table 9.1 above showed that the issues were the main subject of news stories more than twice as often as the party leaders.

Both ITN and *Channel 4 News* planned for a significant portion of their campaign coverage to be devoted to the issues. Unlike the BBC, however, ITN chose not to prepare, in advance of the campaign, lengthy issue 'packages' as they had in previous elections. Instead, ITN used a 'flexible response' approach to the issues – keeping archive film on a variety of issues to be used in pieces on the day if the issue emerged as important in the campaign. The key difference between the public service and commercial channels here is that the former may have aired a pre-packaged story on party policies on the environment or defence, for example, regardless of whether it had emerged as important in the campaign trail that day.

ITN believed that pre-planned issue packages could date rapidly and become not entirely relevant to the debate among the parties on the day. To make them relevant would require as much or more work than putting together a new piece using some archive film.

Public interest or audience interest

The commercial news programme makers firmly believe they offer something distinct from the BBC. The public service (PBS) ethos – 'to inform, educate, and entertain' – is not ignored, but rather interpreted differently. Exactly how this is interpreted can be seen from the way in which the commercial channels planned to cover the party leaders, the polls, and the issues. But clarifying the goal of *News at Ten*, as distinct from the BBC, in concrete terms, sometimes proved difficult:

Semetko: 'To what extent is your mission the same as the BBC's?'
Producer: 'We are not PBS at all, we are much more *news* oriented. We are a commercial organization.'

The producer appears to be denying any special obligation to run election news as the most important story of the day, when other, non-political events, better satisfy 'news value' criteria.

Certainly, *News at Ten* was more willing than the BBC to lead on non-election stories (the royals three times, a helicopter crash twice, an earthquake and a pop star's libel action). The BBC's leads strayed off the election only three times (twice for the royals and once for the helicopter crash). There appears to be a tension between the concern to inform viewers about the important political news, on the one hand and, on the other, to give viewers the 'real news' of the day even though it may be non-political. This was resolved at ITN by changing the running order of the stories, but often the amount of time given to less newsworthy election coverage was not reduced.

The problem was one of balancing an obligation to cover the campaign in full, giving the parties a fair opportunity to state their case, on the one hand, with the duty to deliver the most 'newsworthy' events of the day. This underlying tension of balancing these dual obligations was most clear at *News at Ten* which serves a mass audience. The comments of journalists at every level of the organisation, however, suggest that their most important obligation is to the audience.

Conclusions

Blumler *et al.*'s observation studies at the BBC during the 1983 and 1987 campaigns identified four distinct approaches to election newsmaking. The first is a 'prudential' approach, in which campaign reporting should be politically innocuous and not intervene in the political course of the campaign. The second is a 'reactive' approach, which emphasises the obligation to report the parties' activities each day. TV news, from this viewpoint has a duty to report the parties' activities as the centerpiece of campaign stories. The third is an 'analytical' approach, espoused by the leading political commentators, who believe they have a 'Reithian duty' to 'tease out the central threads of the arguments and the issues involved'.[14] And finally, some at the BBC held a 'conventionally journalistic' view, characterised by the emphasis on professional news value criteria in the selection and placement of election news stories.

The observation study at ITN and *Channel 4 News* in 1992 suggests that reporters in the commercial channels took the conventionally journalistic approach, buttressed by an emphasis on the analytical, in which reporters were to *interpret* developments in the campaign for the viewer. 'News values' were almost always the primary criteria for the selection and placement of election news stories. ITN and *Channel 4 News* possibly felt more free to rely on news values because, after the 1990 Broadcasting Act, they were relatively unconstrained by direct political threats, unlike the BBC, whose future was then unclear with its Charter up for renewal in 1996. The need to attract and hold audiences was far more important than complaints from politicians. Ironically, it was the BBC, despite its more prudential approach, which earned the greater wrath of the politicians. The Conservative *Sunday Times* (5 April) reported 'intense and colossal bitterness' among senior Conservatives at what was regarded as unfair reporting by the BBC.

The 'news worthiness' approach predominated, not only at *News at Ten*, with its mass audience, but also at *Channel 4 News* whose much smaller audience (1 to 2 million), according to one Channel 4 executive, is sophisticated and includes many 'political junkies'. There appeared to be no indication of a 'prudential' orientation to campaign reporting. And a 'reactive' orientation existed only to the extent that the news did report daily on the politicians' activities and, despite the lack of stopwatching, editors remained aware of the amount of time devoted to each party. This awareness, however, did not provoke a rush to correct any imbalance. Viewer interest was uppermost in the minds of news producers, and this resulted in a more 'personalised' interpretation of the campaign characterised by an emphasis on the party leaders, as well as by stories focusing on electors' reactions to the campaign. In short, newsmaking on the commercial channels displayed the characteristics found in observation studies in the United States.

Our content analysis of the *Nine O'Clock News* and *News at Ten* confirmed the commercial channel's far heavier emphasis on the electoral game, the horse race, the conduct of the campaign and a greater willingness to generate stories. But it did not demonstrate a descent from balance on ITN, as measured either by leader appearances or by origin of story. Indeed, by initiation of the main subject of each story, it was the BBC that strayed from balance, to the advantage of the Conservatives. Generally, however, our analysis accords with the audience surveys which show that a large majority of views found television to be well balanced.[15] Neither the BBC nor ITN cut back on election coverage, despite cost pressures and the belief that many viewers were already bored by the 'phoney campaign'. The concentration on substantive issues – especially the economy – on both channels also continues to set British election news apart from the market-driven coverage of US presidential elections.

Thus we can conclude that public service broadcasting fared reasonably well in its sternest test yet. If the BBC remained hyperactively public service-oriented, ITN was not yet overwhelmed by the ratings-matter-more-than-electors philosophy. However, our conclusion does not signal a confident and complacent thumbs-up for British election broadcasting. The emphasis on substantive issues was almost certainly artificially bumped up by the extraordinary episode of 'Jennifer's Ear' which accounted for much of both channels' social welfare coverage. The range of issues aired was also notably narrow, especially on ITN. Subjects not featuring sufficiently to merit attention in our tables include law and order, local government and the poll tax, Europe, Northern Ireland and transport.

Moreover, all the indications are that by the next election, market pressures will be far more intense as cable and satellite expands and the audience continues to fragment across the increasing variety of media choices. News will almost certainly become more sensitive to the ratings and one might expect the 'American' pattern of less emphasis on substantive issues and more on the personalities and horse race. We shall need to recall the jury on public service broadcasting.

Notes

This research project is supported by grants from the Economic and Social Research Council (UK) and the University of Michigan. Grateful thanks to Vincent Hanna at Viewpoint, to STICERD, LSE, and the University of Michigan for providing the additional support necessary for this project. Thanks also to Janet Newcity and David Tewsbury for research assistance.

  1 See T.J. Nossiter, 'British television: a mixed economy', in Jay G. Blumler and T.J. Nossiter (eds.), *Broadcasting Finance in Transition* (Oxford: Oxford University Press, 1991); Tony Prosser, 'Public Service Broadcasting and deregulation in the UK', *European Journal of Communication*, 7 (1992), 173–93.
  2 Barrie Gunter and Carmel McLaughlin, *Television and the Public's View* (London: John Libby, 1992).
  3 See Jay G. Blumler, Malcolm Brynin and T.J. Nossiter, 'Broadcasting finance and program quality: an international review', *European Journal of Communication*, September 1 (1986), 343–64; Jay G. Blumler, and Holli A. Semetko, 'Mass media and legislative campaigns in a unitary parliamentary democracy: the case of Britain', *Legislative Studies Quarterly*, 12 (1987), 415–43.
  4 See Blumler and Nossiter (eds.), *Broadcasting Finance in Transition*.
  5 See Holli A. Semetko, J.G. Blumler, M. Gurevitch and D. Weaver, *The Formation of Campaign Agendas: A Comparative Analysis of Party and Media Roles in Recent American and British Elections* (Hillsdale, NJ: Lawrence Erlbaum, 1991).

6 Martin Harrop and Margaret Scammell, 'A tabloid war', in David Butler and Dennis Kavanagh (eds.), *The British General Election of 1992* (Basingstoke: Macmillan, 1992).

7 Paul Medlicott, media adviser to David Steel in 1987, described television as being 'uniquely vulnerable' to the parties at elections, and believed that this was of especial importance to the Liberal Democrats. Quoted in Margaret Scammell, 'Political advertising and the Broadcasting Bill', *Political Quarterly*, 61 (1991), 200–13.

8 The content analysis covers the period from 16 March to 9 April. Based on variables used in Semetko *et al.*, *Formation of Campaign Agendas*, it coded each news story for up to four main topics; up to ten main actors; as well as story initiation (Conservative, Labour, Liberal, Media, Other Party, Mixed, Other); story format (presenter only, studio interview, etc.); and overall story length (timed in seconds). The general subject categories used in the content analysis include the following:

> *Economy*: tax, inflation, interest rates, jobs, unemployment, privatisation, public spending, industrial disputes, trade unions, balance of trade, the Budget, recession and recovery.
>
> *Social welfare*: NHS, private health care, poverty, homelessness, housing, the elderly, pensions, education. 'Jennifer's Ear', because it played such a significant role in the coverage of the health issue, is listed as a sub-category.
>
> *Opinion polls/horse race*: media polls, marginal seats analysis, results predictions and speculation about the outcome;
>
> *Party leaders*: narrowly refers to Major, Kinnock, and Ashdown and their political or personal qualities, and their individual (as opposed to party) campaigns;
>
> *Constitutional reform*: refers to devolution and the demands to reform the electoral system;
>
> *Conduct of the campaign*: party strategy, spending, advertising, general campaign trail activity, rallies, press conferences, and that which could not be rendered to a particular party leader;
>
> *Defence, Europe, foreign affairs, energy and the environment* do not include any other sub-categories. Subjects which did not feature sufficiently to merit any attention in our tables, though they were coded, include: law and order, local government/polls tax, Northern Ireland and transport. Overall 209 campaign subject categories were used in this content analysis.

9 Observation and interviews at the BBC were conducted by Professor Nossiter, in collaboration with Professors Jay Blumler and Michael Gurevitch (see chapter 8 in this volume).

10 Professor Semetko was based at ITN and Channel 4 for thirteen days during the 1992 campaign, in the first weeks from 19–22 March and then again in the final weeks from 1–9 April.

11 MORI, *British Public Opinion: The British General Election of 1992* (London: MORI, 1992).

12 The origin of stories is often difficult to decipher because a great many use a mixture of party, media and expert sources. Stories were coded for up to four subjects, and

each subject was coded for initiation. The figures used here refer to origin of the main subject only, unless otherwise stated.

13 Compare with Blumler *et al.*, chapter 8 in this volume.
14 Blumler *et al.*, 'Setting the television news agenda', p. 115.
15 See Martin Harrison 'Politics on the air', in Butler and Kavanagh (eds.), *The British General Election of 1992*, pp. 155–79.

10 People-metering: scientific research or clapometer?

John Rentoul, Nick Robinson and Simon Braunholtz

'Elections are determined by three things', according to one American political consultant: 'television, television and television.' So it is surprising how little analysis there has been of the effectiveness of political communications on television.

The 1992 election in Britain was the first in which a new technique was used to monitor the second-by-second responses of voters to political messages on news programmes and party broadcasts. 'People-metering' was imported from the United States by the two main British political parties; first by the Conservatives in 1989, and then by the Labour Party in 1990, as part of their search for political messages that move votes. It was also used by the broadcasters for the first time in a general election campaign as part of our efforts to reveal the calculations of the campaign managers and to assess their impact on voters. We developed a system called Voter Metering for BBC TV's *The Vote Race*, and a rival system was used by ITN's *Channel 4 News*.

People-metering helps the campaign professional do what Brendan Bruce, former Conservative Director of Communications, calls 'pre-editing', that is, ensuring that television news is provided with market-tested soundbites. Dr Richard Wirthlin, President Reagan's pollster, who introduced Bruce and the Conservatives to people-metering, sums up its aim: 'It's to fine tune your communication messages; that is, to develop what we call power phrases – that capture the essence of what you want to communicate in the most compelling and positive way.' Mark Mellman, the Democrat consultant who advised the Labour Party on people-metering, says it is one of the best ways round the 'gut' problem. His argument is that the gut instinct of politicians, their advisers and advertising consultants (and, no doubt, journalists too!) is almost bound to be wrong. Their obsession with politics is such as to make them socially deviant and, in many ways, the people least qualified to judge political advertising or a speech. People-metering helps them watch television through the eyes of 'moveable voters', who generally have an unimaginable lack of interest in politics.

'People-metering' was first developed in the United States in the 1930s, to assess audience response to radio programmes. It has since been turned, by the use of computers, into a flexible, mobile and powerful tool of analysis for television. It has been used in US political campaigns since at least 1980, when a 'very crude' system was used by Richard Wirthlin for Ronald Reagan's

Presidential campaign. It was used by both the Clinton and Bush campaigns in 1992.[1]

Otherwise known as 'feedback', 'perception analyser', 'speech pulse', 'media pulse analysis' and 'realtime response measure', people-metering involves a group of subjects watching speeches and other political messages on video screens. As they watch, each of them uses a handset to indicate whether they believe or approve of what they see and hear. Their responses are recorded continuously, and combined by computer into a moving graph on a screen.

For the BBC's research, MORI recruited a new group of fifty electors to attend a research session on each of the three Saturdays during the campaign. The sample was intended to reflect as closely as possible the national profile of those intending to vote in Great Britain. As they watched party election broadcasts (PEBs), speeches and interviews, each of them turned a hand-held dial as they felt 'more positive' or 'less positive' towards the party concerned. The dial was calibrated to measure strength of feeling. Their responses were combined every second to produce a moving graph.

We divided the fifty people into four subgroups: red, blue and yellow lines represented firm supporters of the Conservatives, Labour and Liberal Democrats. The most important, and largest, subgroup consisted of floating voters – 'don't knows' and those who had considered voting for other parties – represented by a white line (see appendix to this chapter). Our focus was on the movement of this white line. We wanted to see, firstly, which phrase of a speech or portion of a party broadcast produced a reaction among floating voters and secondly, which way it moved them – towards the firm supporters of the Conservative Party (the blue line) or Labour (red) or the Liberal Democrats (yellow). It is this movement rather than any precise level on the graph that we watched for.

Each week we played back the key sections of the metering to our audience and asked them to explain and discuss their reasons for reacting in the way that they did.

Our findings

Despite derisive criticism of John Major's campaign by many commentators, our people-metering identified some of the Prime Minister's hidden attractions for the voters.

The first Conservative PEB, entitled 'John Major: The Journey', showed him going back to his Brixton roots. The 'humble origins' theme was only partly effective. But one of the more unexpectedly well-received passages was that shown in figure 10.1. The floating voters' line rises immediately after 'people are entitled to their own views', and rises steadily throughout this homily on tolerance, based on his experience of Brixton. What is striking about this passage is how different it sounds from Margaret Thatcher while still being firmly based on Conservative precepts. Committed

Labour voters, unimpressed to start with, remained unmoved, while committed Tories, already rating the broadcast very highly, could mark it up only a little.

A repeated theme of criticism of the Conservative campaign was that it was negative. But our metering suggested that John Major's positive message, when it was getting through, was popular. In his Shepton Mallet speech in the last week of the campaign, he defended the government's education reforms: 'My aim is for parents to have that power to choose what is right for their child. They know best what is right for their child, and they should have the opportunity to choose what is right for their child and a Conservative government will give them that right.'

This produced a steady rise in the floating voters line, up to close to the Conservative line, while Labour supporters started off disapproving and remained so. The metering also showed that such concrete illustrations of 'choice' were more effective than attempts to generalise Conservative philosophy. There was no response, for example, to this passage in the same speech: 'I believe that every person wants to have more say, have more choice, be the master in their own private corner of life.'

It is worth noting that education is a 'motherhood and apple pie' issue. People-metering consistently found a favourable response to any promise to improve education. The Labour emphasis on 'education and training' and the Liberal Democrat pledge to put a penny on income tax to pay for education always scored well. But John Major's peroration on parent choice, coming after a general promise to 'level up' standards, gained an *additional* favourable response from floating voters.

The opinion polls confirmed that the Liberal Democrats had succeeded, by the end of the campaign, in identifying themselves with the education issue. Our people-metering picked up the appeal of their position from the start. It was clear in one of Paddy Ashdown's first campaign speeches, when his paean to the gift of learning scored extremely well with all political groups. 'Education is the one gift that you can give that no one can ever take away. They can take away your house, they can take away your job, they can take away your freedom, but they can never, never take away your education.' But the important thing is that the lines remain at the top of the screen when he 'toughens' the message by demanding higher taxes to pay for education. 'That's the gift, the precious gift, that I say it is worth paying a penny on my rate of income tax, to give my children, our children and our country that precious gift.' (See figure 10.2.) Our audience discussions revealed remarkably high awareness of, and support for, the 'penny on tax' promise even in week one of the campaign.

People-metering also revealed some of the weaknesses of the opposition parties' positions. General criticism of the political system was well-received by floating voters as well as Labour supporters and Liberal Democrats. But electoral reform, although surprisingly attractive to committed Labour voters, left floating voters cold. This applied to Paddy Ashdown's extravagant rhetoric attacking first-past-the-post: 'Our old voting system now lies like a dead hand stopping progress in Britain' (figure 10.3). It also applied to Neil Kinnock's retrospectively notorious press conference in which he offered to extend the membership of Labour's electoral systems review committee 'to people from other political parties'. In both cases, firm Conservatives were hostile, Labour and Liberal Democrats responded favourably, and the floating voters' line was neutral and flat.

We also metered Conservative efforts to use the issue of electoral reform to scare floating voters into their camp. For this we had to break down our subgroups further. In the final week we asked the group how they would vote if there were only a Labour and a Conservative candidate standing in their constituency. This enabled us to split the floating voters into 'Labour leaners' and 'Conservative leaners'.

We then looked at how these two groups responded to John Major's 'Trojan Horse' warning: 'Beware of Mr Ashdown – a nice man. But he's the door-keeper to a Labour Britain. I warn you: don't look at the man, look through the door. The most famous door in the world is Number 10 Downing Street. Don't let Mr Ashdown open that door for Mr Kinnock.'

This argument seemed to be successful in driving a wedge into the middle ground, and pulling the Conservative leaners over towards the Conservative camp. The Conservative leaners line rose gently, while the Labour leaners drifted downwards.

It is, of course, much easier to be confident of these judgements with hindsight. At the time, what was much clearer was the effectiveness of Labour (and Liberal Democrat) communications techniques. Labour election broadcasts generally appeared to be more persuasive than Conservative ones. Labour's overall strategy may have been flawed, but its technique was good.

What worked well was Labour's use of 'real people' in their broadcasts. For example, in their penultimate election broadcast on 2 April, Labour front-benchers were intercut with 'vox pops'. A young woman talking about the health service was particularly effective. 'When it comes to health, you can't mix with people's health. That should be – that is something which should be natural, like going to drink a glass of water, you should be able to go to a hospital and get treated, and not have to wait hours and hours to be seen to. That should be something that comes first.' This produced a steady, but increasingly steep rise in the floating voters' line, from just above the firm Conservatives to just below the firm Labour supporters line, as shown in figure 10.4.

In addition to the party lines, described above, the Voter Metering system allowed us to sub-divide our subjects by sex, age, class and other background factors. Surprisingly, perhaps, these were very rarely enlightening – the floating voters' reaction was by far the most productive to watch.

Is it research?

People-metering is controversial. Some campaign managers, pollsters and commentators are dubious about what it measures and whether useful lessons can be drawn from the findings. They see it as an expensive toy.

Shaun Woodward, then Conservative Party Director of Communications, abandoned people-metering in the run-up to the 1992 campaign, preferring to rely mostly on focus groups and 'in-depth' one-to-one interviewing. Chris Patten, who took over as party chairman in November 1990, was sceptical of the technique. However, Philip Gould, of Labour's Shadow Communications Agency, was an enthusiast, and the Labour Party tested rough cuts of its PEBs throughout the campaign.

We believe that, providing it is carefully used, it is an effective research tool – in *addition* to conventional polling and focus groups. From the broadcasters' point of view, it also adds a new dimension to television coverage of the campaign.

People-metering is instantaneous, so it does not rely on recall; it is non-verbal, so there is no bias towards the articulate and extrovert; it is unmediated, so it does not depend primarily on a researcher asking probing questions; and it is phrase-by-phrase, so it allows detailed analysis of the construction of political messages.

We were careful not to make grand claims for people-metering. We never tried to use it to predict how people would vote. It was always intended to provide interpretation of, and add depth to, opinion polls during the campaign. Nevertheless, our metering did point up some Conservative strengths and opposition weaknesses which were not apparent in opinion polls.

Despite the appearance of calibrated precision, people-metering is not a 'quantitative' technique like opinion polling. What matters is not the precise levels of approval indicated by the graph, but movement up or down. People-metering is a qualitative technique, designed to get a feel for public opinion. We only interpreted the people-metering graph in the light of the group discussion after the metering sessions. Movements in the lines could sometimes be ambiguous, in that people were responding to different things or for different reasons from those we had assumed. The constraint of filming the discussion made this difficult, but in political or commercial use the post-metering discussion, a 'focus group plus', is as important as the metering itself.

As well as identifying 'power phrases', people-metering can also identify 'clangers'. Our research showed few examples of these during the election campaign, in stark contrast to our earlier experiments which saw the graph nosedive at unexpected moments. When Margaret Thatcher claimed in a 1989 speech that 'the Thames is now the cleanest metropolitan estuary in the world', all the lines on the graph plummeted. So, too, did the floating voters' line in a Labour PPB in April 1991 in which John Smith, then Shadow Chancellor, endorsed Neil Kinnock in fulsome – but obviously somewhat unconvincing –

terms: 'I think Neil Kinnock turned the Labour Party right round, and gave it a sense of purpose; and was courageous enough to make the Labour Party face up to problems and solve them.' (See figure 10.5).

Negative campaigning

We were well aware in advance that one of the limitations of people-metering is that it cannot properly measure the effectiveness of negative messages. For example, the Conservative campaign theme of Labour's 'Double Whammy' – higher taxes, higher prices – prompts the viewer to respond unfavourably to the message while becoming more favourable to the messenger. This cannot be captured on a simple dial.

We also know from quantitative polling that most voters claim to dislike negative campaigning, and yet negative information can be recalled more easily than positive information. So we were careful not to downplay the effectiveness of negative advertising, and tried to use the studio discussions to assess how these messages were received.

However, there were occasions where there was no doubt about which way to turn the dial. The penultimate Conservative broadcast was an effective mixture of negative and positive, and included an attack on Labour that certainly hit home (see figure 10.6). At the 'sting in the tale' of Labour's spending promises, 'Where is the money coming from?', the floating voters were sharply split from Labour supporters. The white line suddenly turned up, parallel with the Conservatives, while the Labour line turned down. Here was a clue to the potency of the Conservative 'tax bombshell' charge that Labour would put up everybody's taxes, not just those of the better off. Labour had failed to shake off its 'tax and spend' image.

Is it journalism?

That people-metering is a useful research technique is vouchsafed by its continuing use by political campaigns in Britain and the United States. But we still have to justify its use as part of television journalism. Is people-metering serious election coverage, or just entertainment?

Our justification for the journalistic use of people-metering is a response to what David Butler, in the last edition of *Political Communications*, called the 'professionalisation' of British election campaigns since 1979. As Professor Jay Blumler observed in the same volume, journalists had already started to respond to this in the 1987 campaign, borrowing from American political correspondents the idea that they were 'under an obligation to open the viewers' eyes to the manipulation underlying the message.'[2]

This view of the journalist's role dominated the news coverage of the 1992 election, as broadcasters tried to find new ways to report what is, in effect, a professional advertising campaign. But we believe that the single-minded attempt to report the processes of campaigning, rather than the campaign itself, only succeeded in making the election more inaccessible to the voters.

There was an obsession with filming 'behind the scenes', with reporting the activities of campaign managers, and strategy meetings. One Labour campaign manager, Patricia Hewitt, complained afterwards that the broadcasters would rather have a news story showing the party leader discussing a speech with his aides, writing the speech, and then a spin doctor briefing the press after the speech, than use any of the speech itself at all.

This is obviously an exaggeration, but there did appear to be such a determination to prevent politicians from 'dictating the agenda' that broadcasters sometimes felt it their duty to prevent politicians speaking to the voters except through them. This reinforced the tendency of the 'professionalisation' of the political campaigning to distance the election from the people.

We argue that there is another way of tackling the problem of pre-packaged politics, and it is to use politicians' weapons, like people-metering, to open up the campaign to people.

The Vote Race was the innovation in BBC TV's election coverage. People-metering enabled us to 'let the voters in' to the campaign, to have their say through instant electronic response to political messages. It involves the television viewer in an unfolding drama. The viewer fixes on the line as it moves, gauges their own reaction and anticipates how the line produced by the studio audience will move. Instead of journalists telling the viewer how political communication works, viewers can feel and witness it for themselves.

In addition, our studio audience were able to speak out on issues which they had themselves selected for discussion through metering. One of the successes of the 1992 campaign coverage was the role of members of the public on programmes like *Election Call* and *The Granada 500*. The thirst for direct voter contact with politicians was more marked in the US election in 1992, when conventional television journalism found itself usurped by phone-ins, talk shows and the huge audiences for the three presidential debates – watched by around ninety million people, almost as many as voted on 3 November.

Conclusion

People-metering is more than a television gimmick. As a research tool, people-metering is a useful way of assessing different ways of getting a message across by tapping the spontaneous response of the inarticulate majority. It is the closest research can get to the way political messages on television are received at home.

It also helps journalists who are reporting on elections to see them through the eyes of real people. And when it is used to complement other forms of election coverage, especially direct voter contact with politicians, it is a valuable way of 'letting the people in' to a political process which all too often appears closed.

Notes

1 Stan Greenberg, Bill Clinton's pollster, used people-metering in the preparation for the Democratic Convention speech and the televised debates, on samples of Perot supporters and weak Clinton supporters. Bob Teeter used it for the Bush campaign. A version involving a sample of undecided voters using touch-tone telephone keypads at home, was also used by CNN (Cable News Network) in its coverage of the debates.
2 Ivor Crewe and Martin Harrop (eds.), *Political Communications: The General Election of 1987* (Cambridge: Cambridge University Press, 1989), pp. 130 and 164.

Appendix

The BBC/MORI system was designed by IML, who developed the software specially. The groups were recruited by MORI in two phases:

Face-to-face recruitment: a team of interviewers were set recruitment quotas to achieve within constituencies in West London (inner and outer). Each interviewer was responsible for recruiting eight participants from a constituency, with quotas set by sex, age, class, work status and party support.

Telephone recruitment: in addition to the 56 participants recruited from the London region, MORI also recruited around 12 people by telephone from around the country outside the South East of England.

The overall quota was set to be representative of the national population, and the political allegiance was set according to the contemporary standing of the parties in the opinion polls. The categories used were Conservative, Labour, Liberal Democrat, other party, and 'undecided'. Those people who named a party were asked whether they had definitely decided how they would vote, or whether they might change their minds. This 'softness' indicator was then used to define 'floating voters'.

The table below shows the average profiles of the participants over the three weeks.

Conservative	13
Labour	10
Liberal Democrat	4
Floating voters	23
consisting of:	
Conservative, may change	7
Labour, may change	7
Lib. Dem., may change	4
Other (undecided, other party)	5

Participants could not see the traces that they were producing. However, behind the scenes, we were able to watch the video overlaid (simultaneously) with the traces for the responses of the committed Conservative supporters in the group, the committed Labour supporters, the committed Liberal Democrats, and a fourth line for floating voters. In addition to this, we ran an inkjet printer which produced a series of traces splitting the audience into men vs women, people aged 18–34 vs 35–54 vs 55 +, and ABC1 (middle class) vs C2DE (working class). All these data were stored, with the option of using any of these characteristics, or any others, including those based on questions asked during the session, to illustrate variations of response among different sub-groups.

Channel 4 News used a PEAC people-metering system operated by market researchers Pegram Walters, which has handsets with buttons A to E (very positive to very negative) rather than dials. *Channel 4 News* used the same group of about 120 floating voters in Birmingham throughout the campaign, metered in two successive groups of 50 on Thursday nights. The main control was reported 1987 vote, with an approximate 40–40–20 split. The data for the two groups were aggregated, although the findings from each were similar.

The Labour Party research, set up by Washington DC Democratic consultants Mark Mellman and Ed Lazarus, and operated for the party by its polling company, NOP, used groups of 60 floating voters (defined as those who said they might vote Labour), using dials, with separate lines on screen for men and women.

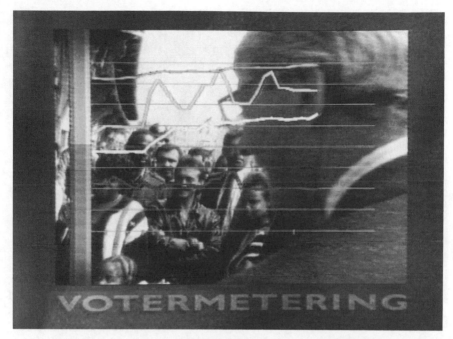

Figure 10.1 *John Major*: 'People are entitled to their own views, to their own instincts, to their own beliefs, and it is quite wrong to try and pigeon-hole everybody into the same beliefs that the majority of people hold. Firstly, it cannot be done because individuality is there and it cannot be changed, and you should not try to change it. But secondly, if you tried to do it, you'd have a very intolerant, very unpleasant, very autocratic society, and not the sort of society I would wish to see.'

Conservative Party Election Broadcast, 18 March 1992.

Key to lines (top to bottom at right): Conservative, Lib. Dem., Floaters, Labour.

Figure 10.2   *Paddy Ashdown*: '. . . but they can never, never take away your education. That's the gift I want to give our children in a society and economy which will be about change and competition and new technologies and knowledge. That's a gift, the precious gift, that I say it is worth paying a penny on my rate of income tax, to give my children, our children and our country that precious gift.'

Speech, 19 March 1992.

Key to lines (top to bottom at right): Lib. Dem., Floaters, Conservative, Labour.

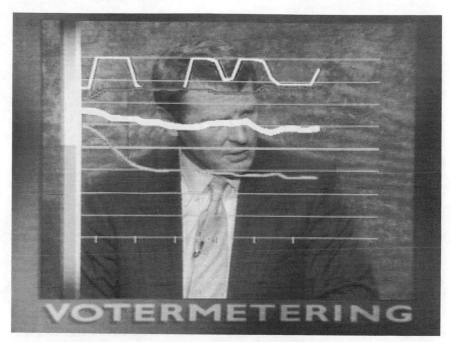

Figure 10.3   *Paddy Ashdown*: 'We now have a system which debases the very idea of justice and democracy. The system makes mistakes. We all pay the price. No one ever says sorry. The system keeps the powerful in power. And it keeps the people out of power. Our old voting system lies like a dead hand stopping progress in Britain.'

Speech, 2 April 1992.

Key to lines (top to bottom at right): Lib. Dem., Labour, Floaters, Conservatives.

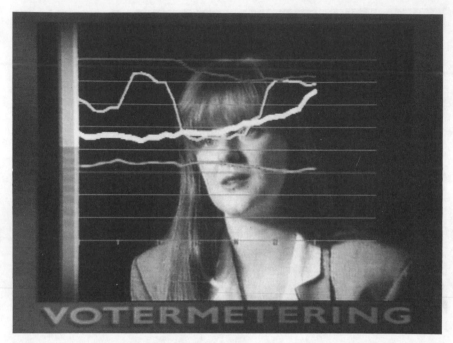

Figure 10.4   *Margaret Beckett*: '... five pounds for a single person, with the full increase going to everybody. By introducing fair taxes and raising benefits, we'll make eight out of ten families better off.'

Vox pop, young woman: 'When it comes to health, you can't mix with people's health. That should be – that is something which should be natural, like going to drink a glass of water, you should be able to go to a hospital and get treated, and not have to wait hours and hours to be seen to. That should be something that comes first.'

Labour Party Election Broadcast, 2 April 1992.

Key to lines (top to bottom at right); Labour, Lib. Dem., Floaters, Conservative.

Figure 10.5   *John Smith*: '. . . we want companies *all* to be investing in training, and we want the most modern technology in our industry. And we need of course to get interest rates and inflation down and keep them down. If we do these things, we create the opportunities, the opportunities for success. I think Neil Kinnock turned the Labour Party right round, and gave it a sense of purpose; and was courageous enough to make the Labour Party face up to problems and solve them.'

Labour Party Election Broadcast, April 1991.

Key to lines (top to bottom at right): Labour, Floaters, Conservative (Lib. Dem. included in floating voters line).

Figure 10.6   *Commentary*: 'Gerald Kaufman – £2.5 billion worth of promises. Gordon Brown had made £460 million worth of promises. Roy Hattersley managed only £270 million worth of promises. So many promises. So many pledges. So many billions of pounds. What they still haven't told you is: Where is the money coming from? Because they suspect you won't like the answer.'

Conservative Party Election Broadcast, 3 April 1992.

Key to lines (top to bottom at right): Conservative, Lib. Dem., Floaters, Labour.

Part IV
The campaign in the press

11 'Fact is free but comment is sacred'; or was it *The Sun* wot won it?

David McKie

In a valedictory press conference on 13 April during which he announced his resignation, the Labour leader, Neil Kinnock said:

I make, and I seek, no excuses, and I express no bitterness, when I say that the Conservative-supporting press has enabled the Tory Party to win yet again when the Conservative Party could not have secured victory for itself on the basis of its record, its programme or its character.

That provokes three questions. Was there bias? If so, did it matter? If it did exist, and if it did in fact have any substantial influence on the outcome, is there anything to be done?

I distinguish here between two doctrines of the purpose of newspapers, one of which honours the words of the great *Manchester Guardian* editor, C. P. Scott – 'It's [a newspaper's] primary office is the gathering of news. At the peril of its soul it must see that the supply is not tainted. Comment is free, but fact is sacred' – while the other thinks that's a load of cobblers.

The first belongs to what might be called the bystander tendency. It watches from the sidelines, taking an intelligent interest in the game, even shouting partisan comments, but nevertheless taking due account of the nicer touches by the other side (or in this case, sides). The other might be called the cheerleader tendency, though given its predilection for storming onto the pitch and kicking the hell out of the other side, that understates it. This kind of newspaper is all out to see its favourites win by all means available, fair or foul. Taking the eleven daily newspapers which account for the great majority of national coverage, these were the bystanders:

> *The Times* (April 1992 circulation: 386,258). 'Even this early in the campaign', it said in a leader on 14 March, '*The Times* would be dissembling to its readers if it did not admit a predisposition towards a new Conservative mandate. (This predisposition will be confined to this editorial column; the news pages of course will remain strictly impartial)'. Leaders on constitutional issues, especially devolution, were hostile to the government, but on the whole *The Times* performed much as it said it would.
>
> *The Daily Telegraph* (April 1992 circulation: 1,038,138). Though anguished, even aghast at the prospect of Labour victory, as its leaders

daily attested, the *Telegraph* employs political writers as straight as George Jones and mostly attempted to tell both sides of the story, if not necessarily in arithmetically equal proportions.

The Guardian (April 1992 circulation: 429,062). A Lib-Lab paper: that is to say, the Liberals complain that it is Labour and Labour that it is Liberal. Again, strict instructions were given to pursue balanced coverage, though certainly some issues could be faulted (see the preponderance of anti-government stories in the election pull-out of 13 March).

The Independent (April 1992 circulation: 389,523) – 'the only paper that will bring you unbiased reporting of the issues facing the nation', it announced on page 1 at the start of the campaign, to the disgust of some of its competitors. It endorsed no one: its last three leaders of the campaign made the case successively for Labour, the Conservatives and the Liberal Democrats.

The Financial Times (April 1992 circulation: 290,204). Gave little hint of any political allegiance: its surprise endorsement of Labour was the late decision by its editor and could not have been predicted from its balanced account of the campaign.

Today (April 1992 circulation: 533,177). Made impartiality its selling-point, contrasting this with the policy of other tabloids, including its Murdoch stablemate, *The Sun*. Its masthead carried the slogan: PROPER NEWS, NOT PROPAGANDA. After several leaders so neutral as to be anodyne, it endorsed the Conservatives, but without ever suggesting that votes in another direction were wicked.

Few could honestly say that these papers achieved complete objectivity, even if such a condition existed. The strength of *The Independent*'s objections to Labour's taxation policy offset an otherwise sympathetic coverage. Sometimes apparent bias resulted from editorial judgement about the point of a story. This was nicely illustrated in the contrast between *Times* and *Guardian* coverage of John Smith's shadow budget (17 March). *The Times* emphasised possible losses for middle-class families, *The Guardian* the gains for families lower down the scale.

For the purpose of this argument, these newspapers may quietly leave the stage. The rest is about the cheerleaders. On the Labour side, *The Daily Mirror* (April 1992 circulation: 3,660,756 including its Scottish equivalent, *The Daily Record*). On the Conservative side, *The Sun* (April 1992 circulation: 3,570,562); *The Daily Mail* (April 1992 circulation: 1,675,453); and *The Daily Express* (April 1992 circulation: 1,524,786).

With those one ought perhaps to include *The Daily Star* (April 1992 circulation: 805,793). This paper is something of a problem. Strictly speaking, it was neutral between the main parties. It advised its readers in its eve-of-election leader that the choice was Conservative or Labour: but they ought not to vote for 'Paddy Let-down'. But its coverage and comment appeared to this observer to display a clear Conservative preference, especially in the choice of stories to splash and stories to relegate – not least in its attempt to revive an ancient tale about Michael Meacher's wife dabbling in private nursing care (26 March). I class it as a hybrid with cheerleading tendencies.

It is of course a mistake to lump together the tabloids as one kind of animal. *The Daily Mail* and *The Daily Express* aim at different audiences from *The Daily Mirror*, *The Sun* and *The Daily Star*. It is also misleading to treat the *Mirror* and *Sun* as equivalent papers on either side of the fence. The *Mirror*, not least because these were Labour issues, honoured its traditions as a paper of social conscience, especially in its final appeal, begging readers to remember the consequences of the election for people less fortunate than themselves. It used its centre spreads for 'state of the nation' surveys – thus reducing its scope for manoeuvre in the light of the news as it broke. The *Sun*, unrestrained by such obligations, campaigned with a style and a brutal wit which the *Mirror* rarely matched. The difference between the panache of the *Sun* and the *Mirror*'s predictability was the difference between the *Mirror*'s election morning 'Time for a change' and the *Sun*'s 'If Kinnock wins today, will the last person out of Britain please turn out the lights?' – illustrated by a picture of Neil Kinnock's head in a light bulb.

MORI's final report on the election contrasts the 'blatant' support which the Conservative tabloids gave the Conservatives with 'the weak support given Labour both in the space devoted and in its content'. MORI's analysis of front-page content shows that *The Daily Mail* gave 48.1 per cent of its front page space during the campaign to election news; *The Daily Express*, 41.9 per cent; *The Sun* 26.1 per cent; *The Daily Star* 24.4 per cent; and *The Daily Mirror* 11.6 per cent.

It needs to be said that the searing partisanship of these newspapers did not begin when John Major named the day. Indeed, as *The Guardian* and *The Independent* noted at the time, *The Daily Mail* and *The Daily Express* were conducting a kind of phoney election at the start of the year. Attempts would be made on Monday to supply a theme for the week. This was the *Mail*'s contribution in January:

Monday, 6th: LABOUR PLANS EIGHT NEW TAXES. (Followed on Tuesday by: LABOUR DOUBLE BUDGET BLOW; including tables on estimated effects derived from Conservative Central Office calculations and based on a 10p increase in basic rate)
Monday, 13th: Leak of planned Conservative attack on Labour defence claims
Monday, 20th: LABOUR PART-TIME TAX SHOCK
Monday, 27th: FORD CHIEF: LABOUR'S CRAZY TAX PLANS. (The Ford chief was Ian McAllister of Ford, who repudiated the story. A similar story presenting Labour as a threat to the car industry led *The Daily Mail* on 4 April.) A second story charted projected effects on Courtaulds and Coates Viyella of Labour's minimum wage. The story was only partially confirmed by Coates Viyella and repudiated by Courtaulds. (Patrick Wintour, *The Guardian*, 29 January 1992)

Table 11.1 *Percentage of news items given to each topic*

	Tabloid front pages	Radio and TV
Economics	30	24
Opinion polls	21	12
Dirty tricks	13	3
Leaders' competence	12	8
Progress of election	7	18
Health	4	6
Proportional representation	3	2
Hung parliament	2	3
Crime, law and order	2	2
Housing	2	1
Role of media	1	3
Constitution exc. PR	1	2
Race and immigration	1	1
Devolution	0	5
Education	0	3
Marginal seats	0	3
Defence	0	1
Environment	0	1
Transport	0	1
Local government	0	1
Energy	0	1
European Community	0	1
Social Security	0	0
Foreign affairs	0	0
Total	100	100

Source: Loughborough University Communications Research Centre; *Guardian*, 11 April 1992.

As their architects hoped, some of these stories were taken up by the broadcasters, prompting Labour deputy leader Roy Hattersley to lodge the year's first complaint. 'Here is a serious democratic problem', he said, 'when one newspaper can tell a lie and the BBC can report it as fact.'

The strident partisanship of the election was nothing new. Even in 1983, when the outcome was scarcely in serious doubt, Labour, and in particular its leader, Michael Foot, had come in for abuse at least as rabid as anything in this election. *The Daily Express* called Foot: 'Half socialist, half politician, half journalist, half ranter, half raver, half baked and half gone.' (See also the comparison of *Sun* judgements on Conservatives/Thatcher and on Labour/

Foot by Martin Harrop in Butler and Kavanagh (eds.), *The British General Election of 1983*, pp. 190–1 – even better read aloud.)

What was different this time was the urgency. The result appeared to be truly in doubt. The crusade for decent values (not to mention the life styles of Fleet Street editors) had never been so essential.

Establishing that the tabloids fought this election on the assumption that, to reverse C. P. Scott, facts were free and comment was sacred, scarcely needs detailed analysis, any more than it needs a forensic examination to show that a man lying face down in the gutter, surrounded by empty cans of Tennents, and beginning his thirteenth chorus of 'Show Me the Way to Go Home', is drunk. But for those who did not have the pleasure of their company throughout the campaign, it may be worth noting a few basic techniques.

The first is the selection and rejection of stories, particularly those on page one whose headlines show on the news stand. The list of lead stories in table 11.1 demonstrates the way on which political preference coloured this choice day after day in the cheerleader papers.

Professor Peter Golding and his team from Loughborough University, who monitored the media for *The Guardian* throughout the campaign, wrote on 11 April: 'In the daily tabloids the Conservatives present and attack, but never defend, while Labour defend far more often than they present or attack, although their proportion of policy presentation (thanks probably to the *Mirror*) exceeds that of the Conservatives. The Lib. Dems and others do not feature.' (This analysis covered English editions only.) Bad news can be lost on an inside page or an inconspicuous paragraph (see for instance, the *Express*'s exuberant coverage of its own Harris poll putting the Conservatives ahead on 17 March, and the downbeat paragraph recording Labour leads the following day). When on the night of 31 March three polls appeared giving Labour winning leads and suggesting the first break in the log-jam, the order: 'Clear the front page' must have failed to go out in some offices. The *Star* led with a story on Libya, the *Sun* on a multi-home-owning shadow minister, and the *Mail* on Labour's allegedly 'coy' response to its splash of the previous day. Next day, however, the *Mail* and *Express* made much of these polls as exemplifying the danger that a Liberal Democrat surge might put Labour in.

In newspaper terms, all news is relative: what will make your splash on a Monday might be pushed to make the front page on a Thursday. So alternative stories to lead on are always a godsend when the party you back is in trouble. The first full week of the campaign was full of grim economic indicators: Central Office was known to be apprehensive, reconciled simply to riding it out. That these damaging figures failed to get the expected prominence was largely due to the breaking by *The Daily Mail* on Wednesday 18 March of a thumping royal story: the impending split-up of the Duke and Duchess of York. The *Mail*, *Express* and *Sun*, and the *Mirror* as well, led on royal stories for the rest of the week. It could have been concidence, but it is hardly surprising that Labour suspected that the *Mail* had timed its 'world exclusive' to take the heat off the Government.

You can also contrive to lose inconvenient detail: the *Sun*'s four-page coverage of the Jennifer Bennett affair failed to include the fact that Jennifer's father backed the use of the story. It simply reported that he had called the Labour election broadcast 'a piece of fiction'. You would hardly have guessed from the way the *Sun* reported it that he had said this in defence of the programme.

You can tailor stories and fictions to ridicule and humiliate. Two examples from the *Mirror*: a front-page cartoon and story after the Budget picturing Norman Lamont as a shifty salesman; or their picture story of 17 March showing John Major in a fish shop. Headed: SPOT THE FISH FACE, it began: 'The sight of a fellow creature as grey, washed out and gutted as himself had a dramatic effect on John Major yesterday'.

You can dabble in false impartiality, as when the *Sun* gave roughly equal space to the Conservative and Labour manifestos, but put hostile headlines on some Labour proposals ('LABOUR GOES FOR GRABS – 11M INVESTORS TO BE STUNG'; 'MORE POWER DEALS WITH UNION BOSSES') while the Conservatives got universally friendly ones. The most blatant example here was *The Daily Mail* of 6 April, which had opened its pages to the three party leaders to answer *Daily Mail* questions. Neil Kinnock refused to take part: his questions were printed, and the space for answers left blank. A leader condemned his pusillanimity: 'how arrogant of him', it said, 'to turn down this perfectly civil request to clarify his views'. Still, reading the questions you could see why he would have been suspicious.

Sample questions to Major: 'Can I ask whether you think Mr Kinnock was wise to admit to grave errors of judgement?'; 'Why don't you make the point that the other two parties will pull us into a federal Europe, and the Tory party won't?'

Sample questions to Kinnock: 'Socialism has been ditched in Eastern Europe and discredited here in the West. What makes you think Britain needs another dose of it?' 'Your manifesto is stuffed with spending promises which Labour won't cost and the nation cannot afford. Is not this manifesto a fraud?'

You can also set out to disrupt your opponents not just by what you write but by how you instruct your reporters to operate. The extreme example of this was furnished by *The Daily Express* which called home its Moscow correspondent, Peter Hitchens, whose pursuit of Neil Kinnock had plainly discomfited the Labour leader in 1987, to resume his harrying. The Conservatives campaign, newspapers had predicted, would concentrate on fears about Labour's tax proposals and distrust of its leaders. That, together with a package of dire predictions about the economy (mortgages up, a shrinking pound, the return of roaring inflation) was also the Conservatives tabloid agenda throughout the campaign. But towards the end other issues were worked up too. The main ones were:

The return of union power. For instance:

Sun, 24 March: THREAT OF RETURN TO PICKET TERROR

Star, 24 March: STRIKES WILL BE BACK: secondary picketing will be legalised.

Star, 25 March: REMEMBER THE WINTER OF DISCONTENT

Mail, 31 March: LABOUR'S SECRET PLANS TO PAY UNIONS MORE (continued on 1 April). *Leader*: public sector would rule the roost under Labour

Mail, 1 April: THE KICKBACK: THIS SECRET TAX WHICH WILL ALLOW LABOUR TO REWARD ITS UNION PAYMASTERS, by Eric Hammond

Express, 1 April: UNION PAYMASTERS IN THE WINGS, by Lord Tebbit

Sun, 8 April: UNIONS WILL EXPECT NEIL TO COUGH UP. LEST WE FORGET: THE WINTER OF DISCONTENT IN WORDS AND PICTURES

Mail, polling day: DEMON KING ARTHUR [SCARGILL] WAITS IN THE WINGS. The winter of shame: this was the face of Britain last time Labour ruled (winter of discontent)

Express, polling day: GIVE SACKED MINERS THEIR JOBS BACK, SAYS SCARGILL: Arthur is back, waiting in the wings

Immigration. For instance:

Mail, 26 March: KINNOCK WON'T CURB FLOOD OF BOGUS REFUGEES. Leader quotes Douglas Hurd as saying that there is no sign the Labour Party understands the problem or can be trusted to deal with it

Express, 30 March: *Leader* – Labour is soft on terrorism and immigration

Express, 2 April: FAKE IMMIGRANTS – AN EXPLOSIVE PROBLEM (Baker warns). Feature: Open door to chaos – stricter controls needed as immigration threatens to swamp Europe's cities

Mail, 2 April: MIGRANT MADNESS – ASYLUM SWITCH 'WOULD OPEN DOOR TO REFUGEES' (Baker warns)

Sun, 4 April, *Front-page spread*: Human tide Labour would let in: bogus refugees will grab state hand-outs: We risk sowing the seeds of fascism, says Garry Bushell.

Express, 7 April *Lead story*: BAKER'S MIGRANT FLOOD WARNING: 'LABOUR SET TO OPEN DOORS'. *Leader*: dangers of uncontrolled immigrant

Mail, 8 April: MAJOR STANDS FIRM AGAINST MIGRANT FLOOD ('John Major stood alone yesterday as the only serious party leader to reject any relaxation of immigration control')

Sun, 8 April: Labour's lukewarm stance on immigration will weaken European resistance to the threat of massive immigration

Electoral reform. For instance:

Mail, 7 April: PR HAS HELPED THE FASCISTS MARCH AGAIN IN EUROPE, warns Baker

Mail, 8 April: ITALIANS WANT TO DUMP PR AND ADOPT FIRST PAST THE POST

Express, 7 April: BAKER DESCRIBES PR AS 'PACT WITH THE DEVIL': COULD HAVE TERRIBLE EFFECT ON BRITAIN, HE WARNS. *Feature*: the politics of chaos – under PR, Nazis and even porn stars have a say in government.

The culmination of all these processes, and possibly the most perfect specimen yet in the history of this art form, was *The Sun*'s penultimate paper on 8 April. This picked up a phrase used by John Major when attacking Labour (and said to have been borrowed by him from a friendly journalist). Across the top of page one was a comment piece asking who would best run Britain. 'Who would you choose?' it asked: 'A solid dependable man with a cool head who has been Chancellor, Foreign Secretary and Prime Minister. An experienced world statesman whose friends criticise him for having the style of a bank manager? Or Kinnock: look at his public image. A nice man, but someone who could be drawn into a punch-up at a curry house.'

Readers were then asked to turn to a sort of journalistic theme park called 'Nightmare on Kinnock Street' on pages 2, 3, 4, 5, 6, 7, 8, 9 and 34. (Since this paper is no longer obtainable, its ingredients are summarised in an appendix.)

The way such campaigns are orchestrated, and the joy with which reporters (even some who declare they intend to vote for the party they are busy demeaning) was described in *The Independent* of 3 February by its political editor, Tony Bevins, once of the *Sun* and the *Mail*. 'The anti-Labour, pro-Tory bias', he wrote,

permeates every level of the Tory tabloids; to the point that political reporters see it as their task to generate their own propaganda . . . Having worked for nine years as a political correspondent of the *Sun* and the *Daily Mail*, I count myself as something of an expert on the insidious nature of the process. To survive and rise in, or on, 'the game', you pander to the political prejudices of your paymasters, giving them the stories that you know will make them salivate. That means putting a sparkling gloss on anything to do with the Conservatives and their policies, while denigrating, or 'ratting', Labour. When I was on the *Sun* and *Mail*, for example that task included taking every possible opportunity to hype every threat from the Labour Left in general, and Tony Benn in particular. The direct assistance of Conservative Central Office was not needed then, any more than it was needed by the *News of the World* yesterday, when it headlined its report on the latest anti-Labour wheeze from Rupert Murdoch's Wapping power-base: 'Kinnoch and the Commies' . . . Their [the rat-packers'] friends recognise their skill as professionalism, their critics as prostitution. The best are rewarded with salaries of between £40,000 and £50,000, generous expenses and big cars. Those who fail do not survive; the attrition rate is high.

Mark Lawson observed the rat-pack at work in the early days of the campaign. On 21 March, he reported in *The Independent*:

For John Major, every encounter with the tabloid press is a home fixture; for Neil Kinnock, each one is a perpetual away match. If Donald Duck led the Tory Party, the *Sun* would praise his distinctive rhetorical style. If Mother Teresa was the Labour leader, she would be presented as a venal careerist and hard-hearted pragmatist . . . The tabloid journalists boarding . . . Labour's chartered campaign train were seeking one or both of two stories: the Gaffe story, in which Mr Kinnock forgets a colleague's name or ad-libs a new policy which contradicts John Smith's, and the Mask Slips story, in which Mr Kinnock talks warmly of Albanian economic policy or is seen meeting former members of Stasi in a Cardiff pub.

The open collusion between journalists and party officials shocked some old hands. According to Bevins, at the 1991 Conservative Party conference the government Chief Whip, Richard Ryder, was seen sitting at a *Daily Mail* keyboard reviewing a story for the next day's paper. During the election campaign, one Central Office official sat next to a Conservative tabloid journalist offering advice on how best to shape the story. A useful example of politicians and journalists in each other's pockets was contained in a *Daily Mail* account of the 21st anniversary celebration of the paper becoming a tabloid:

Sir David [English] recalled how during the election campaign he received an 11.15 pm telephone call from the Prime Minister. He agreed with the PM's suggestion that using a soapbox would be a 'brilliant idea' and would turn things around and bring victory.

There is an extra benefit here for the politician. If the wheeze discussed proved to be a mistake, no editor, having concurred, is likely to blame you for it.

But we also need to remember the dog that did not bark. A lot of personal smears were expected: hardly any materialised. Some came to light later, especially with *The Sun*'s disclosure that an unnamed cabinet minister had tried to interest its editor in a story about Paddy Ashdown having five mistresses as well as the one he had declared. *The Sun* declined to deal with the story which it said was in any case untrue. (There were claims later that the call had been made by a notorious Fleet Street hoaxer.)

That fewer smears occurred than in 1987 reflected two things. One was the fear of retribution now that the press was under notice that if it failed to clean up its act there might be legislation – as in David Mellor's famous warning that Fleet Street was 'drinking in the Last Chance saloon'. Still, they have drunk the place dry since then without any adverse consequences. The main constraint may have been different – a balance of fear, on the basis of 'you spill the beans on Frimpton, and we'll say what we know about Frampton'.

In place of smears came mere hints. From *The Sun*:

Disturbing rumours reach me about one of our political figures . . . It is said that the man, who has a charming wife, has had affairs with different women . . . One newspaper is said to have a tape recording of the politician making a compromising call to a woman friend . . . I do not know if there is a shred of truth in any of the allegations. But if there is, one thing is certain. It will destroy the man's political career. (Column by 'The Whip', 3 April)

Labour's shadow foreign secretary Gerald Kaufman was at the centre of a smear riddle last night. Solicitors for bachelor Kaufman, 61, wrote to the *Sun* warning us not to publish 'fabricated stories' being circulated about him. The London firm of solicitors gave no hint of the allegations – but claimed two Tory MPs were trying to smear Kaufman. He is defending a 14,000 majority at Gorton, Manchester. (News story, 31 March)

Did all of this make any difference? After Neil Kinnock's valedictory outburst, some evidence was marshalled to suggest that it did.

Exhibit 1, called in aid by Kinnock himself in his resignation press conference of 13 April, was a column in *The Sunday Telegraph* the previous day by the former Conservative party treasurer, Lord McAlpine:

'The heroes of this campaign', he wrote, 'were Sir David English [editor of the *Mail*], Sir Nicholas Lloyd [editor of the *Express*], Kelvin MacKenzie [editor of the *Sun*] and the other editors of the grander Tory press. Never in the past nine elections have they come out so strongly in favour of the Conservatives. Never has the attack on the Labour Party been so comprehensive. They exposed, ridiculed and humiliated that party, doing each day in their pages the job that the politicians failed to do from their bright new platforms. This is how the election was won, and if the politicians, elated in their hour of victory, are tempted to believe otherwise, they are in very real trouble next time.'

Exhibit 2, also in *The Sunday Telegraph*, came from an even more eminent source:

She [Mrs Thatcher] told friends that it was the Tory journalists who won the election and that this should never be forgotten. Men like Mr Paul Johnson and Mr Kelvin MacKenzie, the editor of the *Sun*. 'You won it', she said to Sir Nicholas Lloyd, the editor of the *Express*. (Mandrake column, *The Sunday Telegraph*, 19 April)

Some Conservative MPs, who had held on to seats they once looked certain to lose, were said to feel much the same way. Under the heading: 'IT'S THE SUN WOT WON IT', the paper reported on 11 April: 'Triumphant MPs were queuing yesterday to say "Thank you my *Sun*" for helping John Major back into Number 10.' The paper quoted David Amess (Conservative, Basildon) as saying: 'It was your front page that did it'. (This was the front page with the man with his head in the light bulb.) 'It crystallised all the issues.'

But none of that is anything like conclusive. Here we have a disgruntled Thatcherite (Lord McAlpine), out of sorts with the new Central Office regime, reluctant to see Chris Patten, or even John Major, getting the credit; and another disgruntled Thatcherite (Mrs T. herself) of whom much the same could be said. As for *The Sun*'s crowing, it did not really mean it. 'We never tried to force our views down their throats', the paper protested. 'It is flattering for him to suggest we have so much power. Like so much else he says, it is also untrue.' A spokesman for the paper was quoted as saying: 'Neil Kinnock's claim that the Press cost him victory is an insult to the 14 million people who voted Conservative.'

David Amess himself later claimed that the most he had said was that *The Sun* had helped. He had been misquoted. The *Mail* also rebuked Mr Kinnock's naivety. Its editor, Sir David English, told a reporter:

Table 11.2 *Newspaper readers: how they swung in the 1992 election* (%)

	How they would have voted in June–Dec. 91		How far they swung	How they voted 9 April	How they would have voted if typical of their social class
The Daily Telegraph	Con.	72		72	50
(Con.)	Lab.	13	1 to Con.	11	27
	Lib. Dem.	15		16	20
The Daily Express	Con.	66		68	45
(Con.)	Lab.	19	3 to Con.	15	33
	Lib. Dem.	13		15	19
The Daily Mail	Con.	66		65	45
(Con.)	Lab.	16	0.5 to Con.	14	32
	Lib. Dem.	15		18	19
The Times	Con.	61		64	51
(Con.)	Lab.	19	3.5 to Con.	15	25
	Lib. Dem.	17		19	20
Today	Con.	51		43	43
(Con.)	Lab.	31	4 to Lab.	31	36
	Lib. Dem.	18		23	18
The Sun	Con.	39		45	39
(Con.)	Lab.	47	8.5 to Con.	36	40
	Lib. Dem.	11		15	17
The Independent	Con.	33		25	55
(nil)	Lab.	39	3 to Lab.	37	27
	Lib. Dem.	25		35	20
The Daily Star	Con.	26		32	37
(nil)	Lab.	62	7.5 to Con.	53	39
	Lib. Dem.	9		12	17
The Daily Mirror	Con.	20		20	39
(Lab.)	Lab.	67	2 to Con.	63	40
	Lib. Dem.	12		14	17
The Guardian	Con.	12		15	49
(Lab.)	Lab.	59	3.5 to Con.	55	28
	Lib. Dem.	22		25	20

Source: Times Guide to the House of Commons, 1992 based on MORI analysis.

I have no doubt that we helped swing a number of people towards the Tory position and equally turned a few more away from Labour. To suggest, as Mr Kinnock has done, that the *Daily Mail* singlehandedly won the election for the Conservatives and brought about a Labour defeat is very flattering but it ascribes far more influence to us than we could give ourselves.'

Let us turn from this fanciful stuff to calm psephological and academic analysis. The main evidence adduced was figures compiled by MORI showing swings from Labour to the Conservatives among readers of different newspapers up to 9 April, with substantial swings to the right among readers of some of the right-wing/cheerleader papers and Labour gaining ground among readers of the neutral *Independent* and near-neutral *Today* (see table 11.2).

But here too there are reservations. These figures could have been affected by changes in newspaper readership over the period. There are swings to the Conservatives among readers of papers which were opposed to them – 3.5 per cent among *Guardian* readers, 2 per cent among *Mirror* readers. And why should the *Sun* and *Star* (which, remember did not formally endorse the Conservatives) have been so much more persuasive than the equally fervent *Express* and *Mail?* Professor Bill Miller of Glasgow argues that *Mirror* readers are likely to be committed to a political party (70 per cent), *Sun* and *Star* readers less so (41 per cent). *Mirror* readers are interested in politics (75 per cent), *Sun* and *Star* readers less so (55 per cent). In other words, *The Sun* appeals to the uncommitted and the apolitical and one would expect its readers to be more open to influence.[1]

There is some supporting evidence from the polls. Harris's final poll for ITN found that voters who in fact would not have been hurt by the Labour budget or would even have gained from it believed it would harm them. That supports Labour's belief that the constant reiteration of the dubious Conservative claim that Labour would put £1,250 on every tax bill, in the press as well as on billboards, helped turn the election against them. But some of these respondents might have feared for their fate when they had climbed higher up the ladder, rather than what would happen straightaway.

There are also scattered findings in the work of chagrined pollsters who went back to find out what might have gone wrong. ICM, *The Guardian*'s pollsters, quoted these:

I read in the paper about Neil Kinnock having a light bulb in his head and I had strong fears. I also thought Arthur Scargill would raise his ugly head again.

I read the *Sun* . . . Arthur Scargill, what he was going to do with the unions if Labour got in.

I read two or three articles about Labour's tax plans and the implications they would have on me. I had never before seen them so specifically printed.

All had one thing in common: the frighteners had worked.

None of this is conclusive. But it points in the same direction as two academic studies, by Martin Harrop of Newcastle University and Bill Miller of Glasgow University. Harrop found that Conservative voters are more likely to stay loyal if they read a Conservative newspaper (12 per cent more in February 1974, 14 per cent more in October 1974, 15 per cent more in 1979) while uncommitted voters are more likely to choose the Conservatives if they read a Conservative newspaper. Miller calculated the tabloid effect as equivalent to a

Table 11.3 *Election advice of newspapers, by circulation*

	1966	1970	1974 (Feb.)	1974 (Oct.)	1979	1983	1987	1992
Con.	56	55	68	47	66	75	73	66
Lab.	43	44	30	29	28	22	25	25
Lib. Dem.	4	5	5	5	0	0	3	0
Gap	13	11	38	18	38	53	48	41
Majority of winning party	Lab. 97	Con. 31	none	Lab. 4	Con. 44	Con. 144	Con. 101	Con. 21

2-point advantage for the Conservatives. In the year up to the 1987 election, there was a 5 per cent overall swing to the Conservatives; among persistent readers of Conservative tabloids it was 12 per cent; among persistent readers of Labour tabloids only 1 per cent. In a pattern similar to that of MORI's findings, *Express* and *Mail* readers swung right by 8 per cent, *Sun* and *Star* readers by 17 per cent.

The power to reinforce and convert does appear to have limits. The campaigns on taxation and Neil Kinnock's competence exploited existing doubts, partially born of previous press coverage (and particularly by the Conservative tabloid practice of instructing reporters on Kinnock's foreign trips to file only the blunders) but helped out by observation. The concept of Kinnock as garrulous and excitable was more than pure tabloid invention.

At one point the Conservative tabloids tried to drum up support for the poll tax: that fell on stonier ground. On the other hand, how far respondents to the polls were right in seeing John Major at the time of Maastricht as a successful world statesman, and how far they were simply carried along by tabloid euphoria, it is too early to say.

It has also been argued in exoneration (even in *Guardian* leaders) that the Conservative press have always behaved like this, but Labour was still elected when it deserved to be. But Labour has only had two clear victories in the past sixty years, 1945 and 1966. In 1945 Labour had been in coalition, and its leaders were known not to be demons; coverage was also restricted by news-print regulations. In 1966 people had seen a Labour government at work over eighteen months: again, that diminished the effect of the demonology. In 1966 in any case, Labour had an unusually large share of newspaper support, as table 11.3 shows.

Neil Kinnock's indictment cannot be proved, but such evidence as there is seems more in his favour than against him. Perhaps the shrewdest comment on the shy little claims of the *Sun* and *Mail* that they do not make that much difference came from the journalists' trade paper, the *UK Press*

Gazette: 'To claim that they have no influence over the decisions, opinions and attitudes of readers would be a suicide note sent to all advertisers, and it would also mean that their anti-Labour campaign was a preconceived exercise in futility.'

The Conservatives' advantage among tabloid readers, and the unscrupulous way in which these papers behave, seems to this journalist one among several ways in which general elections in Britain are best assessed as contests not being fought on our good old friend the level playing field. Others include party finances and the electoral system; and taking all three cases the Liberal Democrats, lacking any newspaper support, lacking money, and losing out every time on first past the post, suffer more than Labour.

There is one factor, though, which must have reduced the effectiveness of this cheerleader reporting: the counterweight of radio and television. Where 66 per cent say they trust BBC and ITN 'a great deal', and 53 per cent say the same for the broadsheet newspapers, the proportion admitting that they trust the tabloids is only 29 per cent.

Some hammers of BBC 'bias' on the Conservative right like to say that they are not opposed to committed reporting as long as it is openly done. They foresee a world of broadcasting diversity in which party allegiances would be proudly paraded just as they are in the press. Given the motivation of most of those owning such liberated stations, there is little reason to think, and these champions of freedom do not provide any, that the balance between the parties in this new unregulated broadcasting would be very much different from the one that now prevails in the tabloid press.

What can be done about it? Probably very little; and while the Conservative hegemony lasts, nothing at all. A machinery of sanctions which sought to curb these excesses, so that the press might serve democracy better, would need to avoid entirely the risk of making it more difficult for newspapers to print information which inconveniences and embarrasses governments. No one has yet suggested with any persuasiveness how this could be done. Codes of conduct? But we have those already, in terms which ought to preclude much of the tabloid practice we saw in March and April 1992. Take these two requirements, for instance:

Newspapers and periodicals should take care not to publish inaccurate, misleading or distorted material.

Newspapers, while free to be partisan, should distinguish clearly between comment, conjecture and fact.

Apply those to the tabloid coverage of the election and one would not have much of it left.

More honest standards of journalism? Not a hope, while professional pride and generous money buy acquiescence, even enthusiasm. Some of those who deploy their skills in the Conservative tabloid crusade were not so long ago doing much the same thing for the other side on *The Daily Mirror*.

Will it help to sustain even longer the longest period of one-party dominance for over a century? Very probably, yes.

Note

1 See Martin Linton, 'Press-ganged at the polls', *Guardian Guide to the House of Commons*, 1992.

Appendix A
Certified average sale of daily newspapers

	April 1992	Dec. 1991 to May 1992
Express	1,542,786	1,517,697
Mail	1,675,453	1,677,555
Mirror/Record	3,660,756	3,618,875
Star	805,793	803,732
Sun	3,570,562	3,587,724
Today	533,177	483,481
Telegraph	1,038,133	1,046,379
Guardian	429,062	418,296
Independent	389,523	374,172
Times	386,258	389,399

Appendix B
The contents of 'Nightmare on Kinnock Street', *The Sun*, 8 April 1992

p. 1: Leader comparing Major and Kinnock

pp. 2–3: He (Kinnock) will have a new home (No. 10), you won't – Labour will mean misery for new buyers

A threat to our proud history (Labour, the EC and sovereignty)

Watch gas and power prices rocket

Unions will expect Neil to cough up

Labour's lukewarm stance on immigration will weaken European resistance to threat of massive immigration

Apology to Neil Kinnock for an earlier *Sun* claim that he had never held down a real job

pp. 4–5: Gays to rule on planning applications: even loft conversions, home extensions and garages will have to be approved by gay and lesbian groups if Labour are elected

Prices set to jump 17.6 per cent (under Labour)

Housing horrors (under Labour)

Baby Carl would not have lived but for Tory NHS reforms

p. 6: Cartoons and continuation of p. 1 comment

p. 7: Lest we forget – pictures and story on 'Winter of Discontent'

p. 8: I've just begun, trust me, says Major

Woman 'union boss' [in fact, the vice-chairman of the MSF branch in Bridgwater, Somerset] claims she squelched Kinnock on TV

Alan Sugar of Amstrad blasts Labour's 'con trick'

Tories closing poll gap

Tory doc barred as Kinnock visits hospital

TV slur by Leftie [he used a naughty word]

p. 9: It's Mao or never for Neil. A psychic asked some famous dead people how they would vote in this election. The line up was

Conservative – Churchill, Field Marshall Lord Montgomery, Queen Victoria, Elvis Presley, Sid James

Labour – Mao, Marx, Stalin, Trotsky, Brezhnev, Andropov, John Lennon and Robert Maxwell ('I see a lot of me in Neil Kinnock')

p. 10: Full-page advertisement for the Conservatives

p. 34: First day of a Labour government would see billions wiped off shares; pound falling through floor; dealers issuing the worldwide warning – get your cash out of Britain.

12   Characters and assassinations: portrayals of John Major and Neil Kinnock in *The Daily Mirror* and *The Sun*

Colin Seymour-Ure

Major is a banker. But rather his hand on the tiller than the ginger jester's.
We are not amused by him at all.
The Sun, 8 April 1992, attrib. Queen Victoria

Was *The Sun* taking the general election campaign seriously? Of course it was. But this kind of whimsical fabrication, part of a trawl of voting intentions of historical figures, including Genghis Khan (abstainer), Stalin (Labour) and Hitler (Screaming Lord Sutch), complicated the simple purpose with which this chapter started. The idea was to analyse the coverage of the three main party leaders in *The Sun* and *The Daily Mirror*. How much space were they given? How were they characterised?[1] *The Sun* and *The Daily Mirror* were obvious choices. They have similar readership profiles; they compete for circulation, just as they compete in politics; and together they reach a large proportion of the electorate. Tabloid papers were chosen because of the importance of pictures – both in the amount of space these occupy and in their impact on the papers' presentation and style. If visual images have become predominant in the television age, then the campaign pictures in the press deserve clearer scrutiny than they usually seem to get in the academic literature.

TV lies behind the chapter's purpose in a second sense. The claim that 'TV is the campaign', first voiced in the early 1970s, is now in obvious ways axiomatic. It seemed therefore, again, worth looking at how the TV campaign was reported in the tabloids. In particular, would papers treat the leaders' TV performances as news items to be reported alongside (or in conjunction with) hustings speeches and factory visits? Or would they not waste words on programmes their readers could watch for themselves? How far, too, might they report the TV campaign as dominated even more by the party leaders, perhaps, than it actually was? Would their own campaign priorities, finally, appear to be influenced by TV's own agenda?

All these questions remain unchanged by Queen Victoria's doubts about the 'ginger jester', even if they are not all easily answered – and certainly not in a chapter of this length. The truisms about tabloid papers can be amply illustrated from *The Sun* and *The Daily Mirror* coverage of the leaders. Pictures do take up a lot of space (though less than the author had expected). Tabloid prose does exaggerate, simplify, generalise. Leaders do not make mistakes, for instance, they make gaffes and blunders. Also they drop clangers, endlessly, reverberating like church bells.

Paddy Ashdown might have dropped more clangers if he had been reported much at all. This chapter had intended to compare all three leaders. But in most categories his coverage in both papers was tiny. It consisted in occasional news reports and dismissive editorial comments of a few square inches. The most serious treatment was a full-length feature, matching features about Major and Kinnock, in *The Sun*. *The Daily Mirror* even avoided printing a photograph of him. The virtually complete exclusion of Ashdown was the most comprehensive example in this election campaign of the reductive simplicities of tabloid journalism.

The complications illustrated by *The Sun*'s quotations by long-dead figures start with the very process of deciding both what to count as election coverage and, within that, as coverage of a party leader. There are two types of difficulty. In one, a story's relevance to the specific events of the campaign is oblique, though its partisan point may be obvious. In the other, the relevance to the campaign is clear, but the treatment is oblique. The best examples of the former come from *The Daily Mirror* and of the latter from *The Sun*. Much of the *Mirror*'s campaign was given over, as it announced in the early days, to highly illustrated, densely written analysis of issues such as the NHS, unemployment and homelessness. (This helps to account for the small amount of the *Mirror*'s total election coverage, 13 per cent, that was given to the three party leaders, compared with the 28 per cent given by *The Sun*.) These large, double-page features were powerfully presented and full of human interest in addition to facts and figures. Of course they were at the core of the policy issues contested by the parties. But they were background or context, not news. 'Jennifer's Ear' (known among local consultants as Grommetgate) was, in contrast, the biggest NHS news story of the campaign. In this, too, the precise point at which the blanket coverage in the tabloids might be regarded as not strictly about the election could be a matter of argument. Similarly, was the *Mirror*'s feature story about the sad circumstances of former England foot-baller Bobby Smith, dogged by delays in health treatment, too distant from campaign events to be counted as election coverage, despite the political lessons the *Mirror* would expect its readers to draw?

The Sun too had a few stories that were certainly relevant to the election battle but hardly to the campaign. For instance, the paper splashed a feature telling how Kinnock had allegedly become estranged, as he advanced in politics, from the friend who had been his best man. The story included a large photograph of a party in the Kinnocks' student days. More exotically, the *Sun* offered, early on, an illustrated guide to 'Kinnock-flee zones' – places to which appalled voters could retreat in the accident of a Labour victory. They included Outer Mongolia, the Arctic Circle and the Virgin Islands, with facts about climate, population, living conditions, in each. This example illustrates, too, the common ambiguity in tabloid papers about whether coverage is strictly of a

Figure 12.1   Kinnock-flee zones

leader, or whether the leader's name is used as a synonym for his party. 'Kinnock-flee zones'? or 'Labour-flee zones'?

The best examples in the *Sun*, however, illustrate oblique treatment of definite campaign stories. Like the press in general, for instance, the *Sun* seized on Major's hustings soapbox tactic. Its response was a DIY-style, step-by-step photo-feature about how to build your own soapbox. This ingenious treatment highlighted the populist connotations of Major's tactic, while avoiding the risk of taking it too seriously ('John Major revived a crate tradition'). But only in an indirect sense could the feature be regarded as a political story – and about John Major himself.

The *Sun*'s stories, more than the *Mirror*'s, contained frequent elements of fantasy. The story's idea might be practical, but be given an implausible treatment. Or the idea itself might be implausible. Building your own soapbox was practical in one sense, but *Sun* readers were unlikely to rush out and build one, let alone set it up on a street corner. The Kinnock-flee zones were

Figure 12.2   How to build your Major soap box

described with an entirely straight face, but the 'zones' selected were absurd. Speculation about the political attitudes historical figures might have taken in our own times is a fair game; but attributing *Sun*-speak in direct quotation marks to Queen Victoria makes it surreal. Launching an apparently serious hunt for the Chancellor of the Exchequer, Norman Lamont, on the grounds that he has disappeared (a *Mirror* example), is a tease. Obviously the Chancellor had not gone missing. This was the *Mirror*'s way of making a simple partisan point about his credibility.

The tabloid newspaper's scope for using pictures to dominate text on a small page contributed much to the fantasy treatment of election stories. Two examples in *The Sun* were outstanding. The first was the paper's front-page message to voters on polling day. The second, the same day, offered a picture of 'How Page 3 will look under Kinnock' (not under Labour, note). Both stories combine visual and verbal images to great effect.

'If Kinnock wins today will the last person to leave Britain please turn out

Figure 12.3   If Kinnock wins today will the last person to leave Britain please turn out the lights

the lights.' The image is stark. If Kinnock wins (not Labour, again), there is no alternative but to pack up and go. Turning out the lights and leaving the room is a decisive and final act, reinforced as an image by the deadening associations of darkness. Visually this darkness is emphasised by printing the message on a dark background. More important, though, is the framing of the photograph of

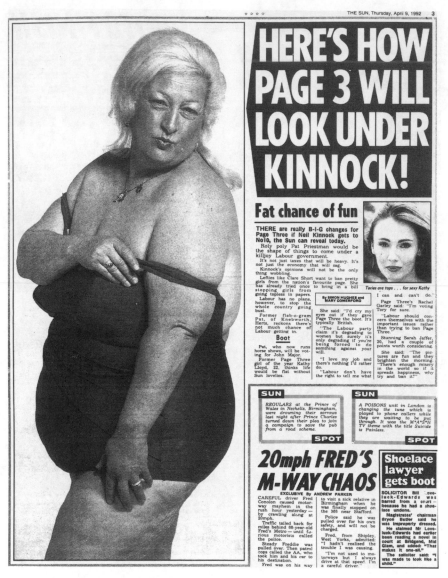

Figure 12.4   Here's how page 3 will look under Kinnock

Kinnock's head in a lightbulb. Turn out the light – and you extinguish Kinnock. With a flick of the switch, a cross on the ballot, the journey to a Kinnock-flee zone can be avoided. The *Sun* signs off with 'Goodnight and thank you for everything', at the end of a short homily reminding readers that 'You know our views on the subject'. The page is a powerful editorial comment, but it is not in the ordinary sense a 'leading article'. It is too short to make an argument. The words are important, but only because they make explicit the idea behind the montage of head in lightbulb.

'Page 3 under Kinnock' used a half-page picture of a former 'flab-o-gram' lady as a symbol of life under a Labour government. The pretext was that 'Lefties like Clare Short want to ban pretty girls from the nation's favourite page'. Half the text quoted former page-3 girls in defence of what they saw as a harmless practice: a Labour government should get on with more important issues. But the first, more prominent, part of the story gave a general warning that 'Roly Poly Pat Priestman would be the shape of things to come under a killjoy Labour government'. The warning was developed in a series of puns playing on the woman's physique. 'It's not just taxes that will be heavy'; 'Kinnock's opinions will not be the only thing wobbling'. Text and picture are mutually reinforcing. *Sun* readers, finding a flab-o-gram lady in place of the usual pin-up, would be likely to get the *Sun*'s point simply from the headline, but the jokey text, backed by the serious points made later on, rammed home the symbolism.

Both the Kinnock lightbulb montage and the flab-o-gram lady are stories using photographs not as direct evidence in support of a point of view but as symbolic evidence. The pictures are intended to evoke feelings on the basis of analogy, rather than to justify reasoned arguments. 'This is what life would be like under Kinnock'; 'If we don't switch off Kinnock today, we'll need to emigrate'. The *Mirror*, by contrast, relied much more heavily on naturalistic photographs, of deplorable housing conditions, schools and health care. Their occasional use of montage was limited to unexceptional examples such as giving John Smith the 'real' Chancellor's dispatch box in a photo of his Shadow Budget. While this might help to establish the Shadow Chancellor's credibility, it was still a form of direct evidence compared with the lightbulb and the flab-o-gram lady. Moreover it was directly political. The flab-o-gram lady has to be read in the context of the adjoining text (which takes up much less space) before she takes on political meaning. Even then, should we really regard this as part of the *Sun*'s coverage of Neil Kinnock's campaign?

The affinity between symbolic evidence and humorous technique, finally, is worth stressing. Since they work by analogy, symbols lend themselves to the *double entendre*. The page-3 story, as we have seen, is built on a visual pun. In the picture, this is strengthened by the lady's pose (with a shoulder strap drawn down over her arm) and by her pout. In the text, the puns start with the heading – 'Fat Chance of Fun'. The Kinnock lightbulb story does not pun in quite the same way. But it involves the incongruous juxtaposition of ideas – one of the staple forms of humour.

Humour is a distinctive part of the *Sun*'s style. Arguably it is intrinsic to mid and late twentieth-century tabloid journalism. Pictures are so easily entertaining; and entertainment has humour as an ingredient – 'light relief' – and is one of the services people have always sought from the popular press. Hugh Cudlipp's memoirs confirm the strength of humour as a feature of the *Mirror* in its heyday in the twenty years after 1945.[2] Perhaps some of the *Sun*'s success in the twenty years thereafter came from its being more fun than the *Mirror*.

The danger of a humorous treatment of an election campaign is that humour can be a strong political weapon yet at the same time can be an excuse for untruth. When the *Sun* quotes Queen Victoria on the 'ginger jester', everyone knows the quotation is untrue, so it does not matter. The *Sun* is teasing Neil Kinnock, while bringing the readers in on the joke (and thereby flattering them). The joke does not diminish the electoral process: at most the *Sun* implies that we should keep a sense of proportion about it. But the joke does tend to belittle Kinnock. (John Major, it goes without saying, is not teased in the same feature.)

'Untruth' is barely the right word in such an example. 'Fantasy', used earlier, is better. But untruthfulness of any kind in a newspaper is dangerous unless it is very clearly signalled by the conventional compartments of newspaper design, through which news, features, reviews and so on are separated from each other. In partisan papers such as the *Sun* and *Mirror*, these lines become confused during an election campaign. 'News' and 'comment' are blurred (as in the page-3 story). 'Fantasy' stories co-exist with hustings reports. In the latter, too, the necessary processes of summary and selection, together with the tabloid style of language, produce a limited and idiosyncratic version of 'the truth', in which a quotation, for instance, may be an encapsulated version of someone's actual words.

There is nothing new in that observation. But it accounts, overall, for the difficulty of doing a simple content analysis of tabloid coverage of the party leaders. Such an analysis is no longer a matter of tracking reports of what the leaders said and did, of pictures of them doing it, and of comments and analyses in feature and editorial columns. (Was it ever? It would be interesting to compare the 1992 style of coverage with one of the post-1945 elections.) Conventional forms survive: leading articles, news reports, editorial features, columnists. But *Sun* editorials in 1992 were often only a few sentences long. A columnist such as Joe Haines in the *Mirror* could sound indistinguishable from an editorialist. The gaffes, blunders and clangers of the leaders – cheerfully tendentious words all – were bandied about in news stories.

One is confronted, in sum, with an integrated package. Pictures and text supplement each other in the ways described. Together, they may fill a page with a story that is neither a 'campaign report' nor an 'issue analysis' in the obvious sense at all. Large amounts of space are given to items such as the DIY soap-box feature, which are not strictly about one of the leaders (and have not here been counted as such) and yet which may have contributed to readers' opinions about them. Neither the *Sun* nor the *Mirror* had a consistent practice of referring to a Kinnock/Major government rather than a Labour/Conservative government. But each attached the leader's name to stories that were not in the direct sense 'about' him.

Table 12.1 *General election press coverage, 12 March–9 April 1992*

	The Daily Mirror	The Sun	The Guardian	The Daily Telegraph
Total election coverage				
Sq. ins.	12,900	11,222	49,256	29,782
Party leaders (%)[1]	1,710 (13)	3,094 (28)	9,021 (18)	4,715 (16)
Coverage of broadcasting[2]				
Total sq. ins. (%)	521 (4)	557 (5)	2,312 (5)	1,775 (6)
Party leaders (%)	108 (21)	261 (47)	767 (33)	630 (35)
Photographs[2]				
Total sq. ins. (%)	2,073 (16)	1,583 (14)	8,521 (17)	3,448 (12)
Party leaders (%)	566 (27)	655 (41)	3,614 (42)	1,460 (42)
Other election coverage[3]				
Total sq. ins. (%)	10,306 (80)	9,139 (81)	38,556 (78)	24,604 (83)
Party leaders (%)	1,036 (10)	2,178 (24)	4,640 (12)	2,670 (11)
Coverage of Royal Family				
Total sq. ins. (%)	5,730 (44)	7,100 (63)	*	*

Note: 'Party leaders' includes Major, Kinnock and Ashdown.
[1] Excludes cartoons of Leaders.
[2] Includes photographs and broadcasting.
[3] Includes campaign reports, features, editorials, letters, etc.
* Not calculated.

This chapter has not quite ended up being about a different topic from what it intended. But scrutiny of the *Sun* and *Mirror* left the author much more interested in the style and technique of those papers during the election campaign than in the quantitative details of coverage. This feeling was confirmed by such obvious factors as, for instance, the distorting effect which a single splash headline can have on the total space devoted to a particular subject otherwise covered only in small items over a period of time.

The tables provide summary data, first, of the three party leaders' coverage, with statistics from *The Guardian* and *The Daily Telegraph* for comparison. Next, a closer look is taken at leading articles. These provide case studies about the selectiveness of the tabloids and, with evidence from feature writers, about the language in which the leaders were characterised. Thirdly, the coverage of broadcasting is examined. Last come observations about photographs, to supplement the analysis which has already been offered.

Total coverage of the three leaders was rather less than had been expected. In *The Sun*, it was more than one quarter (28 per cent) of the total election coverage. This might seem high, on a constitutionalist view of the election as a contest in 651 constituencies, or between rival teams of some two dozen potential cabinet ministers who would share collective responsibility for government. But it is certainly not a figure high enough to justify claiming, say, that the *Sun* conducted a 'presidential' campaign. To put the election in context, table 12.1 includes the coverage of the Royal Family during the campaign. This was mainly about the separation of the Yorks and the death of Prince Diana's father. These stories took up more than three times as much space as the party leaders in the *Mirror* and more than twice as much in the *Sun*.

An exaggerated impression of the amount of coverage given to the leaders might also be gained if they dominated the front page news. This they did in *The Guardian* (although the paper's layout did not present a particular story as clearly 'dominating' the front page). Of twenty-three *Guardian* lead stories, Major was mentioned in twenty-one, Kinnock in eighteen and Ashdown in twelve. In the *Mirror* and *Sun*, however, the leaders featured in the lead story infrequently. In the *Mirror*, Major was mentioned twice and Kinnock once; in the *Sun*, Major three times and Kinnock five times.

The space given to photographs of the campaign would not support an impression that tabloid papers are dominated by pictures, either. Indeed, pictures took up proportionately more space in *The Guardian* than in either the *Mirror* or the *Sun*, and not much more in the *Sun* than in *The Daily Telegraph*. If photos seem to dominate, perhaps it is because of the concentrated power of visual images, compared with the scattered acres of text. Coverage of the broadcast campaign was very much smaller still – and at the same low level around 5 per cent in broadsheets and tabloids alike. The hypothesis (much fancied at the outset of this study) that the broadcast campaign would form a significant proportion of tabloid coverage, seems doomed. Only the frenetic few

Table 12.2 *Coverage of party leaders' activities*: The Daily Mirror *and* The Sun *12 March–9 April 1992 (number of sq. ins.)*

	Items in *The Daily Mirror*						Items in *The Sun*					
	Major		Kinnock		Ashdown		Major		Kinnock		Ashdown	
Reports												
Activity:												
Speech	6	90	10	135	1	1	6	182	2	6	1	2
Press Conference	4	27	2	30	1	14	3	89	4	104	1	3
Visit	3	16	2	14	—	—	13	162	5	54	1	1
Broadcast	7	49	5	10	2	6	3	35	8	146	2	2
Newspaper interview	—	—	3	270	—	—	—	—	—	—	—	—
Other/unspecified	8	152	3	24	2	4	3	18	5	73	3	8
Total	28	334	25	483	6	25	28	486	24	383	8	16
Subject:												
Own policies	11	203	12	229	2	17	8	193	11	149	—	—
Attacking other parties	6	30	11	144	1	1	12	142	3	6	3	5
Total	17	233	23	373	3	18	20	335	14	154	3	5
Comment												
Editorial	12	134	4	13	—	—	13	106	20	259	4	10
Columnists' features	5	100	—	—	1	12	9	200	16	815	5	87
Total	17	234	4	13	1	12	22	306	36	1,074	9	97

Note: 'Items' are separate individual stories and articles. Photographs and cartoons are excluded. Figures for broadcasts include only broadcasts *by* leaders.

days after Labour's PEB about the year-long wait for a non-critical operation on Jennifer Bennett's ear, did TV set the priority of the election agenda.

Within these separate categories, on the other hand, the proportion of space given to the three leaders was certainly much closer to what had been expected. Nearly half the *Sun*'s broadcast coverage was about the leaders – the extreme case. So were two-fifths of the *Sun*'s photos (and those of the two broadsheet papers). In the large residual category of various types of news and feature, the proportions not surprisingly were less.

In table 12.2, the extent to which the tabloids reported the election as a two-horse race becomes plain. Paddy Ashdown received perfunctory treatment in the *Mirror*. He had more in the *Sun*, but most references were along the lines 'A vote for Paddy Ashdown is a vote for Kinnock' (3 April). The table excludes photographs: it is intended to show the limited amount of space for words about the leaders. A consequence of this dearth is that the reported items are too few in each category (speeches, press conferences etc.) to warrant an attempt to compare the number of reports with the number of speeches or conferences each leader gave. More interesting are the indications of bias in the figures and the quite high ratio of space given to comment/interpretation rather than to reportage. The latter is confirmation of the line of argument developed in the first part of this chapter (notwithstanding its claim that comment and news become blurred).

The best indication of bias, in the simple sense of giving more space to the preferred leader, is the aggregate of the various types of report:

	Preferred leader (sq. ins.)	Opponent (sq. ins.)
Daily Mirror	483	334
The Sun	486	383

Similarly each paper gave little space to its opponent's attacks on the paper's preferred party, compared with the coverage of its preferred leader's attacks on the other party:

	Preferred leader's attacks (sq. ins.)	Opponent's attacks (sq. ins.)
Daily Mirror	144	30
The Sun	142	12

It should be noted from table 12.2, however, that more space was given in both papers to the party leaders' remarks about their own policies than to their attacks on each other's.

Under the heading 'Comment', table 12.2 includes those parts of editorials (used here instead of 'leading article' or 'leader' to avoid confusion) and of feature articles, which refer to the party leaders. These were used overwhelmingly as instruments of attack. Indeed, *The Daily Mirror* barely mentioned

Table 12.3 *Politicians named in editorials, 12 March–9 April 1992*

Politicians named	No. (%) of editorials			
	The Daily Mirror	The Sun	The Guardian	The Daily Telegraph
Conservative				
Major	12 (55)	13 (38)	21 (60)	12 (41)
Thatcher	7 (32)	3 (9)	12 (34)	5 (17)
Lamont	4 (18)	—	6 (17)	3 (10)
Waldegrave	3 (14)	—	3 (9)	—
Patten	1	—	5 (14)	—
Heseltine	1	—	4 (11)	2 (7)
Clarke	1	—	—	3 (10)
Baker	1	—	1	—
Tebbit	1	—	1	—
Lawson	—	1	2 (6)	2 (7)
Heath	—	1	—	—
Whitelaw	—	1	—	—
Others	—	—	6	1
Labour				
Kinnock	4 (18)	20 (59)	14 (40)	16 (55)
Smith	2 (9)	2 (6)	6 (17)	10 (34)
Cook	—	2 (6)	3 (9)	1
Hattersley	—	1	2 (6)	5 (17)
Meacher	—	1	1	—
Kaufman	—	—	2 (6)	2 (7)
Beckett	—	—	1	3 (10)
Others	—	—	3	3
Lib. Dem.				
Ashdown	—	4 (12)	14 (40)	—
Steel	—	—	1	—
Beith	—	—	1	—
Total election editorials	22	35	35	29

Kinnock at all – he 'looks every inch a Prime Minister', for instance (2 April). Most of its feature articles, it must be remembered, dealt with 'the issues' of the campaign and made no reference to Kinnock. Instead, the paper gave him space to show his paces in three long interviews that were written up as features but are classified here as reports. The *Sun*, by comparison, wrote more often positively about Major. The proportion of editorials mentioning the antagonist leader was almost identical in each paper: twelve out of twenty-two (55 per cent) in *The Daily Mirror* mentioned Major and twenty out of thirty-five (57 per cent) in *The Sun* mentioned Kinnock. The bulk of comment about the leaders in both papers, in features and editorials alike, was knocking copy.

Table 12.3 provides a simple indication of the extent to which editorials mentioned leaders to the exclusion of their colleagues. The greater scope and depth of broadsheet coverage shows up only in *The Guardian*. The afterglow of Mrs Thatcher is bright: in *The Daily Mirror* and *The Guardian* she was too good an enemy to spurn and ranked easily second after Major. The *Sun*, remarkably, named no other serving Cabinet Minister beyond Major at all. The *Mirror* named only John Smith among Kinnock's team. Laying about them, on the other hand, the *Sun* editorialists attacked four shadow ministers in addition to Kinnock, and the *Mirror* attacked six cabinet ministers – chiefly Norman Lamont and Health Secretary William Waldegrave. The editorial as instrument of attack thus penetrated beyond the party leaders themselves. There was a slight tendency in the same direction in the broadsheet papers, but not nearly so pronounced.

The subjects to which the leaders were linked in editorials were comparatively few. Most common (almost half in *The Sun*) were campaign prospects and issues of leadership. The *Mirror* linked Major to the economy and to the NHS, and the *Sun* linked Kinnock to these issues. The *Mirror* linked Major to employment, and the *Sun* linked Kinnock to defence and the European Community. On a broad range of policy issues, such as crime and education, the tabloid editorials were silent or made no reference to the leaders.

More fun is the study of how the tabloids actually wrote about the party leaders and characterised them. Possibly tabloidese is an artificial language, as is sometimes claimed of BBC English between wars. Its punch and pithiness, in any case, are entirely hidden in the bland polysyllabic categories of table 12.4 – victims of a process of summarisation which turns a 'windbag' into someone 'boring'. The table lists all the cases, in editorials, features and news items, when an explicit characterisation was made of Major and Kinnock in the *Mirror* and *Sun*. Neither paper has more than a passing good word to say for the opposing leader: *The Sun* concedes, for instance, that Kinnock's 'heart is in the right place'. The table is therefore organised on the basis of contrasting terms (Tough/Weak, Determined/Indecisive, etc.).

Most of the characterisation is negative: three-fifths in the *Sun*, three-quarters in the *Mirror*. In the comparatively small number of its positive references to Kinnock (twenty-one), the *Mirror* emphasises his toughness,

Table 12.4 *Characterisation of party leaders, The Daily Mirror and The Sun 12 March–9 April 1992*

	No. of positive mentions		No. of negative mentions		
	The Sun	The Daily Mirror	The Sun	The Daily Mirror	
	Major	Kinnock	Kinnock	Major	
Tough, strong, combative, courageous	15	5	9	11	Weak, panicking, cowardly, pacifist
Determined, solid	2	1	8	1	Indecisive
Trustworthy, honest, sincere	4	2	14	3	Untrustworthy, dishonest, unprincipled
Quiet, cool-headed, good humoured	9	2	10	3	Hot-headed, irresponsible
Experienced	2	—	6	—	Inexperienced
Competent	4	4	15	16	Incompetent, 'clangers', 'blunders'
Confident	4	3	—	7	Unconfident
Effective	9	1	7	12	Ineffective, 'dismal'
Modest	1	—	8	6	Arrogant, power-hungry, vain, sneering
Exciting, interesting, 'vision', positive, 'Man of the People'	6	3	5	16	Boring, grey, uninspiring, ridiculous, negative, unpopular
	—	—	—	1	Sexist
Total	56	21	82	76	Total

competence, confidence and capacity to excite. The toughness category accounts for at least the same proportion of the *Sun*'s references to Major. The *Sun* stresses also his effectiveness, quiet good humour and (somewhat less) his capacity to enthuse. The former two are, notably, not characteristics which the *Mirror* finds in Kinnock.

The leaders do not emerge on the negative side as mirror images either, except in a few categories. Each paper finds its opponent more or less weak, incompetent and arrogant (with particular derision for the clangers and blunders). But the contrasts between them are greater. The *Sun* attacks Kinnock as untrustworthy, hot headed, indecisive, inexperienced – none of them defects picked on strongly in Major by the *Mirror*. Major is slammed, rather, as boring, dismal, unconfident and (once) sexist.

A third way of reading the table is to look for symmetry in particular positive/negative pairs. But the lack of symmetry confirms again the extent to which the leaders are not seen as mirror images. Three pairs perhaps show signs of it. The *Sun*, firstly, sees Major as tough, Kinnock as weak, and the *Mirror* sees Kinnock as tough, Major as weak, on a very roughly comparable scale. There are similar relationships in the competent/incompetent and exciting/boring pairs.

It is worth pointing out finally that both the majority of categories in table 12. 4 and the majority of items within them, concern aspects of personality more than of what might be described as professional skills. If the latter are limited to the categories of experience, competence and effectiveness, the balance falls like this:

Major				Kinnock			
Personality		Prof. skills		Personality		Prof. skills	
Pos.	Neg.	Pos.	Neg.	Pos.	Neg.	Pos.	Neg.
41	48	15	28	16	54	5	28

Table 12.1 showed what a small amount of press coverage was given to the broadcasting campaign. Of this, a very large proportion in the *Mirror* and *Sun* was devoted to the furore following the Labour Party broadcast about NHS waiting lists, which referred to the ear problems of the little girl soon identified as Jennifer Bennett. The details are shown in table 12.5, where the scale is emphasised by the comparison with *The Guardian* and *The Daily Telegraph*. Almost none of the coverage was of the original broadcast itself. Most consisted in reaction stories (including photographs) and editorial comment (including a few cartoons). Very little, too, involved the party leaders. The *Sun* attacked Labour in general ('Labour's Lessons in Lying') and made only a brief comment that Kinnock should put his 'house of lies in order' (27 March). The *Mirror* concentrated its fire largely on 'Wally' Waldegrave, apart, again, from one reference to Major's 'Big Lie'.

Table 12.5 *Press coverage of broadcasting: 'Jennifer's Ear'*

	Labour PEB: 'Jennifer's Ear'	
	Sq. ins.	% of total broadcasting coverage
The Daily Mirror		
Report	15	16
Reaction stories	242	76
Editorial comment	86	78
Total	343	66
The Sun		
Report	4	2
Reaction stories	240	85
Editorial comment	99	89
Total	343	62
The Guardian		
Report	29	5
Reaction stories	547	63
Editorial comment	32	4
Total	608	26
The Daily Telegraph		
Report	18	3
Reaction stories	534	64
Editorial comment	50	16
Total	602	34

Note: 'Reaction stories' include items *about* programmes not necessarily themselves broadcast.

The comparatively small attention to broadcasting makes it matter less that there is room here to look at only a few of its features. Table 12.6 distinguishes party election broadcasts from other programmes. Tabloid papers could be expected to pay special attention to these. Other programmes featuring politicians, including one-to-one interviews, might be regarded as coverage by an alternative medium to newspapers – supplementary, but no more worthy of being reported, necessarily, than the coverage of rival newspapers would be. PEBs, on the other hand, being set-piece productions by the parties, deserve scrutiny like, say, the manifestos. Other programmes

Table 12.6 *Press coverage of party leaders' broadcasting, 12 March–9 April 1992*

		PEBs			Other			% total broadcast coverage
		Reports	Reaction and comments	Total %	Reports	Reaction and comments	Total (%)	
The Daily Mirror								
Major	No.	1	3	4 (33)	4	4	8 (67)	12
	Sq. ins.	4	7	11 (16)	38	19	57 (84)	68
Kinnock	No.	2	1	3 (38)	2	3	5 (62)	8
	Sq. ins.	21	4	25 (71)	6	4	10 (29)	35
Ashdown	No.	—	—	— (—)	1	2	3 (100)	3
	Sq. ins.	—	—	— (—)	3	2	5 (100)	5
Total broadcast coverage	No.	3	9	12 (40)	11	7	18 (60)	30
	Sq. ins.	25	340	365 (70)	66	90	156 (30)	521
The Sun								
Major	No.	1	2	3 (43)	3	1	4 (57)	7
	Sq. ins.	7	5	12 (30)	26	2	28 (70)	40
Kinnock	No.	1	6	7 (47)	8	—	8 (53)	15
	Sq. ins.	4	114	118 (54)	102	—	102 (46)	220
Ashdown	No.	—	1	1 (100)	—	—	— (—)	1
	Sq. ins.	—	1	1 (100)	—	—	— (—)	1
Total broadcast coverage	No.	2	14	16 (46)	14	5	19 (54)	35
	Sq. ins.	11	363	374 (67)	151	32	183 (33)	557

Note: Totals for each paper include other politicians and broadcast coverage. Percentages sum horizontally.

Table 12.7 *Election broadcasts: press coverage of individual leaders 12 March–9 April 1992*

	The Daily Mirror				The Sun			
	No.	%	Sq. ins.	%	No.	%	Sq. ins.	%
Major	12	29	68	13	7	20	40	7
Other Conservative	7	17	86	17	1	8	2	—
Kinnock	8	19	35	7	15	43	220	39
Other Labour	10	24	27	5	5	14	28	5
Ashdown	3	7	5	1	1	3	1	3
Other Liberal Democrat	2	5	2	—	—	—	—	—
Total broadcast coverage	42	100	521	100	35	100	557	100

Note: The 'No.' columns refer to separate mentions in each paper, not to separate stories.

have an interviewer or moderator: the PEBs, deliberately partisan, need the press as moderator.

The total columns in table 12.6 confirm that the majority of *space* in the two tabloids was indeed given to PEBs. But this was largely the 'Jennifer Effect': the distribution of the *number* of broadcasting items was roughly 2 to 3 *against* PEBs. On the other hand, there was more coverage of PEBs in the form of reaction and comment than there was of other broadcast items – which does suggest that editors saw them as especially deserving of scrutiny.

The PEB which received the loudest fanfare and was billed by the party itself as 'Major – the Movie', was John Major's return to his Brixton roots. It was explicitly offered as an attempt to match Labour's successful 'Kinnock – the Movie' in the 1987 campaign. Its importance transcended its content and was intended to symbolise the communication skills and professionalism of the Major Conservative Central Office. The press were encouraged to preview it before broadcast. Anthony Howard, in a press round-up, summarised the reaction as a 'general tone of . . . muted restraint mixed with faint mockery' (*The Guardian*, 19 March). The latter was almost inevitable, given that several of the reviewers were sketchwriters, such as Matthew Parris. Major's purchases of tomatoes and kippers were also a sub-editor's delight. In *The Guardian* (19 March) Hugo Young said the film 'focused, with embarrassing irrelevance to anything very much, on Mr Everyman in search of his roots'.

Why 'embarrassing'? This and the 'faint mockery' confirm the film as a theatrical performance, for most of the press (especially the broadsheets). It was 'embarrassing' (if viewed in a certain light) as a piece of propaganda. In contrast, the tabloid tendency to regard the broadcast campaign rather as parallel to the press campaign, without need of elaborate coverage, may explain why the *Mirror* reported the broadcast in a story of four square inches and took it largely at face value. The report was unsympathetic (and made play with the kippers) but had no undertones about background or context.

The Sun did not report 'Major – the Movie' at all. The Yorks were splitting up that day.

Regardless of the type of programme, how far did the tabloids treat the broadcast campaign as a contest chiefly between party leaders? Table 12.7 shows how little space was given to coverage of other members of the parties. Just as in their non-broadcasting coverage, the *Mirror* and *Sun* both gave less coverage to the leader whom they supported. Not only was Ashdown largely ignored in both papers: other members of the Liberal Democrats were not reported at all in the *Sun*, and barely in the *Mirror*. There is, again, a significant difference between the number of items and the amount of space. Apart from Kinnock's involvement in the 'Jennifer's Ear' fracas, the three leaders took up only a minority of space – but they hogged the number of mentions.

From time to time the tabloids certainly indicate that they assume their readers may be following the broadcast campaign. A few editorials and feature articles refer, almost in parenthesis, to the leaders' performances on the Walden programme, for example. (There are rather more such references in *The Guardian* and *The Daily Telegraph*.) The papers acknowledge that the leader we see on television may be different from the leader they write about in their columns. (The 'real warmth' of Major, the *Sun* said, does not come across on television. The *Mirror* harped on how 'dismal' he was.) But there is a less definite sense in the tabloids than in the broadsheets of an artificially constructed television campaign, which constitutes a different, and implicitly more spurious, kind of reality from the campaign reported in the press. For the reader, both may seem spurious. The campaign in the press is as artificially structured, though subject to different constraints, as the campaign on TV.

The first part of this chapter wrote at length about the content of photographs but said little about numbers. The following paragraphs therefore consider how far the photographs reported a campaign of leaders, and which ones. In fact only one third of the two tabloid papers' pictures were of the three leaders – 'only', because in *The Guardian* and *The Daily Telegraph* the proportion was startlingly higher (45 per cent). The proportion of space they took up was identical, however – about two-fifths – except in the *Mirror*, where they were smaller (27 per cent). (This was largely because of the space taken up by the *Mirror*'s photo features on policy issues.) In both tabloids, Paddy Ashdown was completely ignored except for one picture in the *Sun*. Exactly the same was true for all the minor parties.

The most common activities photographed were the leaders' visits to factories, hospitals, etc. and their hustings performances in the street. The *Mirror* treated both leaders much the same, but the *Sun* concentrated more, for

Kinnock, on visits and for Major, on speeches and hustings efforts (the soapbox factor).

In addition to frequency and size, another measure of prominence is whether leaders were pictured by themselves or with other people. The latter took up roughly twice as much space in both tabloids; but the *Sun* had twice the number of pictures of Kinnock by himself as in company. For Major, the numbers were 50/50 in each paper, and in the *Mirror* Kinnock was shown six times by himself and nine times in company.

In contrast to the coverage of the leaders in the text, the tabloids did not feature their preferred leader less conspicuously in photographs than his opponent. Consistent with this, negative pictures were not used as knocking copy. For the purposes of table 12.8, 'negative' images were defined as showing the leader as grim, undignified, in a defensive posture, being heckled and the like. Positive pictures included leaders smiling, active, making assertive gestures, etc. The result showed a large predominance of positive and neutral photos. The *Mirror* had negative photos of Major that were big (e.g. the egg-throwing incident) but three times as many positive ones of him. Most of the *Mirror*'s negative pictures were part of its 'issues' campaign. The *Sun*, similarly, had far more positive photos of Major than of Kinnock but only three negative Kinnock photos.

Overall, a more revealing impression of the tabloids' use of pictures is gained by the kind of analysis undertaken earlier. Separating pictures from text removes much of their significance.

The strongest impression gained by carrying out this study remains, as stated in the first section, the integrated nature of the contents of the *Mirror* and the *Sun*. Each paper began the election campaign with a predetermined partisan position. They presented an attacking picture of the party leaders, by concentrating chiefly on the leader they opposed. Their direct reporting was blunt and reductive (naturally, given their tabloid format). But the *Sun* in particular used pictures in an indirect way, as symbols rather than naturalistic evidence, to support a case for the Conservative Party based on assertion more than on argument.

The importance of visual argument in both papers puts in question the value of square-inch counting. One Kinnock in a lightbulb may be worth 10,000 words of evidence about inner city squalor. But what sort of reality do the tabloids convey? Newspapers can never be other than one version of 'the truth', because of the necessary processes of selection and interpretation (leaving aside the partisan intentions of an election campaign). Pictures give the reader great latitude in interpretation, notwithstanding the guidance of a caption. What would readers actually make of the lightbulb and the flab-o-gram lady?

An alternative guide to the election campaign is available to readers on television. The lack of coverage in the papers was a surprise. Broadcasting is in the background of the tabloids, in the sense that they give signs of their

Table 12.8 *Election photographs: mood 12 March – 9 April 1992*

	Positive				Negative				Neutral				Total			
	No.	%	Sq. ins.	%	No.	%	Sq. ins.	%	No.	%	Sq. ins.	%	No.	%	Sq. ins.	%
Preferred leader																
The Daily Mirror/Kinnock	12	80	323	91	1	7	18	5	2	13	15	4	15	100	356	100
The Sun/Major	13	68	218	73	1	5	12	4	5	26	67	23	19	100	297	100
Opponent leader																
The Daily Mirror/Major	9	64	87	41	3	21	115	55	2	14	18	4	14	100	210	100
The Sun/Kinnock	8	33	119	37	3	13	28	9	13	54	174	54	24	100	321	100
Other election photos																
The Daily Mirror	12	20	222	15	14	24	557	37	33	56	728	48	59	100	1,507	100
The Sun[1]	5	5	129	13	8	9	202	21	78	86	634	66	91	100	965	100
Total election photos																
The Daily Mirror	33	38	632	30	18	20	690	33	37	42	751	36	88	100	2,073	100
The Sun	26	19	466	29	12	9	242	15	96	72	875	55	134	100	1,583	100

[1] Includes one photo of Ashdown and one photo of a minor party leader.

assumption that readers are watching some of it. But it is not incorporated explicitly into the papers' own account of the campaign, and it did not seem to set the papers' agenda except for the case of 'Jennifer's Ear'.

Because entertainment is their primary purpose, the world represented through the tabloids traditionally contains large elements of fantasy, either in the coverage of TV and showbiz subjects or in that of Royals and superstars whose lives are beyond ordinary reach. This is the context in which they have to report an election campaign. Maybe the *Sun*, especially, should no longer be regarded as a newspaper in the traditional sense. The *Sun*'s style nudges it further along the fact/fiction continuum, on which tabloids have always been nearer the fiction end than have the broadsheets. (The *Sport* is currently the extreme case – and it did report the election.) How much further is there to go before the paper becomes a kind of 'Spitting Image' among papers, conveying a twisted latex view of politicians? It is a perfectly defensible role – provided readers know that that is what they are getting. But it bears little resemblance to the reality which parties and leaders themselves seek to present, and which the citizen as voter needs.

Notes

1 The assistance of a grant from the Nuffield Foundation is gratefully acknowledged.
2 Hugh Cudlipp, *Publish and Be Damned* (London: Andrew Dakers, 1955); *At Your Peril* (London: Weidenfeld and Nicolson, 1962).

13 Failing to set the agenda: The role of election press conferences in 1992

Dennis Kavanagh and Brian Gosschalk

The origins of election press conferences are accidental. In the 1950s they were routine press briefings at which journalists were informed about the details of the party leaders' itineraries. The major change came in 1959 when Labour's General Secretary, Morgan Phillips, was given the task of running the press conferences – largely because the party leaders wanted to keep him out of the way. He quickly realised that the journalists wanted a daily story, even if it was from the Opposition. The Labour conferences were held each morning at 10.30 and in the first week they gained 200 column inches in the nine national dailies, ten times the coverage of that for the Conservatives. Journalists were delighted that they no longer had to charge around the country covering party leaders but could rely on the Labour handout for the day. The Conservatives quickly adapted and brought in ministers, but they found that they were usually replying to Labour's charges and never caught up in terms of news coverage.[1]

Press conferences are now an established part of the ritual of the campaigns. The media invest enormous resources in covering a general election and it is considered essential for political journalists to cover the main press conferences; at the same time, parties are more conscious in their efforts to shape the agenda via the media. The press conference is therefore a marriage of convenience, giving copy to journalists and a platform for politicians. But it is also an uneasy marriage and 1992 graphically illustrated the tensions.

Today's press conference serves various functions. For Morgan Phillips it was a device to steal the press headlines. But by 1970 this aspect had declined; in that election the conferences generated only 1 per cent of total press coverage.[2] Instead, the goal is to gain coverage on the mid-day and early evening television broadcasts and so shape the campaign agenda. The more continuous coverage by television and radio means that the impact of the early morning conference has now usually disappeared by lunch-time. (Ironically, if a press conference item runs beyond then, it is usually because something has gone wrong and this was spectacularly true in 1992.) Campaign managers increasingly try to think strategically and more self-consciously answer the questions: 'What are we trying to say?', 'What do we want the election to be about?' They seek to integrate the rest of the day – speeches, tours and events – with the theme of the morning conference. Secondary functions of the conferences are to provide a vehicle for party leaders to launch a new initiative and make statements, put a favourable interpretation on events (e.g., the announcement of routine economic statistics or an opinion poll), challenge the opposition directly or to suggest awkward questions which journalists will carry across Smith Square. Finally, the early morning pre- and post-conference planning meetings provide an opportunity for party heavyweights to meet and talk (before 1964 or so, this was rare), about tactics and strategy.

In 1992 we analysed the proceedings of the main Conservative and Labour morning press conferences. We were interested in establishing the extent to which the parties managed:

(a)   to stimulate 'friendly' questions from journalists;
(b)   to steer the questions on to their chosen theme; and
(c)   to shape the subsequent coverage in the media.

We conclude that on all three aims the conferences were not successful. There is a paradox. Parties are increasingly ruthless in trying to control the press conferences, but they fail as exercises in manipulating the media. We suggest that politicians need to think about other functions that press conferences perform.

Politics of press conferences

Some of the politics of the press conferences has centred on the order in which the parties will hold them. Is it best to go first and try to set the agenda or to go last and have the last word? With the exception of 1979, when Mrs Thatcher decided to hold her party's conference simultaneously with Labour at 9.30 am, the government has always had the last session. But few party strategists any longer consider that the order of the conferences has much significance; timing is more likely to be affected by the leaders' daily campaign plans. Party leaders usually visit the regions in the afternoon and do not want to be tied down by press conferences late in the morning.

Staggering the timing of the conferences allows the journalists to provide feedback from one conference to the next, carry challenges and counter-challenges, and thereby contribute to the debating functions of an election. Before 1959 there was little debate between the rival party campaigns as the leaders talked about 'their' issues, and journalists rarely had the opportunity to question leaders in public.

Election press conferences are a high-risk exercise and they have no counter-part on a daily basis in elections in the United States or on the Continent. Unlike many other political press conferences, they are 'on the record' and, compared to Question Time in the House of Commons, the minister or Prime Minister is not backed by hundreds of cheering backbenchers, or fed friendly or 'arranged' questions from colleagues. Although spokesmen can anticipate and prepare for some of the questions, journalists are free to ask questions on a wide variety of topics. Labour strategists have for long been nervous about the damage that a largely unsympathetic press may do at the conferences and have feared that the journalists might try and set their own agenda or run 'scares'. Prior to the 1987 election they considered the option of not holding them at all or taking them outside London. In the end a number were held in the regions, although the absence of Mr Kinnock from the simultaneous London conference prompted hostile journalists to complain that he was 'running away' from questions. Parties try to limit their vulnerability by making statements – which take up some of the time available for questions – and by trying to shape the agenda: choosing a firm chairman, selecting platform speakers and themes, preventing journalists from asking supplementary questions, and insisting that the early questions deal with the statement of the day, i.e. the party's agenda.

But for all a party's determination to exercise control, press conferences have often gone wrong, and revealed underlying party tensions and divisions. Once divisions between leading political figures appear, hostile journalists may take over the conference. In 1970 Mr Heath was plagued by the journalists' interest in Enoch Powell; faced by a series of questions asking if he would withdraw endorsement of Powell as a Conservative candidate because of his views on immigration, Mr Heath had difficulty talking about other issues, particularly the state of the economy. In some desperation he refused at one conference to take further questions on Powell and the session ended half way through the normal thirty minutes. Mrs Thatcher's dominance at press conferences left no one in doubt about whose show it was. In 1983 she sharply disowned her Foreign Secretary for implying that Falklands sovereignty was negotiable and two days later again corrected him for suggesting in a television interview that a large parliamentary majority was undesirable. In 1987 she and her Secretary of State for Education were visibly at odds over the likely scale of opting out of grant-maintained schools and the possibility of schools introducing fees and entrance examinations. In the same election Mrs Thatcher played into Labour's hands by highlighting hospital waiting lists as a campaign issue. After Labour had publicised the case of a young boy who faced a long wait for a heart operation, she responded to a press conference supplementary question (from Anthony Bevins) with a defence of her use of private health care on the grounds that she wanted to go into hospital 'on the day I want at the time I want and with the doctor I want'. In October 1974 Shirley Williams from the platform destroyed Harold Wilson's carefully cultivated image of a united Labour Party when she said that if a forthcoming referendum voted against Britain's membership of the European Community she would resign from the cabinet. During Labour's doomed campaign in the 1983 election, journalists were amazed to hear the press conference chairman announce that Michael Foot was still the leader of the party and enjoyed the confidence of the party's campaign management team. In 1983, according to one commentator, 'As the campaign progressed . . . Labour's press conferences became ordeals to be endured with minimal harm, rather than opportunities to gain support'.[3]

Table 13.1 *Politicians appearing most frequently at early morning conferences*

Conservative (16/3 to 8/4)		Labour (17/3 to 8/4)	
John Major	19	Neil Kinnock	15
Chris Patten	18	Jack Cunningham	13
Michael Heseltine	9	Bryan Gould	8
Norman Lamont	4	Harriet Harman	8
Douglas Hurd	4	Robin Cook	7
Kenneth Clarke	4	John Smith	6
		Tony Blair	6
		Margaret Beckett	5
		Roy Hattersley	5
		Sylvia Heal	4

Press conferences in 1992

The main two parties were certainly well practised in the 1992 election. They had already been campaigning intensively from January, holding press conferences three or four times a week. All parties had war books which included information on the press conference speaker and themes and how these would be linked to planned photo-opportunities and other campaign events. The Conservative war book urged candidates and, in particular, senior ministers to look to the party's press conferences for information about the theme of the day and the 'line' to follow.

As usual, the preparations (including the statements and spotting likely questions) for the conferences took up an enormous amount of the time of key campaign figures and headquarters staff. For Labour, the 7.45 conference was preceded by briefings on the press and the opinion polls at 6.45 and then a planning meeting at 7.15, both chaired by Jack Cunningham, the campaign coordinator. The Conservatives started at 7.00 in Central Office to review the press and polls, in preparation for a 7.30 meeting to brief the Prime Minister and other participants in the press conference. After the 8.30 press conference a smaller group assembled in the Prime Minister's suite in Central Office to settle strategic issues and confirm the programme for the next day's conference. Central Office personnel would then prepare slogans, themes and statements for a 18.00 meeting chaired by John Wakeham. This was usually attended by the speaker for the next day and/or his or her special advisors. On some occasions ministers were still rehearsing on the platform in Central Office in the early hours of the morning.

Chris Patten and Jack Cunningham always took the chair in London for their parties, except at weekends when John Major replaced Chris Patten and Bryan Gould took over from Jack Cunningham. As a rule, two Conservative or three Labour spokesmen would make statements, each lasting a few minutes

Table 13.2 *Themes at early morning conferences*

Conservative (16/3 to 8/4)		Labour (17/3 to 8/4)	
Tax, economy, recovery	12	Economy (including employment	7
Schools	1	taxation and recovery plans)	
Foreign affairs/defence	2	Health	6
Industrial relations	1	Manifesto	6
Cities/millennium	1	Poll tax	2
Crime	1	Education	1
Constitution	1	Families and child care	1
Manifesto	1		

(and handed out as press releases), and then answer questions. Both Patten and Cunningham usually began by putting a favourable 'spin' on recent campaign developments or the news of the day and both insisted that the early questions should focus on the platform's statement before allowing questions on other topics. Cunningham was probably more ruthless than Patten in preventing journalists from asking supplementary questions but the latter, according to critical journalists, was more thorough in ignoring the hands of potentially 'awkward' journalists.

What was striking in 1992 was the refusal of the two parties to allow supplementary questions. On 18 March, the day of the Conservative manifesto launch, Chris Patten rebuffed the attempt of *The Independent*'s Anthony Bevins to ask a supplementary, with 'Tony, it is question and answer, not a Socratic dialogue'. Labour followed suit on 19 March, the day after its manifesto launch, when Jack Cunningham established a rule that journalists should ask only one question. At the launch three of the first five journalists had asked follow-up questions. One, Philip Stephens (*The Financial Times*), twice pressed Tony Blair on whether people in Labour's proposed work programme schemes would come off the unemployment register, leading Jack Cunningham to say: 'In the interests of fairness to all your colleagues, we have lots of people trying to ask questions, and we do have limited time, so in the interest of fairness we have to restrict you to one question I'm afraid'. In view of the politicians' talent for not directly answering a question, however well crafted, the denial of a follow-up question is a crucial element in the platform's control.

Conservative conferences

At the nineteen early-morning Conservative press conferences studied, a total of 230 questions were asked, an average of twelve per session. Questions were interpreted as hostile when they were explicitly critical of the Conservative record or campaign, pointed to inconsistencies in statements by party spokesmen, sought comment on negative opinion poll findings or official statistics or events, or appeared designed to embarrass the platform. Questions were regarded as neutral when they sought clarification of policy or statements, or invited comments on the other parties.* The adversarial nature of the sessions is reflected in that 62 per cent (149) of the questions were coded as hostile, only 4 per cent (9) supportive and 31 per cent (72) neutral.

Conservative ministers faced many hostile questions on the perceived failure of their campaign to achieve momentum. Why was the party trailing Labour in the polls? Why was the economy still in recession? Why was the campaign not more positive? Some part of the hostile questioning could be explained by the depressing opinion polls, public criticism of the party's campaign, and gloomy economic statistics. In 1992 the Conservatives suffered the fate of Labour in 1983 and 1987 when many journalists concluded that the party had lost the election and carried out a pre-emptive *post-mortem* at the conferences. Sir Robin Day asked the Conservative platform to comment on *The Times'* assessment of the Tory campaign as 'the apex of undignified ineptitude'.

Anthony Bevins regularly terrorised ministers, bluntly asking 'Why are you conning the voter?' and seeking apologies for broken promises and pledges about no future tax increases.† On 23 March Mr Major was uncomfortable in dealing with a series of questions about whether or not the burden of taxation and level of public borrowing had increased since 1979. This was one of the few occasions when journalists, scenting blood, followed up, and Bevins was able to intervene four times. Some of his other questions tackled the difference of view between Major and Lamont about the scope for tax cuts in the next parliament. Alastair Campbell (*The Daily Mirror*) directly asked Mr Heseltine about his leadership ambitions if the Conservatives lost the next election, and Robin

---

* Examples of hostile questions include:

Surely, Prime Minister, your professions . . . of commitment to the state system [of education] would carry more conviction if more than a handful of your ministers actually used it?

Is it enough to justify winning an election to have a smiling Prime Minister and negative attacks on the opposition?

Is your package for London any more than a cosmetic exercise to win over marginals in the capital?

When are we going to get positive talking by the Conservatives on issues like housing, the NHS, perhaps even policy on Europe, because so far it's only negative copy?

Examples of neutral questions include:

Prime Minister, [do] you see the grant-maintained status reforms opening the way to selection and the reintroduction of grammar schools?

Is the future of the Anglo-Irish agreement guaranteed . . .?

Do you see this [manifesto] as a blend of Thatcherism and one-nation Conservatism?

† Typical of the Bevins interrogatory style was: 'I'd like to see a bit of remorse, a bit of regret, a bit of shame that after thirteen years in office, a whole generation of children have gone through the school system . . . without getting what you call a thorough grounding in essential systems. Will you give me a touch, a smidgen, of shame, remorse or regret for this abysmal record?' And: 'if your policies on the health service are so wonderful, why is it that, persistently in every poll, the health service comes top of the issues of public concern and Labour has a thumping great lead over you? If you are so good, why don't they believe you?'

Oakley (*The Times*) on two separate occasions invoked opinion poll evidence about the low salience of taxation to suggest that the Conservative emphasis on tax was a misreading of the electoral mood. A number of journalists complained that the conference themes were too narrowly concentrated on tax and 'knocking' Labour. It was also significant that the questions by journalists from such 'loyal' newspapers as *The Evening Standard*, *The Daily Telegraph* and *The Yorkshire Post* revealed discontent with the Conservative campaign. According to one BBC reporter, this reflected a fear among Conservative-supporting journalists that a change of government would reduce their access to ministers.[4]

Some Conservatives were also critical of their press conferences, largely because they felt that they did not exercise enough control. They claimed that the journalists were too near the platform and, in the first few days, often grabbed the mobile microphone and shouted further questions. When the microphone was replaced by a 'boom', provided by the BBC, this picked up questions shouted by other journalists. Too often television pictures of the press conferences showed ministers speaking defensively under tough questions (e.g. John Major on 23 March on taxation). Some Conservative managers also regretted the opportunities Mr Patten gave to hostile journalists. One, Michael White (*The Guardian*), was particularly adept at asking extra questions; on 27 March he asked four, all about the furore surrounding Labour's health broadcast. Few reporters showed much interest in picking up the leads suggested from the platform. Mr Patten's attempt on 31 March to draw his audience's attention to the 'shattering disclosure' in *The Daily Mail* that morning about Labour's plans for protecting public sector pay in the future, fell on deaf ears.

Inside the Conservative camp few defended the original press conference schedule of themes, and after heavy internal criticism it was scrapped at the end of the first week. It was decided that future conferences should concentrate even more clearly and narrowly on the themes of taxation and leadership. The draft statement proposed for the daily conference was now called by its authors a *Logic* message, an attempt to supply a quality which strategists felt the conferences had to date failed to deliver. But as the topics and speakers for press conferences were being decided at such short notice, ministers' regional visits and other events prepared for the planned theme of the day had to be hurriedly abandoned or rescheduled. At least two cabinet ministers, Michael Howard and Kenneth Clarke, had only twenty-four hours' notice of their scheduled appearances. Any campaign has to be flexible but the Conservative press conference arrangements had too much of a last-minute air about them.

Labour conferences

In all, Labour held forty-three national press conferences, including three outside London (one each in Nottingham, Salford and Birmingham); of these, twenty-three were the party's main morning press conferences. The decision to

Table 13.3 *Papers following Conservative press conference leads, 16 March–8 April*

	Lead story	Other front	Editorial	One of these
Conservative papers				
The Daily Telegraph	5	1	2	6
The Daily Mail	1	0	4	4
The Daily Express	3	0	5	5
The Sun	1	0	4	4
At least one Conservative paper	8	2	10	12
Conservative-leaning 'neutrals'				
The Daily Star	0	1	2	3
Today	2	0	2	3
The Times	3	0	9	10
At least one 'friendly' paper	11	3	15	17
Labour papers				
The Daily Mirror	1	1	4	4
The Guardian	2	2	3	4
Non-Conservative-leaning 'neutrals'				
The Independent	5	2	4	8
The Financial Times	3	1	5	7
At least one 'hostile' paper	5	3	7	11

hold these at the Millbank Press Centre was taken partly to avoid having Transport House as the venue, which would remind journalists of the link between the Labour Party and the trade unions. Millbank was relatively expensive as a venue, but provided a convenient location for journalists covering all three parties, offered good facilities for up to 200 journalists, and enabled Labour to use it more intensively than originally planned, with up to five events on any one day.

Labour's strategy was to appear governmental, its tactics to play safe. The platform usually had four or five, sometimes six people on it, surely a questionable use of time for some of those present. A woman was usually on the platform, although in some cases she played no part; for example, at the first press conference on unemployment, all the questions were answered by Gordon Brown, Tony Blair and Jack Cunningham, except for one which the chairman referred to Joyce Quinn. Of the eighteen questions asked at the press conference on health on 1 April, none were answered by Harriet Harman (nor indeed by Dr Patel, a doctor on the platform). The single-question policy stopped journalists from developing a line of argument, and thereby strengthened the position of the platform. Robin Oakley's 'Given the number of spokesmen on the platform, could they please restrict themselves to one side of A4?', reflected some of the resentment felt about the time taken in platform statements. In practice, Labour's press conferences tended to last around half an hour, with the first half taken up by statements from party spokesmen, typically leaving around fifteen minutes for questions.

We studied twenty of Labour's early morning press conferences. At these a total of 262 questions was asked, an average of thirteen per session. As with the Conservatives, only a handful (2 per cent) were coded as supportive, 38 per cent as neutral, and 60 per cent as hostile. Categorising the nature of the questions again involved an element of subjectivity, but we applied the same criteria as for the Conservatives. A number of questions were frequently posed in an apparently neutral way, e.g. attempts to seek clarification of Labour policies, but also clearly designed to embarrass. This pattern was established at the outset at the press conference to launch the manifesto, when journalists from the 'quality' press and television asked several questions about the party's policies on secondary picketing, Trident, bringing privatised industries back into the public sector, and the costing of its programme. These were all reasonable questions, but each would have been pursued by Conservatives if they had been asking the questions. We categorised these as hostile.*

Like the Conservatives, Labour tended to give the heavyweight political journalists, particularly those from television, the opportunity to ask questions in the restricted time period. One typical conference (20 March) began with

---

*Some examples of hostile questions include:

Wouldn't it be more honest for Labour to ban private medicine?

Can I put to Mr Kinnock a charge made by Norman Tebbit, that in 1983 you tried to lie your way into office by not making clear your opposition to the then policy of the Labour Party on EC withdrawal? He says we are right to suspect that you might be trying to lie your way into office this time. How can we trust you in light of all the changes you have made in policy?

Under the last Labour Government did any little girls have to wait for operations while others went private and can you give a pledge that it won't happen if there is another Labour Government?

What is the Labour response to the letter from the Chancellor regarding the cost of Labour's programme?

Examples of neutral questions include:

Could you spell out where the extra £1 billion for the Health Service comes from and perhaps more importantly whether there is money out of economic growth to pay for the underfunding?

Is the Labour Party worried about the Tories' attack on tax beginning to stick?

Could you please explain what you mean by the phrase 'the Task Force with its own funds' on page 2 of Robin Cook's handout?

Do you accept that the Liberal Democrats are offering more than you on education, including adult education?

questions from John Sergeant (BBC), Elinor Goodman (Channel 4), Michael Brunson (ITN), Philip Stephens (*The Financial Times*), and Andrew Marr (*The Economist*) – hardly a representative cross-section of the journalists present, but a reflection of the importance of television.

Labour was more successful than the Conservatives in keeping to its planned schedule of conferences and in linking the conferences to strategy. But Labour may still have scored more 'own goals' than the Conservatives did. The Nottingham conference on 26 March was a disaster. Julie Hall, the Labour leader's press secretary, intervened to deny that she had leaked the name of Jennifer, the girl who had featured in Labour's health broadcast. The media ignored Labour's claims about an under-funded health service and now concentrated on the rows over who had leaked the girl's name to the media. Then, on 2 April, Democracy Day, Mr Kinnock was asked a question about proportional representation, by Elinor Goodman. Such a question had been anticipated and his reply about the party's position had been drafted by his staff and agreed with Roy Hattersley. It restated the relevant passage from the party manifesto but added an invitation to Liberal Democrats to join the group studying electoral systems under Professor Plant. There was nothing particularly newsworthy about that. But it happened to coincide with the decision of the Conservatives to turn their fire on the Liberal Democrats as a 'Trojan Horse' which would let Labour into office, with media reports of the Liberal Democrats demanding four seats in a coalition Cabinet, and with the pointers of most opinion polls to a hung parliament. The media, already influenced by the findings of the polls and bored with much of the campaign, seized on the new issue. To the consternation of many Labour strategists, the media thereafter seemed preoccupied with the political and constitutional problems of a deadlocked parliament, and the party was unable to generate much interest in its other issues. It is doubtful, however, if Mr Kinnock's remarks significantly contributed to the interest in a hung parliament: many journalists had decided that this would be the story.

The questions at Labour's conference frequently bore little relation to the subject of the press conference, particularly when the subject was health. By Labour's fourth press conference on health, only three of the eighteen questions related to health, compared with seven on the economy and Labour's spending plans, two on tactical voting, three on the polls, and one each on Neil Kinnock's fitness to be Prime Minister, on defence and on targeting welfare benefits. The two press conferences following Labour's health broadcast were 'wasted' on arguments which detracted from the health campaign ('How long would it take under a Labour Government for there to be no children with the same medical condition as Jennifer?', and 'Wasn't your PPB last night a pretty outrageous way of playing on people's emotions to gain votes?') and, arguably, to the subsequent boredom with which health was greeted as a topic for press conferences later in the campaign ('Oh no, not health again' was the response of several journalists). The Conservatives suffered a similar reaction when they focused on the tax consequences of Labour's spending plans.

Little of the hostility displayed by sections of the press towards Labour surfaced at the press conferences. The tone of questioning was probably more polite than for the Conservatives and Labour's platform dealt with questions without making gaffes or highlighting internal divisions. In interviews with us, two political editors, Michael White and Anthony Bevins, claimed that the Labour conferences were less concerned to exclude hostile questions than the Conservatives' and that, in the interests of fair play, they felt they should therefore hold back on some of their tougher questions. In spite of the limits imposed by the one-question-only-rule, journalists occasionally followed up questions raised by their colleagues, and pursued issues from one day to the next (for example, the cost of the party's programme and how it would respond if resources thought to be available for public spending did not match the Treasury's estimates).

Labour campaign strategists felt that, in terms of presentation, their press conferences were probably better than in 1987 and better than the Conservatives' in 1992. But as long as economic competence, trust and party leadership were key themes, the press conference failed as a platform to reassure the voters about Labour's economic policies, to build trust in the party, or to damage the standing of the Prime Minister. The reason why Labour lost the election so decisively more probably lies in events and social and economic trends which predated the election campaign itself.

To what effect?

Press conferences remain a good indicator of the issues a party wants the election to be about and of whom it judges to be its most effective communicators (tables 13.1 and 13.2). The Conservatives' agenda was tax and economic recovery, with some limited scope for foreign affairs, defence and crime. The most frequent appearances, apart from John Major and Chris Patten, were by Douglas Hurd, Michael Heseltine, Norman Lamont and Kenneth Clarke, the party's so-called 'A Team'. At the main morning conferences there was no coverage of health and no William Waldegrave. For Labour the agenda was the health service and economic recovery. This meant that, apart from Neil Kinnock and Jack Cunningham, the main platform appearances were from John Smith, Roy Hattersley, Robin Cook and Harriet Harman, with Gerald Kaufman appearing at only one major morning press conference.

But the morning press conferences failed to lead the media. Coverage of the daily issue rarely lasted beyond midday broadcasting bulletins or the regional evening papers. By early afternoon attention had switched to new initiatives and the media were looking for a new story. The press conferences, like other campaign initiatives, also had to compete with other news, notably about the opinion polls. Central Office felt particularly aggrieved on this score. On

Table 13.4 *Papers following Labour press conference leads, 17 March–8 April*

	Lead story	Other front	Editorial	One of these
Labour papers				
The Daily Mirror	2	3	3	5
The Guardian	5	3	9	10
Either of the above	5	3	9	10
Non Conservative-leaning 'neutrals'				
The Independent	7	3	5	9
The Financial Times	5	2	4	9
At least one 'friendly' paper	7	5	10	11
Conservative papers				
The Daily Telegraph	3	5	1	6
The Daily Mail	4	0	4	5
The Daily Express	4	0	6	6
The Sun	1	1	5	5
Conservative-leaning 'neutrals'				
The Daily Star	0	0	1	1
Today	2	2	2	4
The Times	4	0	5	7
At least one 'hostile' paper	6	6	10	10

1 April the party's press conference was on defence and officials confidently expected ITV News at 5.40 pm to lead on the issue. In the event the top item was the big Labour lead in the opinion polls. In terms of media coverage the most successful conferences were the most unwanted – Labour's conference on health in Nottingham, and the afternoon health conference for the Conservatives, both on 26 March. The two conferences made news largely because of the unanticipated interventions from the platforms – Mr Waldegrave's confession that Conservative Central Office had advised Jennifer's consultant to get in touch with *The Daily Express* and Ms Hall's denial that she had revealed the girl's name to the media. Journalists had grown frustrated with the news management of the parties and for a brief spell ran the show. The broadcast became enveloped in debates about Neil Kinnock's fitness to be Prime Minister, journalistic ethics, and dirty tricks by Central Office. The chaotic scenes made compelling viewing and the BBC *Nine O'Clock News* on 26 March devoted 10 minutes 45 seconds to the affair, compared to 3 minutes 31 seconds for Labour's presentation on the NHS.

Tables 13.3 and 13.4 report the extent to which the press followed the theme of each party's press conference the previous day. The tables analyse the coverage according to lead story, other front page stories and editorials. They also distinguish the press according to its partisan inclination. What emerges is the very limited extent (particularly when one omits the 'Jennifer's Ear' conferences of 26 March, which were exceptional) to which the press followed the conference lead. *The Daily Telegraph*, with more front-page stories than tabloids, was the most likely to give space to the Conservative conference themes and *The Times* was the most likely to cover them in its editorials. Of the Labour-inclined papers, *The Guardian* was the most attentive to the party's conference themes, both in editorials and front-page stories. *The Daily Mirror* tried to help in other ways. It had lead front-page stories on health on 26 and 27 March and 1 April. At the end it led with the Labour slogans 'It's Time for a Change' and on polling day 'The Time Is Now – Vote Labour'. The Conservative tabloids carried tables on the tax impact of Labour's spending plans on middle income earners and these appear to have been drawn from Central Office. On 24 March, the day after a Conservative press conference on Labour's threat to mortgages and union power, the front page of the *Sun* led with 'Labour Threatens Mortgages', the *Mail* with 'Labour to Ration Mortgages', and the *Daily Star* with 'Strikes will Return Under Labour'. And the *Mail* on polling day echoed the Conservative campaign climax by asking 'WHICH MAN DO YOU TRUST?'

In practice, the press conferences are probably a less useful vehicle for the parties for setting the agenda than, say, granting an exclusive to a particular newspaper or raising an issue on the *Today* programme or a breakfast-time television programme. Parties have many other behind-the-scenes links with the media. 'Friendly' press proprietors and editors were frequently in touch with No. 10 in the 1987 and 1992 elections and early in the campaign a 'white Commonwealth' of sympathetic political editors was invited to meet John Major in Central Office. *The Daily Express*'s link with the Conservative Party was demonstrated by Central Office contacting the paper about the health story. For the politicians, the press conferences have acquired uses other than simply providing another vehicle for attacking the other party and gaining media coverage. By conducting the conferences efficiently the party hopes to convey an image of competence and authority. They remain a useful device for putting on record the party's position on an issue (Conservatives exploited them to gain coverage for their calculations about the income tax consequences of Labour's 'shadow' budget). Gathering senior party figures also provides an opportunity to review strategy and resolve problems; for campaign strategists it is essentially the starting-point for each campaign day. Press conferences have other uses than agenda-setting.

Most politicians and journalists bring different expectations to the press conferences. Politicians want conferences which are 'safe' and from which journalists will report the party's line. But for some journalists a good conference is one in which they bloody the politicians. They know and resent that they are part of the scenery, witnesses to the parties' attempts to manipulate the media. This is part of a larger problem. The set piece television interviews with party leaders have their critics but the interviewer at least can ask supplementary questions. And both the professional interviewers and journalists may look enviously at the freedom with which the members of the public question politicians roughly in phone-in programmes and how voters on *Granada 500* put John Major and Neil Kinnock under pressure. In 1992, perhaps only the intrepid Anthony Bevins managed to break through the platform's defences with his pointed questions on government finances to John Major. After the election, Robin Oakley complained about excessive management:

Both Mr Patten and, even more ruthlessly, Dr Cunningham, suppressed supplementaries. It was particularly irritating at the Labour press conferences which opened up with up to five statements read out by frontbench spokesmen, sharply limiting the question period and allowing Dr Cunningham the excuse that it was 'selfish' for any journalist to seek to come back on an unanswered question in the limited time.

The one time John Major faced any difficulty was when *The Independent*, the BBC and *The Times* all pursued the same question on the overall tax plan during one press conference and repeated a question which was not fully answered. Organised 'gangbangs' are not an attractive proposition. But if all continue to pursue our own separate agendas on these occasions, constantly switching subjects, the politicians will continue to have an easy ride.[5]

However, some of the responsibility for failing to put pressure on the politicians must lie with the journalists. The platform was able to exploit the journalists' competitiveness, which prevented them acting collectively; rarely were probing questions from the floor followed up; some questions were irrelevant to everything that had occurred before; and, in the absence of specialist journalists, ministers often had an easy ride. The journalists' interest, implicit or explicit, in the latest opinion polls, parties' relations with the media and the horse-race aspects of the election had a distorting effect and their questions on the progress and management of the campaigns failed to ruffle the politicians. It is also probable that meeting at the press conferences every morning for three weeks probably contributed to a form of 'group-think' among the journalists. It was difficult to escape the impression that most journalists at the conferences decided that the Conservatives had lost the election and that this affected the tone of their questions. A verdict on the conferences in 1964 remains valid for 1992: 'The assembly of the cream of the political writers every day in the same place produced something of an in-group atmosphere; the nuances of the campaign in Smith Square were far removed from the reality of everyday electioneering in the constituencies'.[6]

After the election campaign managers in both parties regretted the loss of control at their health press conferences on 26 March. Those two conferences were unusual in that they lacked the usual chairman and were not held in London early in the morning. The lesson is that the managers will strive for even more control next time. The growing emphasis by the parties on supplying pictures for television is also likely to lead to more use of video-graphics, background posters and other devices at the press conferences, all aimed at the camera. Substance will probably be a casualty. The danger is that, more than ever, journalists will be reduced to the role of extras.

Notes

1 David Butler and Richard Rose (eds.), *The British General Election of 1959* (London: Macmillan, 1960), p. 53.
2 David Butler and Michael Pinto-Duschinsky (eds.), *The British General Election of 1970* (London: Macmillan, 1971), p. 243.
3 Peter Kellner, 'The campaign', in Howard Penniman and Austin Ranney (eds.), *Britain at the Polls 1983: A Study of the General Election* (Durham, NC: University of North Carolina Press, 1985), p. 74.
4 Nicholas Jones, *Election* (London: BBC, 1991).
5 'The potholes on the campaign trail', International Press Institute (London, 1992), p. 19.
6 David Butler and Anthony King (eds.), *The British General Election of 1964* (London: Macmillan, 1965), pp. 147–8.

Part V
The opinion polls in the campaign

14 The polls and the 1992 general election

Robert Waller

David Butler and Dennis Kavanagh entitle a chapter in *The British General Election of 1992* 'The Waterloo of the polls'. In fact, the widespread immediate conclusion was that the election had proved a 'débâcle' for all the pollsters. A cartoon by Les Gibbard in *The Guardian* a few days after the election depicted a polling company office with a pair of legs in view dangling as their owner hanged lifelessly from the ceiling. By 15–20 April 1992, Gallup reported that 60 per cent of the public felt that polls 'do not reflect British public opinion at present', and only 26 per cent that they do – compared with 36 per cent and 46 per cent respectively in July 1988.[1] Many politicians, journalists and broadcasters treated pollsters to a range of reactions from bitterness to *Schadenfreude*. Serious, detailed, deep and even controversial inquiries were launched within the polling agencies and the Market Research Society.

The reason for all this was clear. The final polls by the five main survey research organisations all failed to predict the eventual national result by margins beyond the commonly accepted range of error, and all in the same direction. The four polls published 'on the day', 9 April, on average underestimated the Conservative vote by 4.5 per cent, overestimated Labour's vote by 4 per cent and underestimated the Liberal Democrats by 1 per cent. This discrepancy was the greatest since British general election polling began. Apparently the unanimous impression, which so wrong-footed the politicians and commentators, was that there would be a hung parliament, and the Conservative government would lose its overall majority. This had been the perceived message from the vast majority of the fifty-odd national polls taken and published during the campaign, and also, almost universally, of the regional, marginal and individual constituency polls too. This impression was reinforced by the initial seat projections from the ITN/Harris and BBC/NOP exit polls, which declared at 10 pm on election day that there would be no overall majority. The national analysis polls featured by both channels also underestimated the Conservative share and overestimated Labour's, though by less than half the extent the final pre-election polls had done, and the projection polls in the marginals, which were used for generating the House of Commons seat predictions, did reflect Labour's better performance therein. Together – at ITN at least – with some fine-tuning judgements which proved ill-advised, this produced the false prediction of a hung Commons.

So, all the polls 'got it wrong'. Gallup found shortly afterwards that over

40 per cent of the general public would now like to see them banned in the run-up to elections.[2] Newspaper editors threatened not to commission polls 'for a very long time to come'.[3] The impression was that the pollsters collectively should be banished to St Helena. Would they ever return?

In fact, the demand for polling evidence has hardly nosedived, still less vanished. Within four months of the election, the British press had commissioned and prominently displayed numerous polls relating to the standing of the Royal Family and many other matters of import. The polling figures from the US election campaigns were fully reported and seriously analysed. Surveys of French public opinion before the Maastricht referendum shifted millions of pounds in the City currency and financial markets, as the 'No' vote was reported to be advancing through August (surely a difficult month in which to poll accurately in any country, most of all France). Three weeks into August it was solemnly announced that a 51–49 per cent poll 'suggests a victory for the Noes'. Whatever the eventual outcome of the referendum, it would seem excusable to ask whether people ever learn!

Given, then, that there is still likely to be much attention paid to polls in future elections in Britain, it is indeed important for the polling agencies to learn from their experiences in March–April 1992. The arguments about the reason for the fairly consistent discrepancy between the pre-election polls and the results have been rehearsed fully, before, and elsewhere.[4] Different pollsters and other commentators have stressed different elements, and will surely continue to differ, but it is generally agreed that there was no one simple cause and there is no single potential remedy. Attempts have been made to quantify the constituent causes of the discrepancy, but no exact figures will ever be agreed.

While trying to avoid covering familiar ground as far as possible, I shall here address some of the issues that have been raised. However, I wish to leave space for the treatment of other questions asked in the pre-election and exit polls, which I believe hold considerable interest, and which have been largely ignored as vast attention has been directed towards expressed voting intentions alone.

When considering the 'failure' of the polls to predict the Conservatives' unprecedented fourth consecutive triumph, we can perhaps divide the potential causes into two types: were the pollsters talking to the wrong people (for whatever reason) or were they talking to the right people who then expressed a different preference when they actually voted?

The latter possibility is the simpler to explore, although even it has more than one distinct element. There is evidence that there was a very late swing to the Conservatives which could not have been fully registered by pre-election polls: recall polls suggest that those making up their minds or switching party at the last moment were predominantly Conservative voters on the day.[5] The Conservatives probably benefited from differential turnout between party supporters. The exit polls' superior (if imperfect) predictive quality lends further weight to this theory. The Market Research Society inquiry after the election concluded that 'late changes of mind' accounted for just over a third of the discrepancy they were seeking to explain, and differential turnout nearly another quarter.

A plausible case for the existence of such a late swing can easily be constructed. The voters reacted negatively to the very clear possibility of a Labour government (albeit probably without an overall majority in the Commons) with a triumphalist Neil Kinnock in No. 10. *The Sun* claimed, and is claimed, to have influenced working class electors with an effective final scare against the Labour Party and its leader. Many voters intending to cast their ballot for Liberal Democrats, especially in rural and middle-class areas, decided that given the apparent closeness of the contest they would have to make a choice between two potential national governing parties; and more plumped for Mr Major's Conservatives.

Late movement in opinion tends to be the pollsters' own favourite explanation for such discrepancies as that of April 1992: pre-election polls surely cannot be expected to register events after the time they were in the field. Rather more uncomfortable for pollsters, however (though still absolving them of culpability), is the idea that some at least of the apparent late swing would have occurred whenever the election had taken place: that is, if it had been on, say, 2 April, the Conservatives might still have won.

This speculation is based on the argument that voters behave in a different way when they enter the genuine polling booth from when answering unpriced questions posed by an interviewer. In the latter case they are free to give the 'morally correct' answer, or to express protest, knowing that the identity of the government is not actually at stake. The assumption here is that it is (or at least, was in March–April 1992) easier to admit to intending to vote Labour, with their strengths on caring issues such as the NHS, than Conservative, widely believed to be a selfish 'economic' choice. As shall be demonstrated below, there is much evidence from other polling questions to demonstrate the power of the pressure to answer 'correctly'.

There must surely be a connection too with the undoubted fact that, at least in marginal seats, relatively few Conservative posters appeared in electors' windows compared with Labour or Liberal Democrats posters. For example, Richmond and Barnes was decked with a sea of posters supporting the Liberal Democrats' Jenny Tonge, but on 9 April the Conservative Jeremy Hanley was re-elected with over 50 per cent of the total vote. Nearby in Hayes and Harlington, West London, approximately every fourth house carried a Labour poster, while far fewer proclaimed I LOVE DICKS. Yet the Conservative, Terry Dicks, was returned by fifty-three votes. I do not know if any academic study of poster display has been made in this or previous general elections, but my impression was that the willingness to admit to Conservatism was even rarer in 1992.

The notion of the differential between real voting and expressed voting intention in opinion polls has led some commentators to suggest that Britain has become a nation of liars,[6] concealing their true cynical self-interest behind a caring public facade. It is not necessary fully to accept such a view, itself morally charged. Many, indeed most, of those who changed their mind between interview and poll would genuinely have believed in their expressed intention at the time. However, if such voters' minds would have been 'concentrated' by the prospect of a Labour victory even if the election had been two days, or a week earlier, it does cause concern for the pollsters. If people cannot be relied on to predict their future behaviour, why commission polls to ask them about it? Late swing is thus an occupational hazard for the purveyors and buyers of the voting intention questions. There may well, however, be ways of combating the problem of the 'moral' expressed preference, as elaborated below – look at other questions!

Let us now turn to the variety of possible reasons for the 'discrepancy' which suggest that the pollsters had been talking to the 'wrong people', that is, an unrepresentative selection of voters. Clearly the implication if such causes were significant was that all the pollsters (almost equally) had not been doing their job properly, since all were just about equally inaccurate and all in the same direction.

Several suggestions may be discounted, others measured. Overseas voters uncontactable by pollsters were minimal in number. Certainly some individuals would have participated in polls while not being on the electoral register, and it may be assumed that many of these would be missing because of attempted evasion of the Poll Tax, and that relatively few would express a Conservative preference. However, even by applying a maximal set of assumptions[7] the MRS inquiry could not ascribe more than about a tenth of the discrepancy to this cause, and the organisations which did consistently try to screen out non-registered respondents (MORI and ICM) did no 'better' than anyone else. NOP commenced the campaign screening out non-registered voters, but their initial analysis suggested too little difference in political preference on the basis of registration to be significant and the screening was dropped. Difficulties in interviewing postal voters may also have made a small contribution to the discrepancy.

Nor can inadequate sample sizes be blamed: polls of just over 1,000 respondents produced no worse findings to those of just over 2,000 or even than ICM's 10,000 sample survey for the Press Association. Indeed, Harris's polls of 2,000 for ITN consistently produced that agency's most pro-Labour results and may well have suffered, initially at least, from over-hurried interviewers fulfilling quotas of twenty-two respondents each in little more than a day. Polling agencies continue to differ over the merits of street and in-home interviewing, and one- and two-day polling, but in the final analysis the similarity of the aggregated voting intention figures from all the major agencies suggests no clear and consistent lessons concerning technical superiority emanating from these sources. It is interesting to note that Harris's two polls for *The Daily Express* which were conducted solely in-home over the weekends, on 14–15 March and 21–22 March, produced 3 per cent and 5 per cent for the Conservatives, the latter of which contrasted embarrassingly with another Harris poll for ITN taken largely on Monday, 23 March in the same sampling points and by many of the same interviewers, which gave a 4 per cent Labour lead. The next Tuesday Harris released a 1 per cent Conservative lead (the *Express* – solely weekend interviewing) and a 6 per cent Labour lead (ITN – Monday and Tuesday morning interviewing).

There do not appear to have been any other published weekend polls apart from the three apparently aberrantly pro-Conservative ones by Harris/*Express*, which were on the receiving end of criticism and suspicion at the time: and after two glaring gaps on the successive Tuesdays Harris decided to conduct both ITN and *Express* polling partly over the weekend and partly on Mondays. The overall figures came together, although in the *Express* poll of 28–30 March the interviews which took place at the weekend showed a 3 per cent Conservative lead and those on Monday a 4 per cent Labour lead.

This does not add up to sufficient evidence to claim superiority for weekend polling in home, though there may be *a priori* grounds for believing that this could well be the best time and place to contact a representative sample of voters, especially on dark spring days before the clocks have gone forward. However, long-term analysis of weekend and weekday polling does not find significant differences in party support.

The MRS inquiry team, however, did suggest that possible failings in the methodology of the polls on this occasion may have resulted in an element of the anti-Conservative pro-Labour discrepancy, amounting to a little over a third of the whole.

It is a plausible hypothesis that Conservative voters are a little harder to find than Labour supporters, and that even with class quotas interviewers might be less likely to find the more affluent of the ABs, say, or those who work the longest hours. Quotas and weights are not usually set on criteria such as car and two-car household ownership, telephone ownership and newspaper readership, all of which may reveal a slight skew in favour of the less affluent in poll samples.

There are distinct differences in the sample profiles between the random Harris/ITN and NOP/BBC exit polls and the pre-election polls by Harris, NOP and other agencies. Of the Harris/ITN exit poll respondents to whom a social grade was ascribed, 47 per cent were in the 'middle class' ABC1 groups compared with 41–42 per cent in Harris pre-election polls. Only 13 per cent claimed in the same exit poll to live in local authority rented housing, though some, perhaps most, of the 9 per cent claiming 'other types of tenure' may in fact better be classed in that category; this still represents a lower proportion than found in pre-election polls (23 per cent in the ICM/PA sample of 10,000, for example). It should be remembered that the respondents were filling in self-completion questionnaires and it is known that this leads to an ascription of higher job status than coding by trained interviewers. However, past voting recall also varied between the two types of polls. The Harris/ITN and the NOP/BBC exit poll respondents both registered an 11 per cent lead for the Conservatives in their recollection of how they had voted in the 1987 general election. In the four weekly NOP polls for *The Mail on Sunday*, the Conservative lead on recall varied from 5 per cent to 7 per cent. The MORI panel recruited for *The Sunday Times* recalled a 6 per cent Conservative lead at the initial interview. All these figures include don't knows/refusals/didn't votes.

These differences do not necessarily imply that the pre-election polls erred in their generation of a representative sample of the national electorate and were shown up by the random exit polls. They may be due partially at least to differential turnout, for example (although the predictive quality of last minute pre-election polls would presumably be improved by the success of identification of likelihood of turnout and subsequent weighting). Nevertheless, it remains a strong possibility that the samples contacted in pre-election polls were more working class and less affluent than the electors who actually voted on 9 April.

It is true that the final pre-election polls on average had underestimated the Conservative lead in the 1987 general election as well, by about 3 per cent (although MORI alone were almost spot on) and almost all general election and by-election exit polls in and since 1987 have very slightly overestimated the Labour vote and underestimated the Conservative share. This led the Conservative MP Robert Hayward, a keen amateur psephologist, to circulate a paper as early as January 1992 to the effect that the polls could be expected to underestimate his party's chances.[8]

The Market Research Society's initial inquiry ended in controversy and wrangling as a press release associated with its report suggested that there may have been 'fundamental' errors in sampling which had created a pro-Conservative bias in opinion polling since 1959. The word 'fundamental' did not appear in the report itself and there have been occasions such as 1983 in which the Conservative vote was overestimated and Labour's underestimated. In addition, polling techniques were significantly changed after 1970 and since that time the pollsters have usually produced results which proved acceptable to all. There was no fundamental change in polling practice in 1992.

Yet the 'discrepancy' appeared in 1992, in the form of a pro-Labour and anti-Conservative bias, and it was to be found to a lesser extent in the large scale, random exit polls too. It cannot be fully explained by the factors discussed above – late swing/'moral' expression and some possible sampling of 'wrong' respondents in 1992. Neither of these would apply to exit polls in any case. Another element needs to be explored. It fits in a way into the second category of explanation, that the pollsters talked to the wrong people, except that it might better be stated another way. The right people would not talk to the pollsters. They refused.

The MRS inquiry team believed that there were a higher number of respondents in the pre-election polls who refused to express a voting intention than usual, about 5 per cent. This figure was, however, apparently based only on ICM data and other polling organisations report a lower refusal date. ICM post-election research has shown, though,[9] that there is considerable evidence that these 'refusers' were actually predominantly Conservative voters – certainly a very high proportion of them believed the Conservatives to have the best economic policies, a critical question.

ICM conducted a very interesting piece of research after the election in which they divided their sample into two, and offered half a secret ballot (as in exit polls) while the other half was asked the voting intention question in the conventional manner. They found a 7 per cent increase in the level of Conservative preferences, almost entirely at the expense of refusals, among the 'secret ballotees'.[10]

Reallocation of refusals on the voting intention question on the basis of likely preference would have made some difference to the polls' performance in the 1992 general election. But surely the question must also be raised about the much larger group of voters who refused to take part in the interview at all. ICM research post-election is again useful here, suggesting that of the order of 35 per cent of all attempted contacts refused to be interviewed when the survey was introduced as a political poll and 37 per cent when told it was a market research survey. These non-participants were disproportionately from the older and more working-class groups: 26 per cent were aged 65 plus (compared with 20 per cent in the National Readership Survey) and 62 per cent C2DE (56 per cent).[11] ICM could not find any direct evidence that those who refused the interview were disproportionately Conservative, as in the case of those who refused the voting intention question, but on the other hand over half of non-participants would not respond even to a question on economic competence. It cannot be disproved that they were refusing disproportionately on political lines.

The best evidence for differential political refusal lies with the exit polls, which are free of most of the other potential sources of discrepancy which have been suggested, and which have very large sample sizes and large numbers of sampling points, yet have consistently shown a slight bias to Labour since 1987 in general elections and by-elections (most of all in the Langbaurgh by-election of 1991, where the Labour candidate was Asian).

Differential refusal (both to take part in the interview and to the voting intention question) should then be added to 'late swing' as a single major explanatory factor in the discrepancy between all polls and the result of the 1992 British general election. There may well indeed be a connection between these two elements. Why were Conservatives less likely to express, or admit to, an intention in an interview, and less likely to participate in all kinds of polling?

It could be that the refusals simply belonged to groups which were more likely to support the Conservatives in any case – women, and the elderly, for example. But the exit polls go to great lengths to substitute for refusals with those of the same age and sex (and class as far as it can be ascertained by observation). Of pensioners in the Harris/ITN exit poll, 94 per cent were substitutes compared with an overall figure of 26 per cent. Also, it must always be borne in mind that the size of the discrepancy in 1992 was unique in the history of British opinion polling. That must be explained: what was different this time?

In the discussion of late swing, above, the idea of the 'moral' answer has already been introduced. Ivor Crewe describes it as the 'shame' factor: a Conservative vote was widely identified with selfishness on issues such as taxation and public spending, while Labour seized the 'high moral ground' on health, education and unemployment. The same 'shame' as might have led voters to mislead pollsters (and perhaps themselves) before the election may well have discouraged them from agreeing to an interview in the street or on their doorstep, or, perhaps, put up Conservative posters.

One very speculative point is this: Conservative Party canvassers and their reports to the Central Office organisation were consistently more optimistic than those who relied on opinion polls. While there really is little evidence to abandon the gross distrust that has been placed in any canvass returns, they can at least be compared with previous figures from the same source. Reports from several parts of the country proved more accurate predictions of the results than the opinion polls. Were voters willing to admit their 'guilt' in voting Conservative to partisan visitors but not to independent interviewers?

Why should the 'shame factor', if indeed it was involved in both 'late swing' and differential refusal, have arisen as a problem for opinion research in 1992? If it had been present before, surely it would have contributed to similar discrepancies as that discussed here? Yet once again it should be noted that all elections are fought in different circumstances. In 1992, for the first time since 1974, Labour had a real chance of winning. The polls showed a desperately close struggle, maybe with Labour's nose in front but with a strong likelihood of no overall Commons majority. After thirteen years of Conservative government there was plenty of pressure for a change, especially since the country was mired in an economic recession for which no other political party could be blamed. NHS policy had often been a bone of contention before, but never quite so emotively presented through the television channels. The Conservatives had managed to convince a very large number of people that Labour's taxation proposals would directly take money out of their pockets. Dislike of Mr Kinnock, for whatever reason, was especially serious given his well-favoured chances of entering Downing Street.

It will never be possible to prove or quantify with certainty the elements which made the 1992 election so much harder for the pollsters (and the pundits) to read. Arguments will continue about the strength of the different causes. It is also unlikely that all polling organisations will take the same measures to reduce the chances of suffering further 'débâcles'. Yet there are approaches to ameliorating almost all of the problems.

The polling companies will continue to experiment with the collection and use of extra demographic variables to refine the quotas given to interviewers and weighting procedures, to answer criticisms that they had been talking to the wrong electors. Car ownership, telephone ownership, work status and newspaper readership are among the data which will be examined. Consideration should be given, especially with the publication of the details of the 1991 Census, to switching class quota controls from the 'market research' AB C1 C2 DE classification to census-compatible socio-economic grading.

Further research on telephone interviewing will undoubtedly continue, as its ease of supervision and lack of clustering are very attractive if a representative sample can be assured among phone owners. However, even a radical change of methodology such as the adoption of telephone polling would not in itself confront any biases caused by differential refusal and 'late swing', including the 'shame factor'. Nor would a return to random sampling for face to face polls, which would also demand extra resources of time and money which would be unlikely to be available, in a general election campaign at least.

In August 1992 ICM announced that they would in future no longer ask the voting intention question orally but would give the respondent a secret self-completion ballot paper replicating the ballot box approach of exit polls. This was intended to reduce to almost nil the refusals of the voting intention question. Other pollsters are certainly thinking along the same lines. Those who still refuse the voting intention question and 'don't knows' can be ascribed a party in line with the party which they think would best handle the economy.[11]

If the problem of refusal does indeed extend to those who decline to be interviewed (or take part in an exit poll), even if offered a secret ballot, it may be thought that there is little that can be done. Pollsters are looking at ways of reducing interviewer refusals, but in the end they cannot of course be anywhere near eliminated. One possible, if risky, remedy is at hand, though.

In many other countries the problems caused by voters who are reluctant to 'own up' to their intentions are well known. Unweighted polls have historically underestimated the support for the Communists and the Front Nationale in France, for Sinn Fein in all parts of Ireland, and overestimated the centrist vote in the new democracies such as Poland. Candidates accused of racist appeals have 'flown below radar' in the United States, while in states such as North Carolina some voters have denied that they will vote on racial lines.[12] In some of these countries, such as France, political weighting on the basis of recall of previous voting patterns is applied; it can be strong enough to double the reported Front Nationale share, say from 7 per cent to 14 per cent.[13]

Study of the national and by-election exit poll results over the past ten years suggested beforehand that the Harris/ITN exercise at least might be expected to underestimate the Conservative vote by 1–2 per cent and to overestimate Labour by the same amount. Ironically, if such a 'political' adjustment had been made, both national/analysis and marginals/projection poll figures would have been almost exactly correct.

Given the expectations stimulated by conventional polls, though, no such weighting was seriously considered: on the day, the Harris/ITN exit poll figures seemed surprisingly and, indeed, suspiciously good for the Conservatives.

Political weighting is used outside Britain to counter long-standing and well-proven biases caused by voters lying and differential refusal. It must now be considered in this country, but it is as well to recall that as recently as 1983 the polls overestimated the Conservative position. Perhaps then the 'shame factor' operated against Labour because of the appalling image presented by the divided party tainted with extremism and led by Michael Foot. 'Shame' does not and will not always work only in one direction, against one party. That is why any political weighting adopted in the aftermath of 1992 would be highly risky and far from easy to justify on a historical basis.

I wish to stress that the phrase 'shame factor' is here meant only to represent differential refusal to participate in opinion polls on party political grounds. It does not carry any element of moral condemnation or criticism of the non-respondents themselves.

So, as with any genuine late swing, pre-election polls (at least) will always risk suffering from influences which cannot be eliminated which may disable their use as reliable predictions. Is there anything more that can be done?

As indicated at the beginning of this chapter, it seems to me that far too much attention has been paid to the voting intention question and too little to other questions which might also serve as the basis for guessing the outcome of the election. Much interesting and informative research was in fact carried out, by all major pollsters, which has been overshadowed by the polls' alleged overall failure. In particular, we now have even clearer evidence than before as to which polling questions generate worthwhile answers that can be related to the basis on which people actually do vote, and those which simply elicit the 'moral' or 'expected' reply.

One question which certainly does not act as a useful predictor of voting is to ask the respondents which issues are the most important when it comes to making their electoral decisions. When Harris asked this question for ITN (23–24 March) the two 'top' issues were the NHS and unemployment. During the campaign every polling agency found that Labour was better trusted to handle the Health Service and unemployment issues than the Conservatives – in the case of health, by 47 per cent to 30 per cent in Harris's final ITN poll (4–6 April). This was still the case on election day: the NOP/BBC exit poll found 49 per cent trusting Labour to make the right decision on the NHS and only 37 per cent the Conservatives. This exit poll gave the Tories a 4 per cent lead overall. Labour's lead on being trusted to handle unemployment was 16 per cent in the final Harris/ITN pre-election poll, and 18 per cent in Gallup's final poll (1–6 April). At the end of the campaign, Gallup gave a 25 per cent Labour lead on policy on the NHS, a 14 per cent lead on education and a 15 per cent lead on women's affairs. None of these figures had shifted

Table 14.1 *Issues affecting voting behaviour (%)*

	%
NHS	41
Unemployment	36
Education	23
Prices	11
Taxation	10
AIDS	0
Nationalisation	0
Northern Ireland	0
International peace	0

Source: Gallup.

significantly during the campaign. Even in their post-election survey (10–11 April) Gallup still found substantial Labour leads on all these issues (17 per cent on the NHS) and when at that time they asked about the two most urgent problems that had affected the respondents' voting choice they discovered the results presented in table 14.1. Little comment needs to be made about the value of interpreting this question literally.

Indeed, the polling evidence reveals a large amount about what did not win the Conservatives the election. MORI's panel study respondents, for example, were on balance clearly decided even in the final pre-election wave of interviews that a Conservative government would not keep its promises, nor cut income tax, help improve their own living standards, reduce the crime rate, improve welfare state services, encourage greater racial harmony or improve the way local councils were run. It would, however, make the rich richer and the poor poorer and increase VAT![14]

The campaign made little difference to the parties' images on various policy issues. Nor did it seem to matter who 'won' the campaign. Gallup's final poll asked which party had campaigned most 'impressingly' (*sic*). Labour was named by 36 per cent, the Liberal Democrats by 34 per cent and the Conservatives by only 10 per cent. Similarly, assessments of the leaders' performances during the run-up have no relation to the outcome of the election: Ashdown 'won' with 41 per cent, Kinnock was named as most impressive by 30 per cent and Major by only 17 per cent.

One question did reveal a marked and consistent change during the campaign: 'Irrespective of how you yourself will vote, who do you think will win the next general election?' The initial expectation that the Conservatives would retain power gave way to a belief that Labour were going to win (presumably based largely on the voting intentions expressed and reported in polls themselves). This is clear in the Gallup data presented in table 14.2.

Table 14.2 *Party expected to win (%)*

	11–17 March	18–23 March	25–30 March	1–6 April
Conservative	48	39	35	24
Labour	31	37	37	47
Hung	5	14	18	18

Source: Gallup.

In the same polls every time over 90 per cent thought the election would be close.

Minds were thus concentrated on the genuinely key issues. Admittedly with the benefit of hindsight, we can now see what they were. Consider the polling evidence.

Even in their darkest moments of the campaign, the Conservatives retained a lead on the issues of which party would be best to handle the economy, inflation and taxation. In MORI's final *Sunday Times* panel wave pre-election, the government led by 11 per cent on taxation and 5 per cent on managing the economy. Harris's final poll (4–6 April) for *The Daily Express* gave the Conservatives a 14 per cent lead as the party most trusted to handle the economy and 15 per cent as most trusted to handle taxation. The connection between the use of the word trust here and aspects of Conservative campaigning phraseology should not pass unnoticed. Harris gave the Conservatives a 6 per cent lead as the party most trusted to get Britain out of the economic recession in *The Observer* poll carried out on 19–20 March; even the mention of the recession or an economic crisis did not wipe out the Conservatives' lead. MORI's final panel wave agreed that 'the Conservative government is responsible for the current economic recession' by 59 per cent to 36 per cent, but Gallup found that 'the Conservative government' was associated in this context with Mrs Thatcher, not Mr Major – only 4 per cent blamed Mr Major's government for the recession in their final poll (7–8 April) whereas 43 per cent blamed Mrs Thatcher's regime (and 48 per cent the world recession).

While it was clearly accepted that the economy was in poor shape in March–April 1992, Labour's problem was that it was felt that things would be even worse under them. MORI's fourth and last pre-election *Sunday Times* panel survey agreed that 'the country cannot afford Labour's spending plans' by 52 per cent to 36 per cent. In particular the electorate was largely convinced that they would lose money directly from tax increases introduced by the likely Labour government: MORI again: 'Most people will pay more in taxes if Labour wins the election' – agree 70 per cent, disagree 24 per cent.[15]

Labour's weakness on taxation was particularly clear. NOP (*Independent on Sunday* Recall 1, 19–21 March), found 56 per cent agreeing with the statement that 'Labour will put up income tax a lot for people on average earnings' and

Table 14.3 *Outcome expected to make respondent best off (%)*

Conservative win	41
Labour win	29
Hung parliament	8

Source: Harris.

only 37 per cent disagreeing. By 'Sindy Recall 3' (2–3 April), no fewer than 81 per cent agreed that Labour would put up taxes on those with average earnings. People might say they didn't care about the level of taxation: even in Gallup's post-election survey (10–11 April) 63 per cent claimed to agree that 'government services such as health, education and welfare should be extended, even if it means some increases in taxes', but this only demonstrates the leading nature of such questions.

The overall economic preference of the electors polled during the election was clear throughout.

Harris asked on 15–16 March under which party the respondent would be best off financially: the Conservatives led Labour by 43–32 per cent. When asked which party would bring most prosperity to the country in general, the Tory lead was 16 per cent. This was one of the 'weekend' polls which showed the Conservatives ahead on voting intention (3 per cent), but even in the final *Express* poll (4–6 April) with its 1 per cent Labour lead, the Conservatives were ahead on these two critical economic questions by 7 per cent and 10 per cent respectively. In Harris's final poll for *The Observer* (2–3 April) a 2 per cent Labour lead was recorded but the answers to the question on which result would make the respondent best off, were as shown in table 14.3.

The exit polls confirmed the critical areas of Conservative advantage: Harris/ITN found taxation was only rated as seventh in the list of most important issues in the election (the NHS and unemployment were first and second), but 49 per cent admitted they would be worse off under Labour's tax policies and only 30 per cent thought they would be better off. Among the C2 social group the figures were almost identical to the average – 32 per cent believed they would be better off and 48 per cent worse off. Only 14 per cent of all respondents in the NOP/BBC exit poll regarded income tax as one of the three most important issues – but more than twice that figure, 29 per cent, of 'switchers' to the Conservatives did. In the past year, twice as many NOP/BBC respondents said they had become worse off as better off; but Gallup had found in their final poll (7–8 April) that 30 per cent thought their financial situation would get better in the next six months and only 14 per cent that it would get worse. It was felt at the same time that both the respondents and their families and Britain as a whole would be worse off under Labour.

There is much to be said for the argument that elections in Britain in recent years have been strongly influenced by the voters' 'instrumental' perceptions of their economic interests – see for example the article by Studlar and McAllister in the summer 1992 issue of WAPOR's journal, the *International Journal of Public Opinion Research*.[16] The Conservatives clearly benefited from a lead on the crucial economic issues in April 1992 and interpreters of polls would be well advised to observe such questions, as well as the voting intention figures, when predicting the results of future elections in Britain. Next time we should take note of whether Labour can convince the electorate that it is best placed to put money in its pocket, and remain sceptical of the party's prospects – whatever the expressed voting intention – if it cannot at least draw level in poll questions on economic competence.

The Conservatives' other advantage in the field of public opinion, despite his lacklustre performance during the campaign, was their leader. In the NOP/BBC exit poll, John Major led Neil Kinnock by 15 per cent as 'best Prime Minister'. Although other party leaders have entered 10 Downing Street while less popular than their opposite numbers, they have clearly been liabilities for their cause – and in 1992 the election was as 'presidential' as ever before, with relatively little ideological difference being visible between the parties. Neil Kinnock clearly featured as the biggest single obstacle to voting Labour in Harris's polls for *The Observer*. In NOP's exit poll, twice as many people thought another candidate, John Smith, would be the best Labour leader as thought Kinnock would – an unprecedented situation.

The polls of the 1992 election illuminate many other fascinating and important issues not directly connected with voting intention. There is no space here for most of them. One point which might be made concerns the fashionable topic of electoral reform. The electorate's view of voting reform and proportional representation depends largely on how the questions are phrased.

On 24–25 March NOP asked whether its respondents would approve or disapprove of the idea that we should 'scrap the present system and introduce PR'.[17] As the public is well disposed to most new ideas, the sample approved by 46 per cent to 20 per cent. NOP's exit poll for the BBC asked a more neutral question which mentioned the alternative: only 39 per cent opted for PR against 43 per cent saying they preferred the present system. Harris/ITN found a similar proportion in favour of the status quo (52 per cent to 43 per cent for PR). The differences were largely due to 'Don't know' being offered as an option on the NOP/BBC self completion questionnaire but not on Harris/ITN.

For those who were surprised on 10 April by the Conservatives' victory, one compensation is that they were in the vast majority. In Harris's final poll for *The Observer* (2–3 April) only 19 per cent of respondents expected a Conservative overall majority. More expected a hung parliament than any kind of overall majority. Presumably these respondents were basing their expectations largely on the message being conveyed by the polls themselves; or at least by the expressed voting intention figures. At the next general election, undoubtedly the polling companies will have introduced modifications to the techniques designed to minimise the chances of publishing such misleading 'top line' figures. However, it is to be hoped that it is also true that the whole content of polls, their other questions, will be examined and interpreted with thought and intelligence. This may involve the movement towards some more sophisticated 'modelling' of predictions of the election result based on a multiplicity of data generated by demographic classifications and questions other than the simple voting intention. Even the opinion polls of 1992 cast new light on the bases of electoral decision-making and preference and repay close study, despite the calumny heaped upon them.

Notes

1 Gallup, Political and Social Index 381, May 1992, p. 6.
2 *Ibid.*, pp. 2, 17.
3 Andreas Whittam-Smith of *The Independent*, Saturday, 11 April 1992.
4 See, for example, Ivor Crewe, 'A nation of liars', *Parliamentary Affairs* (October 1992); David Butler and Dennis Kavanagh, *The British General Election of 1992*, chapter 7; Robert Worcester, MORI, British Public Opinion, The British General Election of 1992, Introduction, June 1992; Market Research Society, Research Enquiry into the Performance of Opinion Polls in the 1992 Election, June 1992.
5 ICM, MORI and NOP surveys in MRS Enquiry p. 7.
6 Robert Harris, *The Sunday Times*, 12 April 1992.
7 The assumptions were: 900,000 voters failing to register to vote because of the poll tax, 65 per cent of them would have turned out, and 75 per cent of those would have voted Labour, 15 per cent Liberal or SNP and 10 per cent Conservative.
8 Robert Hayward, 'Bias to Labour in polls' (Tory Vote Underestimated), privately circulated January 1992.
9 ICM, 'Results of tests to improve voting intention polls', August 1992, pp. 8–9.
10 ICM, 'Results of tests', p. 10.
11 ICM, 'Results of tests', p. 16.
12 See, for example, the Senate context in North Carolina in 1990 between Jesse Helms, the incumbent white Republican, and the black Democrat Harvey Gantt who led in pre-election polls but lost the contest by 53 per cent to 47 per cent.
13 Interview, Pierre Weill/Jerome Jaffre (SOFRES), 22 June 1992.
14 MORI, *Sunday Times* panel, Wave 4.
15 *Ibid.* MORI, *Sunday Times* panel, Wave 4.
16 Donley T. Studlar and Ian McAllister, 'A changing political agenda? The structure of political attitudes in Britain 1974–1987', *International Journal of Public Opinion Research*, 4, 2 (Summer 1992), 148–76.
17 *Independent/Newsnight* poll II.

15 The use of panel studies in British general elections

Robert M. Worcester

The use of panel studies to assist marketing and readership research is well known in the market research world. John Parfitt has written extensively about their use in the commercial sector.[1] There is also extensive use of panel studies in political and social research, and in the area of the specific interest of this conference, best known is the SSRC-sponsored election studies referred to in the Nuffield series of British general election books co-authored by Dr David Butler and in his co-authored (with Donald Stokes) *Political Change in Britain.*[2]

The Conservative Party used panel studies in the 1960s, carried out by the British Market Research Bureau while other research was being conducted, first by National Opinion Polls, later NOP Market Research Ltd, and after its founding in 1967, by Opinion Research Centre, later Harris. Starting in 1966, the Conservatives spent approximately £30,000 a year with ORC and on the BMRB panel. There were continuous panel operations starting with 4,500 electors first interviewed in 1965, reinterviewing 700 or so each seven months to detect and determine causes of changes in voting intentions. One startling finding was that at least 30 per cent of the electorate had changed their voting intention in some way between 1964 and 1966, and these tended to be C2s (skilled working class), under 35s and women. This finding affected party policy, election strategy and advertising. It also brought a sense of proportion to Conservative leaders, reminding them in the mid-term period when record anti-government swings in both the polls and in by-elections were running their way that the tide of public opinion went down as well as up.[3]

The Labour Party's MORI panel studies[4]

The use of panels by the Tories was discontinued after 1970, but was reintroduced into private polling for the political parties by MORI in 1973 for the Labour Party, as the vehicle for both simulation modelling and for multivariate analysis in aid of the Labour Party and its leader, Harold Wilson and his media advisers, the 'shadow communications agency' of the time.

In February 1973, MORI conducted a confidential survey on behalf of the Labour Party among a sample of 2,131 respondents in Great Britain (fieldwork 19 February – 1 March). The findings of this study were presented to the Party in May 1973. This study established a base-line for future recall studies and the first of these was conducted during the February 1974 general election campaign. The panel base-line was based on the Voter Model used by MORI for its polling for the Labour Party from 1973 to 1979 and is described in the 'Red Books' published under the title 'British Public Opinion' of the MORI work for the Labour Party.

The findings from the February 1974 studies and those of the October 1974 general election were lodged by direction of the National Executive Committee of the Labour Party at the SSRC Archives at the University of Essex, embargoed until after the 'next' election. This practice continued until after the 1987 general election, so that all work conducted by MORI for the Labour Party from 1973 to 1987 is lodged at the ESRC Archives.

The MORI/*Sunday Times* panel study

In 1976, *The Sunday Times* political team, editor Harry Evans, political editor Hugo Young, and political correspondent Peter Kellner, met with the MORI team to plan polling strategy for the next general election. It was agreed that the objective for the polling would be explanatory rather than be predictive, in that its objective would be to explain throughout the campaign and following its conclusion on election day, *why* what happened was happening and *who* among the electorate was being affected by the campaign itself.

Two reasons were behind this decision: one, the fact that there was substantial evidence to indicate that the previous three general elections were determined in the final week of the campaign, certainly this was true in both 1970 and in the February 1974 campaigns and probably was the case in October 1974; this clearly precluded the thought that fieldwork necessarily carried out a week before polling day for publication on the Sunday before election day itself could in any way be considered 'predictive'. Second, that the nature of *The Sunday Times* itself was one of 'insight' and analysis, and thus a panel study had a unique ability to examine with absolute precision that an individual's voting intention had indeed changed between week 2 in the campaign and, say, week 3, because the same individuals were recalled each week and their answers recorded throughout the campaign.

Peter Kellner wrote in an explanatory article in the *New Statesman*,[5] 'by reinterviewing the same voters, the volatility of the electorate can be measured. If one million voters switch from Labour to Tory, and another million switch from Tory to Labour, the overall result will appear as no change: the substantial shifts below the surface can only be detected by panel polling.'

We were aware that any panel study could introduce bias into attitudes and behaviour, and thus the panel itself might be corrupted and become unrepresentative, especially in something as intensive as an election campaign with the tremendous focus of the media on this event. To guard against this, weighting procedures were employed in the computer analysis to ensure representativeness by demographic classification data, and daily tracking polls were monitored to measure the extent of any political 'drift' that panel

Table 15.1 MORI/*Sunday Times panel studies*

Year	Base-line	Recall II	Recall III	Recall IV
1979				
Dates	4–6 April	17–19 April	24–26 April	4–5 May (post)
Sample size	1,087	928	894	883
Success rate	100%	85%	82%	81%
1983				
Dates	21–25 April	17–18 May	24–25 May	1–3 June
Sample size	1,216	960	1,023	942
Success rate	100%	79%	84%	77%
1987				
Dates	12–14 May	20–21 May	27–28 May	3–4 June
Sample size	1,521	1,328	1,188	1,305
Success rate	100%	86%	77%	85%
1992				
Dates	11–12 March	18–20 March	25–27 March	1–3 April
Sample size	1,544	1,257	1,292	1,265
Success rate	100%	81%	84%	82%

involvement might introduce. It was also agreed that a significant effort to achieve a high recall success rate needed to be made, as some panellists inevitably drop out (and some drop back in) due to illness, holidays or other unavailability or lack of interest. As indicated in table 15.1, the first, 1979, panel resulted in a continuing eight in ten or better response rate, something that has continued to be achieved at that level ever since.

On 3 May 1979, at the general election, 92 per cent of the panel members voted, according to the results of the recall survey conducted on the Friday and Saturday following election day. As the actual turnout was only 76 per cent, it is apparent that the experience of being interviewed repeatedly throughout the campaign had the effect of heightening interest in the campaign and increasing turnout among panellists. It did not, however, much affect voting behaviour other than to slightly overstate the Conservative and Labour shares and understate the Liberal vote somewhat. One interesting finding is that two-thirds (65 per cent) of those who said at the outset of the campaign that they were 'absolutely certain they would *not* vote' reported they did so on the day. Another is that nearly a quarter of the electorate, as represented by the panel, did in fact change their minds (at least once, and some even more often) during the period of the campaign itself.

The 1979 election began with the Labour Party well behind the Conservatives, even though Mr Callaghan was preferred as Prime Minister to Conservative Party leader Mrs Margaret Thatcher. According to both the tracking polls

Table 15.2 *Certain to vote in general elections, 1979–1992*

'Absolutely certain'	Week 1	Week 2	Week 3	Week 4
1979	70%	78%	81%	—
1983	71%	76%	77%	77%
1987	75%	80%	84%	84%
1992	72%	77%	81%	85%

Source: MORI/*Sunday Times* panel studies.

and the panel there was very little net change during the first three weeks of the campaign, followed by a narrowing of the Conservative lead in the fourth week and then a widening back again in the final few days of the campaign.

One factor that helped the Conservatives (yet again) was their effectiveness in getting the postal vote organised. This is a difficult thing for tracking polls to measure and of course impossible for the exit polls. In our 1979 panel, 2 per cent in the recall said they had voted by post or proxy (admittedly only fourteen people) and of these, ten said they had voted Conservative, three for Labour and one Liberal. Of those few in the panel who did not vote, the two principal reasons were illness (16 per cent) and lack of interest in the outcome (also 16 per cent); of the rest, they had moved recently (15 per cent), were not convinced that any of the parties represented their views (14 per cent) or had the answers to the country's problems (11 per cent). Of those who did not vote, 10 per cent blamed the weather.

Unlike the February 1974 campaign and more typical of other elections, the colder and rainier, the greater the Conservative lead. The Conservatives were also more likely to vote earlier – and later. The Conservatives had a 15 per cent lead among the 23 per cent of voters who cast their ballots before 11 am, and a 6 per cent lead among those who voted after six, while a Labour lead of 2 per cent was recorded among voters who said they went to the polls between 11 am and 6 pm.

Week after week the panel showed just how volatile it and, by projection, the British electorate was during the campaign. In October 1974 the Harris panel for *Weekend World* found that 23 per cent of their respondents changed their voting intentions between dissolution and election day while 33 per cent of the smaller ORC/*Sunday Times* panel reported that they had changed their minds, less than the 43 per cent they had found in February 1974 but much more than the 20 per cent recorded in comparable studies a decade earlier.

While tracking studies measure the aggregate net change from week to week, a panel study, uniquely, measures the individual change. To take part in interviewing a 'switcher' whom you had interviewed the week before and recorded a Labour intention, and to have that person tell you they now intended to vote Tory, and when asked 'What has happened to make you

Table 15.3 *1979 general election change matrix*

	4–6 April		45%	36%	8%	2%	9%
		%	Con.	Lab.	Lib.	Other	DK
3 May	Con.	41	81	3	9	0	26
	Lab.	36	5	82	7	12	33
	Lib.	10	4	5	67	0	14
	Other	3	2	1	5	52	1
	None	(10)	(8)	(7)	(12)	(6)	(26)

Source: MORI/*Sunday Times* panel studies.

Table 15.4 *Changes on the issues: week 1 to week 3, 1979*

Change	Prices %	Strikes %	Jobs %	Taxes %
From Con.	8	11	8	10
To Con.	11	9	11	9
Net	+3	−2	+3	−1
From Lab.	6	6	5	4
To Lab.	12	13	14	12
Net	+6	+7	+9	+8
Labour Gain	+3	+9	+6	+9

Source: MORI/*Sunday Times* panel studies.

change your mind?' then says 'Oh, I haven't, I've always intended to vote Tory', says something important about the electorate generally, and the surprise in 1992 specifically.

Tracking studies disguise the underlying turmoil in the body politic, many people not that interested in the campaign, yet bombarded on all sides by the parties' and in many cases the newspapers' propaganda about the importance of voting in the first place and for the party supported in the second.

In the 1979 election, as shown in the change matrix table 15.3, one in five original Conservative and Labour intenders did in the event defect elsewhere, as did a third of the Liberals. The Conservatives lost 5 per cent of their support to Labour and 4 per cent to the Liberals, Labour 3 per cent to the Tories and 5 per cent to Liberals; the Liberals, from a much smaller base, of course, lost

9 per cent of their original supporters to the Conservatives and 7 per cent to Labour.

Panel studies tell a rich story of the underlying effect of the campaign. On the key issues of that campaign, prices (55 per cent), strikes (52 per cent), taxation (39 per cent) and unemployment (36 per cent), the Tories began the campaign with leads on three, + 3 per cent on prices, + 9 per cent on unemployment (!), + 24 per cent on taxation and only on strikes and industrial relations did Labour have a one point lead. Between week 1 and week 3 Labour gained ground on all four key issues.

Unfortunately for the Labour Party in the 1979 general election, the last week of the election focused some minds in the other direction, and they lost nearly all of the gains on the issues they had made. Over the campaign from beginning to end, they lost one point on prices, losing four in the last week, broke even on strikes, losing all nine of the points they had gained up until then, were behind by three on jobs by the end, losing six points in the final week, and lost all nine they had gained on taxes, to remain twnety-four points behind the Tories on that, even then, key issue.

MORI/*Sunday Times* panels in 1983 and 1987

In 1983 and again in 1987, *The Sunday Times* again commissioned MORI to undertake panel studies. They believed that it was the most effective way of monitoring the movements of perceptions, attitudes, voting intentions and behaviour during the campaign, especially considering that whilst recorded changes between *ad hoc* surveys can easily be within the bounds of sampling error, changes within the panel are 'real', because the same people are interviewed each time.

The 1983 panel was larger than 1979, 1,216 respondents. The initial base-line was set up two weeks before the date of the election was announced by the Prime Minister on 9 May. The recalls followed in the three weeks of the election period, as noted above. It was also larger in scope, as questions were added to assess the impact of the campaign on the main parties' images, and 'one-off' questions were added at each phase, to look at, among other things, recognition of leading politicians, images of party leaders, attitudes to the media and newspaper bias, and expectations of the incoming government.

During the course of the campaign, some 17 per cent of the electorate (at least) changed their minds, some 7.1 million electors in all *up to the final week* (no post-election recall being done, it is impossible to say what the entire election period switching was in the 1983 election). Switching between parties was much less, mainly between the Alliance and other main parties.

In 1987 the panel was enlarged again, to enable more detailed analysis of sub-groups, switchers and 'churners', who moved back and forth as the parties' arguments persuaded them one way or another or as they became 'fed up' with

Table 15.5 *Switching in the 1983 election campaign*

Switching in weeks	1–2	2–3	3–4	1–4	1–2–3–4
Switched between panels	6.0%	3.5%	3.5%	8.5%	11.0%
Switched VI/DK/WNV	10.5%	5.4%	6.0%	14.6%	17.0%

Source: MORI/*Sunday Times* panel studies.

Table 15.6 *1983 general election change matrix*

	17–18 May		42%	27.5%	21.5%	1.5%	7.5%
		%	Con.	Lab.	SDP/Lib.	Other	DK
	Con.	43.5	95	2	7	11	26
1–3 June	Lab.	27	*	85	7	0	14
	SDP/Lib.	24	4	11	86	11	14
	Other	1	0	1	*	67	0
	None	(4.5)	(1)	(1)	(*)	(11)	(46)

Source: MORI/*Sunday Times* panel studies.

the election campaign. More analytical work was done, and the panel saw the expansion of open-ended questions and even the introduction of follow-up interviews by a *Sunday Times* journalist (Edward Welsh) who visited panellists in their homes and watched party election broadcasts with them to gauge reactions on the ground.

The 1987 election saw the introduction of the graphic change matrix, introduced by Geoff Sims of *The Sunday Times'* Graphics Department, which became the major feature of *The Sunday Times'* write up of the campaign movement. It also saw the percentage change matrix give way to extrapolation of the data into millions of voters (and non-voters), using the weight of the lines to represent the churning of the electorate during the campaign.

Former *Times* editor, then *Sunday Times* columnist, Simon Jenkins was the author of the 1987 panel reports, and the caption of the final graphic stated 'How 7.5m voters have switched since May 13'. The copy read 'voting intention has hardened since the panel was first interviewed, 9% have actually switched parties (nearly 4m people) and the churners (people who move in and out of the 'don't know' category) are 7.5m'.

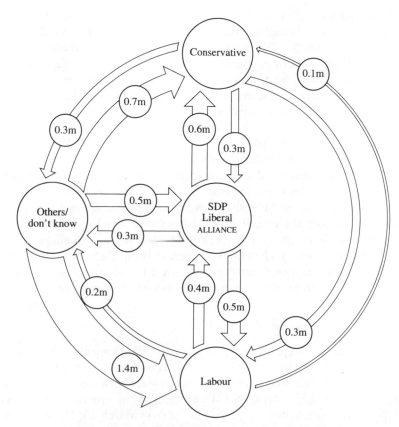

Figure 15.1   How voters have switched since 13 May. The voting switches during an election campaign are more complex than simple 'swings' between parties. Most polls show a net shift in the totals. *The Sunday Times*/MORI panel indicates the total amount of change, which is far greater than the net figure. Labour's recent gain has been mostly drawn from 'don't knows'.

Panel studies in the general election of 1992[6]

In the immediate run-up to the 1992 general election, thirteen out of the fifteen polls conducted by the major pollsters kept to the close contest call: Conservatives 39 per cent (± 2 per cent), Labour 40 per cent (± 2 per cent), Liberal Democrats 16 per cent (± 2 per cent).

But one thing that these snap-shot polls, either during the campaign or as exit polls, do not show is the movement of the electorate between parties, which largely cancelled itself out. Only panel surveys provide information as to what is really going on in the electorate.

The most instructive analyses should come from the two major panel studies which were conducted throughout the election, both by MORI, one for *The Sunday Times*, the other for BBC's *On the Record*. Both were recalled immediately after the election. Both post-election recalls were done by telephone on people interviewed throughout the campaign. In the recall interviews for *The Sunday Times*, the interviewing was done by FDS, an independent market research firm who were sub-contracted to undertake the recalls, the MORI telephone survey subsidiary, On-Line Telephone Surveys, being fully stretched with recalls on the panel for the BBC. FDS, on MORI's behalf, contacted 934 panellists on Friday, 10 April, between 10 am and 9 pm. This represented a 60 per cent recall of the original panel, not bad for a one-day recall, especially when it is borne in mind that some 10 per cent of the original 1,544 panel were unavailable because they were not on the telephone. The data were weighted to both the demographic and political profile of the original panel. Over one thousand (1,090) of the *On the Record* panellists were interviewed by On-Line, who had the advantage of being able to interview not only on Friday, but also on Saturday up until 3 pm, because of the later deadline of the BBC programme which was broadcast at 1 pm on Sunday.

MORI/*Sunday Times* panel

The MORI/*Sunday Times* panel base-line consisted of a nationally representative sample of 1,544 adults aged 18 + in 65 constituency sampling points throughout Great Britain, first interviewed face-to-face between 11–12 March 1992. Subsequently, 1,257 members (81 per cent) of the original panel were reinterviewed on 18–20 March, 1,292 (84 per cent) on March 25–27, and 1,265 (82 per cent) on 1–3 April, as noted in table 15.1. Re-interview responses were weighted by first-week voting intentions to ensure comparability. After the election, telephone recalls were made on the Friday and Saturday.

Each week, *Sunday Times* deputy editor Ivan Fallon met with the MORI team to go over the findings of each survey, and thoroughly and carefully absorbed the findings and our analysis of them. He then drafted his copy and it was checked by MORI executives as were the graphics, drafted by MORI and executed by the paper's Graphics Department.

The panel found, and reported each week, a higher level of 'don't knows' than had been found in 1979, 1983 or 1987. Each week the graphics and copy alike conveyed a greater degree of churning and switching than in any previous election. The vivid 'switching' graphic was originally developed for use in the 1987 election by *Sunday Times* graphic artist Geoff Sims and continued in the 1992 contest. It graphically represented the change matrix. A valuable addition introduced in 1992 at the suggestion of executive editor Tony Bambridge was the summary of net voter movement during the campaign, designed to underscore just how massive the changes were that were taking place, in the millions of electors switching and churning underneath the surface of the static

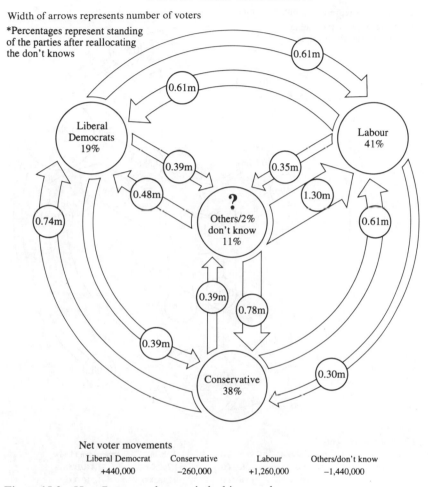

SUNDAY TIMES–22 MARCH 1992

Width of arrows represents number of voters

*Percentages represent standing
of the parties after reallocating
the don't knows

Net voter movements

Liberal Democrat	Conservative	Labour	Others/don't know
+440,000	−260,000	+1,260,000	−1,440,000

Figure 15.2   How 7m voters have switched in a week

election appearance being given by the media interpretation of the tracking polls.

One in eight Conservatives and nearly one in five Labour supporters at the outset of the campaign in fact defected to another party by polling day. Only three-fourths of Liberal Democrats remained faithful to their party. In the final week, 8 per cent of Conservatives defected, but 12 per cent of Labour and 18 per cent of Liberal Democrats went astray, the latter defecting to the Conservatives three votes for every one to Labour.

Just over three million electors switched in the final week of the campaign, according to the movements in the panel findings.

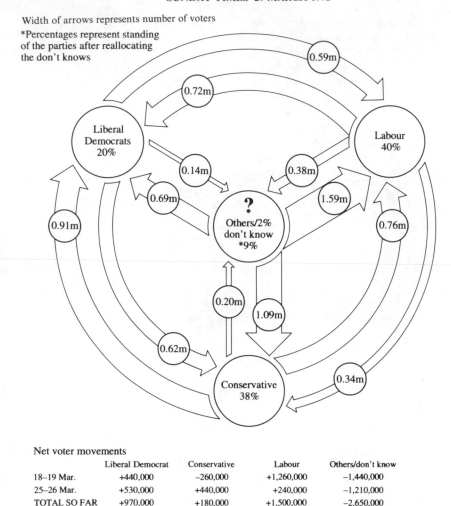

SUNDAY TIMES–29 MARCH 1992

Width of arrows represents number of voters

*Percentages represent standing
of the parties after reallocating
the don't knows

| Net voter movements | | | | |
	Liberal Democrat	Conservative	Labour	Others/don't know
18–19 Mar.	+440,000	−260,000	+1,260,000	−1,440,000
25–26 Mar.	+530,000	+440,000	+240,000	−1,210,000
TOTAL SO FAR	+970,000	+180,000	+1,500,000	−2,650,000

Figure 15.3   How 8m voters have switched so far

The MORI/*Sunday Times* panel recall found that only 63 per cent said they had made up their minds before the election had been called, down nearly 20 per cent from the more usual 80 per cent that we have measured in previous elections. And, as noted below, 8 per cent said they had only made their mind up in the last twenty-four hours, and 21 per cent during the last week of the campaign.

As deputy editor and panel report author Ivan Fallon reported week after week, the amount of movement in the electorate – people who switched from one party to another ('switchers') or in and out of 'don't know' ('churners') –

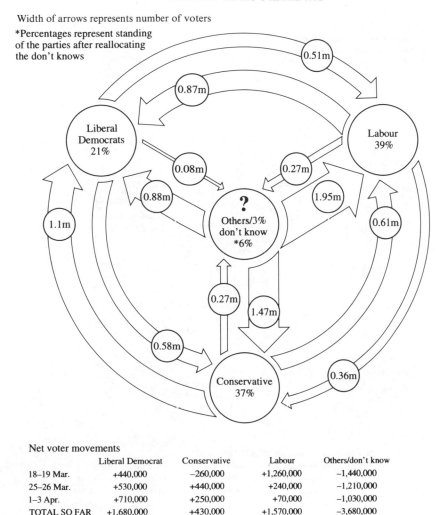

SUNDAY TIMES–5 APRIL 1992

Figure 15.4   How 9m voters have switched so far

was higher than ever before, and as reported in the final article, some 11.1 million electors changed their minds during the campaign out of the 42.58 million in the electorate. The week before polling day, the panellists indicated their voting intention at the time as a Labour lead of two; a week later the country voted in the Conservatives by a 7.6 per cent margin, a swing of between 4 per cent and 5 per cent.

The recall of the panellists showed a 2.5 per cent swing in their voting intentions between the week before and the day after the election. Before the

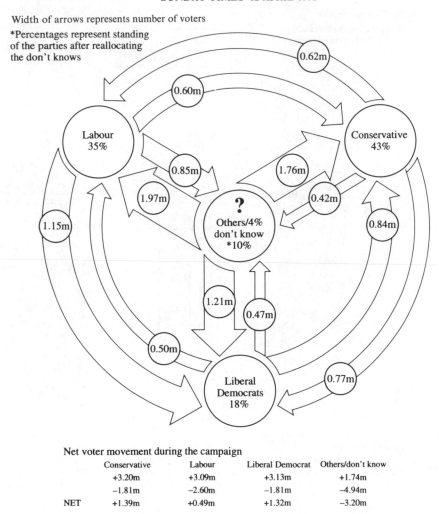

SUNDAY TIMES–12 APRIL 1992

Width of arrows represents number of voters

*Percentages represent standing
of the parties after reallocating
the don't knows

Net voter movement during the campaign

	Conservative	Labour	Liberal Democrat	Others/don't know
	+3.20m	+3.09m	+3.13m	+1.74m
	−1.81m	−2.60m	−1.81m	−4.94m
NET	+1.39m	+0.49m	+1.32m	−3.20m

Figure 15.5   How 11.1m voters changed their minds

election the panel registered a 37 per cent Conservative, 39 per cent Labour, 20 per cent Liberal Democratic voting intention, right in line with other polls – no 'panel bias' evident. Still, it was three points short of the Conservative final figure and two points up on Labour (and two points too high on the Liberal Democrats). Any argument that there was an in-built bias throughout the campaign is best fought on this evidence, yet the unweighted profile was close to what we would have expected, no skew by gender, but a younger, more middle class, more owner occupier (77 per cent owner occupier, 16 per cent

Table 15.7 *The switching of the electorate in the final week*

Wave V–post-election	Wave IV (millions)			
	Con.	Lab.	Lib. Dem.	Other/DK
Con.	14.24	0.39	0.77	0.67
Lab.	0.50	13.42	0.23	0.61
Lib. Dem.	0.35	0.78	7.08	0.20
Other/DK	0.32	0.69	0.60	1.70
Total	15.41	15.28	8.68	3.18

Source: MORI/*Sunday Times* panel studies.

Table 15.8 *The switching of the electorate in the 1992 campaign*

Wave V–post election	Wave I (millions)			
	Con.	Lab.	Lib. Dem.	Other/DK
Con.	12.63	0.60	0.84	1.76
Lab.	0.62	11.56	0.50	1.97
Lib. Dem.	0.77	1.15	4.84	1.21
Other/DK	0.42	0.85	0.47	2.38
Total	14.44	14.16	6.65	7.32

Source: MORI/*Sunday Times* panel studies.

council tenant) response. Of course it was weighted, by gender, age, class and housing tenure, by region, to the national profile; interestingly, this moved an 8-point Conservative lead into a 3-point Conservative lead. In other words, weighting destroyed a near perfect (if too high a Liberal Democrat share) recall, at least for the gap between Conservatives and Labour.

Only 10 per cent of the panellists, some of whom having been interviewed four times during the election, said they were still not certain they would vote for the party they said they supported on election day. Afterwards, of those who admit they switched, one each of the Conservative intenders went to Labour and to Lib. Dem., but three Labour switched to Conservative and six to the Lib. Dems. while seven of the Lib. Dem. intenders voted for the Conservatives and only one Labour. Within the net change of the undecideds, the Conservatives lost two and gained ten for a net + 8; Labour gained two but lost nine for a net − 7; the Liberal Democrats gained seven, lost eight for a net − 1.

Among those working in the private sector in the panel, 34 per cent of the

Table 15.9 *Floating voters*

	Campaign week			
	1	2	3	4
	%	%	%	%
May change				
1983	29	17	14	10
1987	25	18	12	7
1992	28	22	16	11
Undecided				
1983	10	10	8	6
1987	11	9	7	6
1992	14	9	9	6
'Floating voters'				
1983	39	27	22	16
1987	36	27	19	13
1992	42	31	25	17

Source: MORI/*Sunday Times* panel studies.

electorate, the Conservatives had a 9 per cent lead but among public sector workers, 17 per cent of the panellists, the two main parties were level pegging. Of the panel, 20 per cent were trade unionists; among these, Labour's share was 48 per cent to the non-trade unionists' 27 per cent, but among non-trade unionists, the Conservatives led Labour by 43 per cent to 34 per cent.

Week after week we reported that the undecideds ('won't vote', 'refused to say' and 'don't know') and the percentage who said they might change their mind were abnormally high, as table 15.9 illustrates.

Participation in the panel seemed to break down any reservation anyone had in revealing their voting behaviour after the vote; of the nearly 1,000 individuals we were able to contact the day after, only seven refused to say for whom they voted and, when pressed, three of these, two Labour and one Lib. Dem., admitted their inclination, leaving only four people from whom voting preference was not obtained.

Table 15.10 indicates the answers from the MORI/*Sunday Times* panel to the question 'Which two or three issues were most important to you in helping you decide which party to vote for at the general election?', indicating that one in four of those who eventually voted Conservative admitted that tax cuts was a deciding factor.

Other findings of particular note from the panel for *The Sunday Times* included the fact that four in ten said they voted after 5 pm, and that 8 per cent

Table 15.10 *Issues in 1992*

	All	Con.	Lab.	Lib. Dem.
	%	%	%	%
Health care	51	36	67	57
Education	41	26	48	58
Unemployment	25	13	37	25
Tax cuts	14	25	7	7
Economy	12	16	8	10

Source: MORI/*Sunday Times* panel studies.

said they had made their mind up on for whom to vote in the final twenty-four hours of the campaign, that one in five Labour voters (19 per cent) said that John Major would make the most capable Prime Minister and that a quarter (25 per cent) of those who voted Conservative said that tax cuts were one of the two or three most important issues determining their vote.

MORI/BBC On the Record panel

The MORI/BBC panel was of a different design, a compromise between the BBC client team, their advisor, John Curtice, and MORI. It consisted of 'floating voters', and comprised those who after expressing a voting intention said they might change their minds between the time interviewed and polling day, plus the full category usually described as the 'don't knows', which is the 10 per cent who said they would not vote, the 4 per cent who were 'undecided' and the fewer than 1 per cent who refused to say how they intended to vote.

In all, the 'floaters' represented some 38 per cent of the base-line survey from which the panellists were recruited, so some 62 per cent said they were sure of their party loyalty, within a point of the stated firmness of party commitment in the base-line panel survey for *The Sunday Times*.

The BBC invited MORI to set up this panel of 'floating voters' for its *On the Record* programme broadcast each Sunday during the election campaign. Initially, a representative quota sample of 6,843 adults 18 + was interviewed face-to-face throughout Great Britain between 5 and 7 March, in anticipation of the election call. Of these, 2,650 were classified as 'floating voters', defined as those who did not name a party at the voting intention question, or named a party but then said they might change their mind during the campaign; in addition, those who said they would not vote were also included. It may have been better to have excluded the 'would not votes' altogether, since they have a high propensity not to vote, and include many people who are generally indifferent to politics. Certainly, this would have alleviated some of the difficulties (and cost) that arose in setting up the panel because more people had to be screened to find sufficient floating voters who were willing to take part in subsequent waves than had originally been estimated from experience on other panel recruitment exercises.

For the purposes of the recall surveys, which were conducted by telephone by On-Line Telephone Surveys, the MORI telephone survey subsidiary, further 'floating voters' who had previously been interviewed in our omnibus surveys were recruited into the panel. In total, MORI recruited 1,721 floating voters who were available for recall after the initial base-line survey and booster, although after those without telephones had been excluded, this dropped down to 1,509 for the second recall. Thereafter, around 50 respondents dropped out at each recall and the response rate of those available at each stage remained a healthy 80 per cent up to recall five. The surveys were conducted 12–14 March, 19–20 March, 26–27 March, 2–3 April and 0–11 April. The same sizes for the telephone recalls were 1,072 (Survey 2), 1,219 (Survey 3), 1,173 (Survey 4), 1,146 (Survey 5) and 1,090 (Survey 6). Data were weighted by Survey 1 voting intention within social class. In all, 38 per cent of the electorate were defined for the purposes of this panel as 'floating voters'. In addition to their being broadcast by *On the Record*, BBC consultant John Curtice wrote up the results for, variously, *The Times*, *The Guardian* and *The Financial Times*, which are included in the MORI 'Green Book'.[7]

From the outset, the purpose of the panel was not to reflect national voting intention, but rather to provide a basis for interpreting what was going on in the minds of those responsible for the changes observed in regular ad hoc surveys. It did this by asking a series of questions which were identical week on week and varying some of the other questions as issues or personalities appeared to be playing a more prominent part in the campaign. One thing it did *not* do, except in the final wave (which might be a matter of some debate), is to ask those who changed their voting intention during the campaign *why* they had done so. Rather, reliance was placed on looking at the different types of switchers – Con./Lab., Lab./Con., Lab./undecided, etc and interpreting their views on key issues such as taxation or, indeed, how their views had changed on such issues, to suggest what was responsible for the shifts in voting intention. Significantly, this panel also showed evidence of the late swing shown by the more traditional *Sunday Times* panel findings. The Conservatives, it seemed, attracted their vote fairly early on with a base-line of 24 per cent rising to 32 per cent of the floating voters in the first recall and staying at around 31 per cent until the fourth recall before rising to 34 per cent in the post-election recall. Labour's vote started at 19 per cent in the base-line, rose to 25 per cent, then 27 per cent and 29 per cent by the fourth recall, then dropped to 26 per cent in the post-election survey. The Liberal Democrats started at 13 per cent, rose to 20 per cent, then 22 per cent, 26 per cent and 28 per cent before declining slightly to 27 per cent in the post-election survey.

In the final analysis it seems, while one might be tempted to conclude that the undecideds switched to the Conservatives, as did a few Labour voters, the final recall of the panel shows, not surprisingly, that the pattern was rather more complex. True, the Conservatives attracted more of the undecideds than the other two parties, but a large number of Liberal Democrats also switched to the Conservatives, twice as many as switched the other way. Labour seemed to lose out to both Liberal Democrats and Conservatives, in each case losing more votes than moved in the other direction.

The suggestion that the Kinnock factor may have been a major factor was reinforced by the reasons given by respondents for switching. Switchers disproportionately preferred Major to Kinnock. They also preferred Conservative policies generally, and/or to dislike Labour policies and to like the Conservative Party and/or to dislike the Labour Party. Although the base was small, some 12 per cent of those who switched to the Conservatives from anywhere mentioned tax as a reason. The health issue seemed to benefit Labour but no one else, and the Liberal Democrats probably gained a little on tactical voting.

The post-election recall also showed marked swings on the question of which party had the best policies in key areas; it is interesting to reflect on whether these really are post-election changes in attitude which resulted in the late change of mind in voting intention, or a *post hoc* rationalisation as a result of knowing that the Conservatives had won. Nevertheless, it was significant that the proportion who thought the Conservatives could best handle the economy changed little during the campaign, then shot up from 41 per cent in the survey before the election to 59 per cent immediately after the election, at the expense of both Labour and the Liberal Democrats. Support for the Conservatives on taxation also shot up, this time from 44 per cent to 59 per cent, with Labour declining from 25 per cent to 19 per cent, having shown steady gains throughout the campaign. While Labour gained slightly on the health issue from 49 per cent to 51 per cent, immediately pre and post the election, the Conservatives also gained a little ground here, going up from 26 to 29 per cent. The Conservatives also showed marked gains in terms of being best at controlling inflation, rising from 48 per cent to 60 per cent immediately pre and post election and on unemployment, rising from 18 per cent to 24 per cent.

As with the results of other surveys, John Major showed a relative strength compared with Neil Kinnock when voters were asked who would make the most capable Prime Minister. While Mr Kinnock remained at around the 15 per cent to 16 per cent mark throughout the campaign, John Major had recorded at least twice this level throughout, although had drifted down between Recall 3 and Recall 4, as Paddy Ashdown gained in popular support. However, the post election survey showed Major leaping ahead to 48 per cent, Kinnock and Ashdown declining to 12 per cent and 32 per cent respectively on this measure reflecting, one suspects, the respective euphoria and disappointments of the party leaders. Major also leapt forward on the measure on who had been the most impressive during the campaign from 14 per cent to 26 per cent, having actually trailed Neil Kinnock a week earlier at 21 per cent, though both were surpassed at each wave by Paddy Ashdown.

The evidence on tax as the cause of the last-minute swing is somewhat enigmatic. While it is true that those who switched to the Conservatives were more likely than those who switched to Labour or Liberal Democrats to believe the Conservatives would cut the overall level of taxation, the difference was relatively small and there is no indication in the research that taxation was necessarily the key issue to these switchers. Nonetheless, it is true that throughout the campaign, at least seven out of ten floating voters thought Labour would raise the basic rate of income tax if it was elected, although six out of ten also believed that the Conservatives would raise or extend VAT.

In the early part of the campaign, Labour did well to keep the health issue on the boil, and benefited by boosting its rating as the party with the best policies from 50 per cent in the first recall up to 54 per cent in the second recall, although in the third recall in the aftermath of the 'Jennifer's Ear' broadcast, its rating declined to 46 per cent only to recover a week later to 49 per cent at the expense of the Conservatives.

These figures suggest that 1992 saw an electorate who made up their minds later, and shifted their ground in greater numbers, than we have measured before. It is interesting to note just who the 'switchers' were. Upon examining the voting intentions of the *On The Record* panellists interviewed in week 4, the week before election day, and reinterviewing those same people the day following the election, several interesting patterns emerged:

Among trade union members, there was a 2.5 per cent swing to Labour, *against* the trend to the Conservatives, and possibly in reaction to the millions of pounds spent by the trade unions on advertising in the final few days of the campaign;

A bigger, 4 per cent, swing among the eight in ten of the electorate who are *not* trade union members, possibly in a backlash against the same advertising;

A small, 1 per cent, swing *against* the Conservatives among people employed in the private sector;

A 4 per cent swing from the Liberal Democrats to the Conservatives among people employed in the public sector – civil servants, health workers, teachers, policemen and the like. The week before, 24 per cent of public sector workers said they intended to vote Lib. Dem., 38 per cent for the Tories; the day after the election, 20 per cent said they had finally voted Lib. Dem. while 42 per cent said they voted Conservative;

A 4.5 per cent swing to the Conservatives among women, and among the over 55s and an 8.5 per cent swing among council tenants;

A 4 per cent swing favouring the Conservatives in the South of England;

Finally, among regular readers of *The Daily Express*, the swing from the week before to the day after the election was 9.5 per cent!

As late in the campaign as 2–3 April a third of the panellists of the BBC 'floaters' still said they might switch their vote, the Conservatives had a 41 per cent to 23 per cent lead over Labour on handling the economy then, a 48 per cent to 19 lead on dealing with inflation, and a 59 per cent to 19 lead on taxation. Three-quarters (76 per cent) of these 'floaters' said they expected Labour to raise the basic rate of tax, if elected, while 72 per cent of them said they thought Labour would increase government spending too much, and two-thirds (68 per cent) said they expected Labour's election would lead to a rise in mortgage interest rates.

One telling post-election finding was that when asked 'Thinking about the way you voted, which was stronger, your liking the party you voted for, or your dislike of the other parties?', by 55 per cent to 37 per cent, it was dislike rather than like that drove voters to vote the way they did in 1992.

Conclusion

Methodologically there is no substitute for longitudinal panel research. As the data in this chapter show, cross-sections are no substitute for the certain knowledge of individual shifts afforded by panel data. Interviewers report that when switchers and churners are asked why they have done so, a few respondents will have forgotten or even deny their own voting intention recorded the previous week.

Panel studies show that massive switching and churning goes on beneath the surface of 'snapshot' polls. It is clear that, at least in the case of short-term panels, that non-response in subsequent waves can be controlled effectively by weighting and that in any case an 80 per cent level of contact is the norm. It is clear that panels closely replicate voting intentions as measured by cross-sections and that neither attitude nor general behaviour is seriously affected by 'panel conditioning'.

What does happen is that turnout increases. People who take part in these panel studies do turn out to vote in general elections at a higher rate than they think they will when first recruited, at the beginning of the election, or than do people not part of the panel. Panel studies are a useful, indeed unique, contribution to a scientific understanding of electoral attitudes and behaviour.

Notes

1 J. Parfitt, 'Panel studies', in R. Worcester and J. Downham (eds.), *Consumer Market Research Handbook*, 3rd edn (Elsevier: North Holland, 1986).
2 D. Butler and A. King, *The British General Election of 1966* (London: Macmillan,

1966); see also D. Butler and A. King, *The British General Election of 1964* (London: Macmillan, 1965); D. Butler and M. Pinto-Duschinsky, *The British General Election of 1970* (London: Macmillan, 1971); D. Butler and D. Stokes, *Political Change in Britain* (London: Macmillan, 1969).

3 R. Worcester, *British Public Opinion: A Guide to the History and Methodology of Political Opinion Polling* (Oxford: Basil Blackwell, 1991).

4 R. Worcester, 'Campaign polling presentation', Confidential Research Studies conducted for the Labour Party, Market & Opinion Research International, 5 March 1974, *British Public Opinion*, February 1974 'Red Book', see also October 1974, 1979, 1983 and 1987 'Red Books'.

5 P. Kellner, 'The voters who switch sides', *New Statesman*, 27 April 1979.

6 MORI, *British Public Opinion: The British General Election of 1992, 'Green Book', Volume I of IV*, 15 June 1992, contains full code frames; data are lodged with ESRC Archives, University of Essex, England, and Roper Center, University of Connecticut, USA.

7 MORI, *British Public Opinion: The British General Election of 1992*, vol. 1, 1992.

16 Forecasting the 1992 election: the BBC experience

John Curtice and Clive Payne

Forecasting the number of seats each party will win in a British general election on the basis of an exit poll is one of the riskiest research exercises imaginable. It demands methodological innovation. One cannot simply lift off the shelf and adapt methods whose validity has been tried and tested elsewhere. On the other hand opportunities to develop and test one's methodology are rare.[1] Meanwhile, the task is inherently demanding. Because the objective is to forecast seats rather than votes, one not only has to estimate correctly each party's share of the vote, but also how that vote is distributed between constituencies. Yet the results of the enterprise are broadcast to a large and attentive public, to whom the accuracy or otherwise of the forecast is apparent in a matter of hours.

One consequence of all this is that it is difficult to make methodological progress. Getting the election night forecast right has become an invaluable weapon in the battle for credibility between the various broadcasting organisations and the different polling companies – and getting it wrong a potential source of endless political embarrassment. This battle means that published assessments of the forecasts tend to generate more heat than light. But given the rarity of the opportunities to learn from experience, it is essential that those opportunities which do occur, are grasped through dispassionate analysis of what happened. The aim of this chapter is to provide such an analysis.[2]

The chapter has three main tasks. It is evident from both public and professional commentaries after the event that there was widespread misunderstanding as to the sources of the information on which the forecast was based. So the chapter's first task is to describe the methodology used by the BBC to forecast, at the close of the polls, the number of seats that would be won by each party, and then to update that forecast as the first individual constituency results were received. The BBC made a number of changes to its methodology in 1992 following what was widely regarded as its disastrous performance in the 1987 election[3] and particular attention is paid to describing these.

The chapter's second objective is to evaluate the success or failure of the BBC's operation. In particular, it attempts to identify the reasons for the discrepancy between its initial forecast of a hung parliament in which the Conservatives would just be the largest party, and the actual outcome of a Conservative majority of twenty-one. In so doing we attempt to identify ways of improving such an operation in future.

Table 16.1 *The BBC central forecast*

	Seats		
	10 pm forecast	11 pm forecast	Actual result
Conservative	301	305	336
Labour	298	296	271
Liberal Democrat	24	22	22
SNP	7	7	3
Plaid Cymru	3	3	4
Others	18	18	17

Finally, in the light of our conclusions we consider the utility of exit poll based forecasting. What should be the objectives of exit polling? Can these be achieved given current methodological knowledge? And is such an enterprise a worthwhile feature of election journalism?

The forecast

The BBC's first forecast of the outcome was broadcast on the stroke of 10 pm when the polling stations closed. This forecast underestimated the number of seats the Conservatives would win by 35 seats (see table 16.1). This was only slightly less inaccurate than its 1987 forecast which underestimated the Conservative total by 38 seats. In placing the Conservatives (narrowly) ahead of Labour, the forecast did signal that the result would be more favourable for the Conservatives than the pre-polling day polls had indicated, but even so it suggested that it was highly unlikely that the Conservatives would be able to win any kind of overall majority. The central forecast was presented within a 'confidence band' whose upper boundary was that the Conservatives could win 316 seats, still 20 seats short of the eventual outcome.[4]

This 10 pm forecast was based on the data supplied by NOP, the polling organisation responsible for the exit poll, at 9.45 pm. Further updates of the exit poll's results were received thereafter. As a result of these updates the forecast was revised at around 11 pm; this forecast put the Conservatives 4 seats higher, leaving the upper boundary of the 'confidence band' still 6 seats short of an overall majority.

The 11 pm forecast was then subsequently updated on the basis of the results as they came in. But it was not until approximately 150 results had been received that the central forecast put the Conservatives at 326 seats or above. Indeed as table 16.2 illustrates, the forecast took longer to come into line with the actual result than on any previous occasion.

Table 16.2 *Updating the forecast*

Election	Error in lead of winning party over second party						Actual lead
	Results declared						
	0	5	10	50	100	300	
1974 (Feb.)	6	2	16	12	4	2	4
1974 (Oct.)	28	13	15	7	8	4	42
1979	4	13	2	0	9	3	70
1983	2	3	7	10	16	6	188
1987	70	39	46	20	20	5	147
1992	62	49	40	30	36	10	65

Sources of information

The widespread confusion which surrounded the exit poll based forecasts was aptly demonstrated in one of the contributions made by Bob Worcester, the head of the polling company MORI, to the post-election debate about the performance of the opinion polls at the general election. 'The exit poll results', wrote Worcester in a letter to the editor of *The Independent*,[5] 'would have forecast about a 16-seat majority for the Conservatives on a national swing if their 10 pm results had not been subject to such jiggery-pokery by the psephologists'. Worcester's comments were based on the results of two exit polls published by the BBC and ITN. ITN's poll gave the Conservatives a lead of five points over Labour while the BBC's gave a lead of four; in both cases the Liberal Democrats' support was put at 18 per cent. If we assume that the movement since 1987 represented by these results was replicated uniformly across the country then indeed both these polls point to a Conservative lead very close to the actual outcome of a Conservative majority of 21.

However, these polls were not the polls upon which either the BBC's or ITN's seats forecasts were based. Further, Worcester's comments assume that information published after the event was necessarily available at 10 pm, a crucially inaccurate assumption as we shall see. In any case the accuracy of such a hypothetical seats forecast rests entirely on the good fortune that two errors in its methodology happen to cancel each other out.

The major change in the BBC's methodology in 1992 compared with 1987 was that it relied upon an exit poll to provide an estimate of how the nation had voted rather than a large opinion poll obtained using normal quota sampling methods.[6] In so doing it decided to adopt the same strategy that ITN had used in elections since October 1974. But the BBC (like ITN) conducted not one but two exit polls. One was designed to produce a representative national sample of voters. Its aim (in contrast to the equivalent poll conducted by ITN) was not to produce any kind of forecast, be it of seats or votes. Rather, it was designed to produce material which would be able to help explain the reasons why the electorate voted as it did. Accordingly it was known as the 'analysis poll'.

Indeed, there were two key features of this poll which suggested it should not be relied upon to give a precise estimate of the parties' share of the overall national vote. Firstly, it had a fairly lengthy questionnaire which could easily take respondents ten minutes to complete. Previous experience in by-elections had indicated that such a lengthy questionnaire would engender a high refusal rate, thereby undermining the representativeness of the sample.[7] This is precisely what happened; one in three of those approached to participate in this exercise refused to do so. Secondly, the poll was highly geographically clustered. Polling took place in two polling locations within 75 constituencies across Great Britain with a sample size of 4,639.

Because of these considerations the editorial decision was taken well before polling day not to publish any estimate of the national share of the vote at 10 pm on the basis of this poll. Further, because the poll was not intended to be a 'forecast' poll it was given a low priority during the day in the queue for data processing and no attempt was made to have the most up-to-date results available by 10 pm. In the event when the data was finally available – by which time the real result was largely known – this poll gave an accurate estimate of Liberal Democrat support, but overestimated both the Labour and the Other vote by just over 1 percentage point and underestimated the Conservatives by nearly 3 points.

The exit poll which was designed to help produce a forecast of the distribution of seats in the House of Commons was an entirely separate exercise. Like the equivalent poll at ITN this poll was focused on marginal constituencies alone. It was therefore not capable of producing an estimate of the parties' share of the overall national vote. But, as was amply demonstrated in 1992, an accurate estimate of the overall national share of the vote can be a poor guide to the number of seats each party will win. If anyone had had available to them at 10 pm on election day, 9 April, a wholly accurate estimate of the main parties' share of the overall national vote, and assumed that the change this represented from 1987 was distributed uniformly across all constituencies, the resulting forecast would have overestimated the Conservative figure by as much as 25 seats – almost as large an error as in the forecast that the BBC did produce. This was because Labour did significantly better in marginal constituencies than in the country as a whole.[8] It was precisely in order to avoid such an error that the BBC opted to undertake its forecast on the basis of information of what was happening in those constituencies which were most likely to change hands. The ability of commentators such as Worcester to claim that an accurate forecast of the distribution of seats could have been derived from the BBC and ITN 'analysis' exit polls rests on the fact that both of these

Table 16.3 *The analysis poll*

	% vote (GB)	
	Poll	Actual result
Conservative	40.0	42.8
Labour	36.3	35.2
Liberal Democrat	18.3	18.3
Other	5.4	3.8
Swing from Con. to Lab.	4.1	2.1

polls underestimated the Conservatives' national lead in votes. This error compensated for the poorer Conservative performance in marginal seats.

Further, in contrast to the 'analysis poll', the methodology of the marginals poll was geared to producing as accurate an estimate of the parties' shares of the vote as possible. Thus, the questionnaire was limited to just two questions – how did you vote and how did you vote in 1987 (both administered on a mock ballot paper) – together with a record of sex and age group. The shortness of the questionnaire and the use of the mock ballot paper were both designed to reduce the refusal rate, which at 16 per cent was less than half that of the 'analysis' poll. In addition the sample was far larger and less clustered. Interviews took place in four polling locations in each of 100 constituencies in order and on the day 18,686 interviews were conducted.

However, the design of such a poll of marginal seats is not unproblematic. One cannot assume that there is a single universe of such seats. As already indicated, the rationale of any poll that concentrates on marginal seats is that these seats may behave differently from the country as a whole. This may be because of their distinctive social character or regional location, or perhaps because of tactical voting. But if this is the case, such factors could also result in differences in behaviour between different kinds of marginal seats. For example, if Conservative/Labour marginals behave distinctively because of tactical voting by Liberal Democrat voters, then they are also likely to behave differently from other kinds of marginal seats where the local tactical situation is different.

In theory, indeed, each combination of parties in first and second place produces a unique tactical situation for which separate estimates of party performance are required. But some such combinations may be so rare that it is uneconomical to produce such estimates by conducting an exit poll. For example, there were just six seats where the Conservatives and the SNP were in close contention with each other in 1992. Other kinds of marginal seat were known to contain a large proportion of seats where local factors, such as the popularity of the local MP, were particularly important. This was true, for example, of most of the seats defended by the Liberal Democrats. Meanwhile, those seats where the Conservatives were challenging Labour were of little interest because if the Conservatives were doing well enough to make significant gains amongst these it would be readily apparent that they had won the election.

So, in practice, the BBC's exit poll concentrated on two specific sets of marginal seats in which the outcome would be most crucial to answering the key question: could the Conservatives retain power, in the event of a swing away from the Conservatives since 1987? The larger set consisted of those seats which the Conservatives were defending against Labour. Labour would probably have to win all those seats where the Conservatives' lead in 1987 was less than 8 per cent to deny John Major his overall majority, while they would need all those seats where the lead was less than 16 per cent if Neil Kinnock was to secure the narrowest of overall majorities. In order to cover the possibility that Labour might secure a substantial majority, symmetry suggested that a Conservative/Labour marginal should be defined as a seat where the 1987 Conservative lead was less than 24 per cent. Of the 100 seats covered by the BBC's exit poll, 83 fell into this group.

The smaller set of seats covered the Conservatives' second flank against the Liberal Democrats. The poll covered 17 seats where the Conservatives' 1987 lead over the Alliance was less than 15 per cent. Given the Liberal Democrats' poor showing in the polls between 1987 and 1992, this seemed to be the outer limit of their realistic ambitions.[9] Given the rationale of the poll, in many respects the two sets of seats can be considered as two separate polls designed to give estimates of party performance in two independent universes.

How, then, did we cope with other kinds of marginal constituencies? And what about those constituencies where idiosyncratic local factors might well be more important than the national scene, such as seats where there had been a by-election or the sitting MP had been deselected and was standing as an Independent?

Such constituencies were defined as 'special seats'. No attempt was made to forecast the outcome in these seats on the basis of the marginal exit poll. Rather, the likely outcome was forecast on the basis of expert judgements. The views of a range of journalists and academics were canvassed as to the chances of each party in each seat. Those judgements were of course heavily influenced by the evidence of polls published prior to polling day, and especially by any polls that may have been conducted in the relevant constituency. In Great Britain, 45 seats were placed in that category in 1992, together with 17 in Northern Ireland.

Thus it is important to be aware that the BBC's forecast was not wholly based on the evidence of its marginals exit poll, but also upon expert judgements in the special seats. The use of such judgements was in no sense an innovation but rather has long been a standard feature of the BBC's forecasting procedures,[10] while a similar procedure is also adopted by ITN. In assessing

Table 16.4 *The accuracy of the marginals poll*

	Mean change in % vote since 1987	
	Poll estimate	Actual
Conservative/Labour marginals		
Conservative	− 3.1	− 0.9
Labour	+ 8.4	+ 6.9
Liberal Democrat	− 6.5	− 6.9
Swing from Con. to Lab.	− 5.8	− 3.9
Conservative/Lib. Dem. marginals		
Conservative	− 4.2	− 0.8
Labour	+ 4.9	+ 3.2
Liberal Democrat	− 1.5	− 3.2

Note: Seats in Scotland and Wales have been downweighted in calculating the poll estimate to compensate for their overrepresentation in the sample of Con./Lab. marginals. All seats regarded as special have been excluded from the calculation of the actual change.

the accuracy of the information upon which the forecast was based we have to look not only at the exit poll but also at the forecasts made for the special seats.

How accurate were these sources?

The exit poll

As the marginals exit poll was designed to estimate party performance in two different sets of seats – Conservatives/Labour marginals and Conservative/ Liberal Democrat ones – we should assess its accuracy by comparing its findings with what actually happened in the two universes the poll was attempting to estimate separately. Where one's objective is to forecast seats rather than just votes, the key figures supplied by any poll are not the level of support for any party, but the change these represent in each party's support since the previous election. Table 16.4 shows the poll's estimates of the mean change in party support since 1987 and the mean change in all marginal seats in the relevant universe.[11]

The poll underestimated Conservative performance and overestimated Labour's in both universes. Although the underestimate of the Conservatives' performance (just over 2 percentage points) in Conservative/Labour marginals was less than that of the analysis poll, the overestimate of Labour's vote (one

Table 16.5 *The special seats forecast*

	Seats	
	Forecast	Actual
Conservative	7.0	16
Labour	12.1	9
Liberal Democrat	18.4	16
Others	7.5	4

and a half points) was slightly greater, leaving the estimate of the crucial swing from Conservative to Labour equally astray (two points).

Given that this poll was invested with considerably more resources than the 'analysis' poll, it is clearly disappointing that it should have proved no more accurate in its estimate of party performance. But the poll did correctly identify two crucial parts of the election night story. One was that the swing to Labour was indeed higher in marginal constituencies than in the country as a whole. The other was that the Liberal Democrats would do better than average in a number of their target seats.

The special seats

The special seats were a significant source of error in the final prediction. The methodology used did not require that the winner in each seat be identified correctly. Rather, for each seat the prediction consisted of the estimated probability that each party would win (with the sum of the probabilities equalling one). The predicted total number of seats for each party was simply the sum of its probabilities in all these seats. Thus, for example, if in two seats it was predicted that the Conservatives had a 50 per cent chance of winning and Labour 50 per cent, the prediction was that in the aggregate the Conservatives would win one seat and Labour one seat. However, in the event, as table 16.5 shows, the sum of the probabilities in the special seats substantially under-estimated the Conservatives' performance.

Indeed, of the 31 seat underestimation of the number of Conservative seats in the 11 pm forecast, nearly one-third or nine seats can be accounted for by errors in the expert judgements.

Sources of error

The exit poll data

So both the exit poll and the judgements made about the special seats contributed to the inaccuracy of the forecast. How can we account for them? So far as the exit poll is concerned, can any methodological weaknesses in its conduct be identified that might help account for its underestimate of the Conservative performance? This is not an easy task, for the errors in the poll are not large. But there are some important clues.

One obvious possibility is that the selection of sampling points was biased. The selection was a three-stage process. In the first instance a two-in-three sample[12] of parliamentary constituencies was systematically selected from a list of Conservative/Labour marginals arranged in order of 1987 marginality and stratified by region. An analogous procedure was adopted in the case of Conservative/Liberal Democrat marginals. Then at the second stage, the component local government wards within each of these constituencies were rank ordered on the basis of the most recently available local election results and four wards were systematically selected in each constituency, so that in each case one ward was one of Labour's strongest (or in a Con./Lib. Dem. marginal one of the Liberal Democrats' strongest), another was one of the Conservatives' strongest, while two were more marginal.[13] Then at the final stage within each ward a polling district was selected as the one in which interviewing would be conducted with the probability of selection being proportional to electorate size. Some pragmatic adjustments to this final selection stage had, however, to be made to take account of the logistics of the polling stations concerned.[14]

Thus a key feature of the selection procedure was that considerable use was made of stratification variables so as to maximise the chances that the eventual selection of polling locations was representative of marginal seats. But did it succeed? Not surprisingly, given the high proportion of seats sampled, the selection of parliamentary constituencies amongst Con./Lab. marginals was not evidently biased. As table 16.6 shows, party performance in the selected constituencies was little different to that in all seats in the same universe.

The selection of Con./Lib. Dem. seats was, however, less successful. The Liberal Democrats did noticeably better in the selected seats – indeed sufficiently well to account for all of the error in the estimate of the Liberal Democrats' performance and a third of the error in the Conservative estimate. A smaller sampling fraction (one in two rather than two in three), together with the greater variation in party performance in these seats, clearly made the selection of a representative sample more difficult than amongst the Con./Lab. seats.

But the more difficult stages in the selection procedure were the second and third. In particular, given the lack of information in the United Kingdom on the distribution of party strength by polling district, no stratification could be imposed in the selection of individual polling districts. Although stratification by local government electoral strength was used in selecting the wards, because wards are frequently by no means politically homogeneous, it is still quite possible for the final selection of polling districts to have been biased.

There is, however, no clear benchmark against which the success of this

Table 16.6 *The selection of constituencies*

	Mean change in % vote since 1987 in	
	Sampled constituencies	All marginal constituencies
Con./Lab. marginals		
Conservative	− 1.2	− 0.9
Labour	+ 6.9	+ 6.9
Liberal Democrat	− 6.6	− 6.9
Swing from Con. to Lab.	4.1	3.9
Con./Lib. Dem. marginals		
Conservative	− 1.7	− 0.8
Labour	+ 2.3	+ 3.2
Liberal Democrat	− 1.4	− 3.2

Note: This table compares the mean change in party support since 1987 in those constituencies where polling was conducted (the sampled constituencies) and the change in all constituencies that lay within the definition of marginal seats used to select the sample (excluding special seats).

stage of the selection procedure can be judged. True, an inspection of the figures for individual polling stations within each constituency does reveal some individual cases where the selection appears to have gone astray. But some such cases are only to be expected, and are of no consequence so long as the 'errors' cancel out.

In table 16.7, however, we show separately for Con./Lab. and Con./Lib. Dem. marginals the percentage of respondents who reported voting for each of the three main parties broken down by the partisanship of the ward to which each selected polling location vote belonged. It will be seen that the stratification procedure certainly succeeded in identifying strong Conservative and strong Labour areas within Con./Lab. marginals, but was less successful amongst Con./Lib. Dem. marginals (a reflection no doubt of the much more even geographical spread of Liberal Democrat support and perhaps also a weaker correlation between the pattern of Liberal Democrat local election success and its general election support than for the other two parties).

But there is also one clue that something may have gone systematically slightly astray. Amongst Conservative/Labour marginals the average reported Labour lead over the Conservatives in polling locations from the strongest Labour wards was 20 per cent. This was counterbalanced by a virtually identical Conservative lead in the strongest Conservative wards. But whereas Labour had an average lead of 10 per cent in polling locations from less strong Labour wards, the Conservative lead in polling locations in less strong Con-

Table 16.7 *Estimated vote share by type of ward*

Type of ward	Mean % vote			Con. lead (%)
	Con.	Lab.	Lib. Dem.	
Con./Lab. marginals				
Strong Labour	34	54	10	− 20
Less strong Labour	38	48	12	− 10
Less strong Conservative	45	39	14	+ 6
Strong Conservative	53	32	13	+ 21
Con./Lib. Dem. marginals				
Strong Liberal Democrat	40	19	38	+ 2
Less strong Liberal Democrat	40	20	36	+ 4
Less strong Conservative	45	19	34	+ 11
Strong Conservative	46	13	39	+ 7

Note: Type of ward is defined by the results of local government elections held in each sampled constituency between 1987 and 1990. A strong Labour ward is one where the Labour lead over the Conservatives in those elections was amongst the highest 25 per cent of such leads in its parliamentary constituency. A less strong Labour ward is one where the Labour lead over the Conservatives was among the highest 25 per cent of such leads. *Et simile* for the remaining categories.

The figures quoted in the table are the mean percentage of the vote recorded in the polling stations belonging to that type of ward.

Source: Weighted data from NOP marginals exit poll.

servative wards was just 6 per cent. These figures by no means prove that the selection of polling districts had a small pro-Labour bias, but they are suggestive.

A second possible source of error is differential refusal. One of the most difficult tasks in conducting any form of exit poll is minimising the number of people who refuse to cooperate. The vote is, of course, a secret ballot; asking someone how they have voted immediately outside the polling station will obviously be seen by some people as a violation of that secrecy. Experience suggests that even if an exit poll is conducted in the most sensitive manner possible that at least one in seven of those leaving the polling booth will refuse to disclose their vote.

This refusal rate becomes a particular problem should those of one political persuasion be more reluctant to declare their position than others. In order to attempt to monitor possible political bias amongst refusers, NOP's interviewers kept a record of the gender and estimated age group of those who refused to cooperate. If we compare this with the age and sex profile of those who did cooperate we can see that, on these criteria, refusers were indeed different from those who cooperated. Refusers were more likely to be male and

Table 16.8 *Refusal and participation by age and gender*

	% of refusers	% of participants
Males		
18–29	13.8	12.3
30–49	12.8	16.1
50–64	13.2	10.4
65 +	14.2	8.5
Females		
18–29	6.8	13.7
30–49	13.0	17.5
50–64	10.1	10.6
65 +	16.0	10.6
	100	100

Source: Unweighted data from NOP marginals exit poll.

Table 16.9 *Reported vote by age and gender*

	Con.	Lab.	Lib. Dem.
	%	%	%
Males			
18–29	41	41	16
30–49	39	40	18
50–64	42	40	16
65 +	43	42	13
All	41	40	16
Females			
18–29	38	40	19
30–49	42	37	19
50–64	49	35	14
65 +	50	36	13
All	44	37	17

Source: Unweighted data from NOP marginals exit poll.

more likely to be elderly. Of refusers, 54 per cent were male compared with 47 per cent of those who cooperated. And 30 per cent of refusers were aged over 65 compared with just 19 per cent of those who participated.

These categories, however, correlate only weakly with vote – and not in the same direction. True to stereotype, elderly women were more likely to report voting Conservative. Fully 50 per cent did so compared with 43 per cent in the sample as a whole. But, as table 16.9 shows, elderly men were only just more likely to say that they had voted Conservative than younger men. Meanwhile, men in general were less likely to report voting Conservative than women.

Such weak and inconsistent correlations mean that knowledge of the age and sex of refusers is of little help in identifying whether they are politically atypical. True, it does mean that if age and gender were the only socially discriminating characteristics of refusers, it would be highly unlikely that refusers were politically atypical. But other evidence suggests that in small measure at least refusers were different. Aggregate data analysis is helpful here. We not only have information on the age and gender of refusers but also on their geographic location. If refusers are politically atypical then we might anticipate a correlation between the refusal rate and the political strength of a constituency. Although given the design of the poll the variance in Conservative support is not large, this is precisely what we find. There is a statistically significant positive correlation ($+ 0.34$) between the Conservative share of the vote on polling day and the refusal rate. Regression analysis indicates that for each one per cent increase in the Conservative vote the refusal rate increased by 0.38 per cent.[15] Analysis of the refusal rate by polling location tells a similar story. Here, of course, we have to use the poll's own (possibly biased) estimate of the strength of the parties at each location rather than the real outcome. But again we find a statistically significant correlation between the refusal rate and the reported Conservative vote at each location. At $+ 0.11$ the correlation is though rather weaker than at constituency level. The politics of local voters was at most one factor, albeit a peculiarly important one, in determining a location's refusal rate – doubtless differences in the effectiveness of interviewers, of whom there was never more than one pair at any single location, played a role as well.

Attempts were made by NOP to compensate for the possible impact of differential refusal. Weights were applied to the results at each polling station so that the weighted total of interviews at each polling location was equal to the number of interviews that should have been obtained in the absence of refusals.[16] This should have helped reduce the slight systematic under-representation of voters from more Conservative areas in the total sample, but does nothing to correct any error in the estimate of Conservative strength within those areas. In addition, the poll was weighted so that the age and sex profile of respondents matched that of respondents and refusers combined. But as we have seen this will have done little to correct for any under-representation of Conservative voters.

Indeed, both weights had relatively little impact. Weighting those who participated to the age and sex profile of all those who were approached simply increased the estimated mean Conservative performance by 0.1 per cent in both Con./Lab. and Con./Lib. Dem. marginals and reduced the Liberal Democrat estimate by 0.2 per cent in Con./Lib. Dem. marginals. Weighting for differences in the refusal rate between polling stations was only a little more useful. This increased the mean Conservative share in Con./Lab. marginals by 0.4 per cent and reduced Labour's vote by the same amount. But in Con./Lib. Dem. seats it shifted 0.2 per cent from the Conservatives to the Liberal Democrats.

Might an alternative weighting scheme have been more effective? As an exploratory attempt we applied Thomsen's method for ecological inference to the available data.[17] For each constituency, we have information on the percentage of people who voted Conservative, Labour, Liberal Democrat, etc., and the number of people whom were interviewed, who refused and who were not approached at all. What we do not know is the number of people who, for example, voted Conservative and refused to take part. Thomsen's method takes the constituency by constituency variation in vote share and participation and attempts from this to estimate this missing information.

The results are instructive. The method estimates that 47 per cent of refusers voted Conservative, 35 per cent Labour and 15 per cent Liberal Democrat.[18] If we take these figures and combine them with the figures for those respondents who did participate, the error in the estimate of the Conservative vote falls to 1.8 per cent in Con./Lab. marginals and in Labour's vote to 0.5 per cent, thereby nearly halving the error in the estimate of the swing. We should not wish to argue that this analysis is sufficient to demonstrate that Thomsen's technique should be adopted as a weighting strategy in future, but it does indicate that alternative methods of monitoring and allowing for differential refusal may be more successful than the procedure adopted by NOP in 1992 and should be investigated.

Translating the exit poll data into a seats forecast

Inaccurate estimates of party performance are only one possible source of error in producing an exit poll forecast. The other is that the estimates are mistakenly applied in forecasting how many seats each party would win. How successfully was this achieved?

We have already seen the potential pitfalls of assuming that change in party support is uniform. To guard against this possibility the BBC implemented a system which enabled it to analyse the estimates of change for each constituency interactively on the day. This made it possible to try and identify systematic differences between types of constituencies in the way that they were behaving. The system permitted analysis of the data not only according to the tactical situation and geographical location of a constituency, but also according to a wide range of social and economic features.

The BBC's 10 pm and 11 pm forecasts were based upon quite a detailed regional categorisation of marginal constituencies. Full details of these categories and the estimates of party performance that the exit poll gave for them at 10 pm, are given in table 16.10. It will be seen this categorisation identified

Table 16.10 *The basis of the 10 pm forecast*

	Estimated mean change in % vote since 1987			
	Con.	Lab.	Lib. Dem.	Swing to Lab.
Con./Lib. Dem. – South	−7.1 (−2.1)	+7.5 (+2.8)	−1.3 (−1.4)	7.3 (2.5)
Con./Lib. Dem. – North	−3.1 (+2.2)	+4.0 (+4.9)	−1.0 (−7.6)	3.5 (3.6)
Con./Lib. Dem. – Wales and Scotland	−7.5 (−2.6)	+3.2 (−0.4)	+2.5 (+0.3)	5.3 (1.1)
Con./Lab. & Con./Lib. Dem. – London	−5.0 (−1.0)	+9.3 (+6.4)	−5.0 (−5.9)	7.2 (3.7)
Con./Lab. – South	−4.6 (−1.4)	+7.7 (+7.3)	−4.4 (−7.0)	6.1 (4.4)
Con./Lab. & Con./Lib. Dem. – Midlands	−3.8 (−1.3)	+10.4 (+7.7)	−7.3 (−7.1)	7.1 (4.5)
Con./Lab. – North	+0.1 (−0.2)	+6.3 (+6.0)	−6.7 (−6.3)	3.1 (3.1)
Con./Lab. – Wales and Scotland	−3.4 (+1.0)	+10.4 (+5.9)	−11.0 (−9.4)	6.9 (3.5)

Note: The main cell entries are the poll estimate. Figures in brackets are the actual outcome in all seats in the relevant category.

(correctly[19]) a higher swing to Labour in London, the South and the Midlands than in the North of England. Given the relatively large number of marginal seats in those areas this was potentially an important finding. In contrast, the poll failed to identify the relatively strong Conservative performance in Scotland or the fact that the Liberal Democrats did better in their target seats in most of the South of England than in the North. In both these cases, however, the sample sizes were relatively small, itself a reflection of their relative unimportance in determining the outcome.

Thus the BBC's forecast of what would happen in each seat was based upon the exit poll's estimate of what would happen in the particular category of seats to which it belonged.[20] But how effective was this categorisation? At 10 pm it had a marginal but crucial impact. If the prediction had been undertaken by assuming that the only difference in behaviour was between Con./Lab. and Con./Lib. Dem. seats, the forecast would have been Conservative 299, Labour 300, Liberal Democrats 24. Thus although the effect of the categorisation was only to transfer two seats from Labour to Conservative, it made all the difference to which was favoured to be the largest party.

Further, if the exit poll had provided a completely accurate estimate of party performance in each of the categories, the forecast would have been very close to the final outcome, viz. Conservative 338, Labour 265, and Liberal Democrats 24. There would have been slight underestimation of the number of Labour gains but this would have been compensated for by the errors in the prediction for the special seats.

But it might be felt that the differences in estimated party performance between many of the categories are rather small, and indeed they are. Can the use of such a detailed categorisation possibly be defended given the sampling error attendant upon subsets of such a poll?

On the basis of the data presented so far, the answer to that question is undoubtedly no. The categories were however derived not upon the basis of the results received immediately before 10 pm but on the basis of data received earlier during the evening. For the data upon which the 10 pm forecast was based was in fact available just ten minutes before the programme went on air, leaving insufficient time to analyse that data to see if the categories should be changed. Indeed, the computing necessary to produce a forecast was only just completed before Big Ben struck 10 pm![21] But in fact the data made available just before 10 pm differed crucially from the data which had been analysed during the evening. And not least of the differences was that the 10 pm data told a rather different story about the extent to which different kinds of marginal seats were behaving differently.

This can be seen clearly in table 16.11 which analyses the exit poll data which had been received by 9 pm, just an hour before the first published prediction had to be made and the last data for which there was any opportunity for reanalysis. The figures look very different. In nearly all cases the estimated differences between the categories were greater than they were in the

Table 16.11 *The picture at 9 pm*

	Estimated mean change in % vote since 1987			
	Con.	Lab.	Lib. Dem.	Swing to Lab.
Con./Lib. Dem. – South	−6.7	+7.3	−1.6	7.0
Con./Lib. Dem. – North	−0.3	+2.6	−2.3	1.4
Con./Lib. Dem. – Wales and Scotland	−4.5	+0.9	+0.2	2.7
Con./Lab. & Con./Lib. Dem. – London	−8.0	+12.6	−5.1	10.3
Con./Lab. – South	−6.0	+9.3	−4.4	7.7
Con./Lab. & Con./Lib. Dem. – Midlands	−5.4	+11.8	−7.0	8.6
Con./Lab. – North	+0.2	+6.9	−7.4	3.3
Con./Lab. – Wales and Scotland	−4.5	+12.2	−11.4	8.4

data received an hour later. Thus, for example, the swing in Conservative/ Labour seats in London was estimated to be 2.5 percentage points higher than in the South of England and 1.5 points higher than in the Midlands. At 10 pm these figures fell to one point and 0.1 per cent respectively.

But the astute reader will also have noticed something else. Not only were the differences between the categories generally greater, but so also was the overall estimated swing from Conservative to Labour. Across all 100 constituencies the mean estimated swing at 9 pm was 7.1 per cent to Labour; at 10 pm this fell to 6.0 per cent! This change was produced by an increase in the (weighted) sample size of just 2,400 cases, that is from 13,318 to 15,748. As might be anticipated this change had a dramatic impact upon the forecast. Just after 9 pm a briefing was held of all the main presenters, editors and producers to advise them – in most cases for the first time – what the poll was saying. The prediction at that time, as it had throughout the day, pointed clearly to Labour being the largest party with 311 seats.

We shall return to this late swing in the exit poll later, for it also plays a crucial role in the way in which the flow of actual results affected subsequent updates of the forecast.[22] But for now it is important to appreciate that the expectations which had been built up during the day, expectations which were largely in line with the conclusions of the final opinion polls, were shattered just moments before the BBC went on air.

Special seats

Why did the judgements made of special seats go so far astray? In table 16.12 we divide the special seats into the various situations that gave rise to their being classified as a 'special' seat. It is immediately apparent that the error in estimating how well the Conservatives would do largely arose from three particular sets of seats.

The most important source of error was the estimate of what would happen in seven seats which had changed hands in a by-election on a large swing. Such by-elections commonly have a residual impact on the subsequent general election outcome, producing an above average performance (compared with the previous general election) by the winning party. Indeed, the two largest increases in Liberal Democrat support occurred in Ribble Valley and Eastbourne, two of the three seats they won in by-elections; Glasgow Govan produced by far the best SNP performance; while both Mid-Staffordshire and Monmouth appeared in Labour's top ten.

But in the event, none of these exceptional performances proved to be enough. For the first time ever all seats lost in the previous term's by-elections returned to their former loyalty at the general election.[23] This gave the Conservatives six seats in this group, in sharp contrast to the prediction that they would recapture only two.

The second important source of error was in the prediction of what would

Table 16.12 *The errors in the special seats*

	Seats				
	N	Con.	Lab.	Lib. Dem.	Others
Rebel MP standing	4	0.6 (1)	2.7 (3)	0.7 (0)	—
SDP seats/Plymouth	5	1.8 (2)	2.6 (3)	—	0.6 (0)
SNP target	5	1.0 (3)	1.2 (2)	—	2.8 (0)
Lib. Dem. defending	18	0.4 (1)	2.1 (0)	15.1 (16)	0.4 (0)
Plaid Cymru defending	3	—	—	—	3.0 (3)
By-election change 1987–1992	7	1.9 (6)	2.7 (1)	1.7 (0)	0.7 (0)
Alliance loss 1987	3	1.3 (3)	0.8 (0)	0.9 (0)	—
Total	45	7.0 (16)	12.1 (9)	18.4 (16)	7.5 (4)

Note: Main cell entries are the number of seats it was estimated each party would win. Figures in brackets represent the actual outcome.

happen in the three seats where the SNP were close challengers to the Conservatives. It was anticipated that the SNP would capture two of these. The Conservatives in fact held all three.

The final source of error was in the predictions made for three seats which the former Alliance had lost in 1987. The Conservatives were given just a 20 per cent chance of holding Portsmouth South (where the Liberal Democrats were fancied) and a similar chance of holding Stockton South (where Labour were fancied). Again the Conservatives proved to be the victors in both cases.

What were these faulty judgements based upon? In part they were guided by the evidence of local election results, the known popularity of particular candidates and what had happened in similar situations in the past and, where available, the results of polls in the individual constituencies. All of these were measures of relevant local factors. But in addition they were also guided by the message of the opinion polls as to the national popularity of the parties (and indeed, as the final judgements were only made on the afternoon of polling day, by the early results of the exit poll). For the ability of Labour to defend any particular by-election gain clearly depended not only on the size of any local 'by-election bonus' it may have retained, but also on the party's national popularity. In short, the forecast was unable to escape wholly from the expectations that had been generated by the opinion polls during the campaign.

Updating the forecast

Just after 11 pm the first actual result was declared – in Sunderland South. The swing to Labour in this safe Labour seat was just 2.5 per cent, less than half the exit poll's prediction for the marginals. More spectacularly, at 11.20, the first results came in from a marginal constituency – Basildon. The seat remained in the Conservatives' grasp; the swing to Labour was just 1.3 per cent. Yet it was not until after 1 o'clock in the morning, by which time 150 results had been received, that the BBC forecast a Conservative overall majority. Why, it has been asked, did it take the BBC so long to see what was obvious to its viewers with the declaration at Basildon?

There are two main answers. The outcome was not in fact so obvious from the early results as the Basildon result alone implies. But in addition, changes made to the BBC's methodology for updating the forecast in 1992 meant that it was slower than on previous occasions at bringing the forecast into line with the flow of results.

In updating a prior forecast on the basis of early constituency results, an important judgement has to be made. How much weight should be attached to the findings of the exit poll and how much to the early results? The early results have the merit of being real votes, but those constituencies which commonly declare early are by no means a representative sample of the country. They tend to be constituencies which are centred on provincial market towns or are part of a provincial city. Results from both London and rural constituencies are few and far between. With the increased variation in party performance at recent elections, it is rash to assume that the early results will be representative of the final outcome.

The evidence of the exit poll, by contrast, comes from a scientifically designed sample that is intended to be representative of the electorate in the crucial marginal seats. On the other hand, even a perfectly designed poll is subject to sampling error sufficient in a close contest to make the difference between predicting an overall majority or a hung parliament.

Thus, as the first results come in the forecaster may be faced with two pieces of information which contradict each other. But he cannot be sure which (if either) is giving him the information he wants. If, in updating the forecast, considerable weight continues to be placed on the evidence of the exit poll, and its results are wrong, then the forecast will be slow moving into line with the outcome. On the other hand, if the evidence of the exit poll is wholly or largely ignored and attention is focused on the evidence of the early results – and these prove to be atypical (and perhaps variable) – then a perfectly acceptable initial forecast may move around substantially and obscure the clear message initially broadcast.

The balancing act was weighted in 1992 heavily in favour of the exit poll. This emanated in part from the experience of rehearsals when in the absence of the measures which were adopted the forecast could, for example, increase Labour's estimated number of seats despite the fact that the early results were less good for Labour than the exit poll had been predicting. It was felt that editorial considerations demanded that the forecast should not move violently up and down; when this did happen in rehearsals it proved confusing for some of the presenters and thus (it was presumed) the audience. Further, it was felt that having committed substantial resources to the conduct of the exit poll the forecast should place a fair degree of confidence in its findings.

This reliance upon the exit poll was operationalised by two related decisions. The first was that the findings of the exit poll should be regarded as the equivalent of three constituency results. The second was that this weighting should be applied separately to each category of seats identified by the analysis of the exit poll and used in the production of the prior forecast. A crucial side effect of this latter decision was that the results of the exit poll continued to be the sole source of information upon which the forecast in a particular category was based until a result came in from that category. Thus the eggs were firmly placed in the exit poll basket.

The impact of these decisions is demonstrated in figure 16.1, which compares the forecast that was produced on the night with what would have happened if we had operationalised the use of the exit poll in two different ways. The actual forecast produced is the continuous line at the bottom of the graph; this corresponds to a weight of three results, applied separately to each category (e.g. actual results in Con./Lab. marginals in the South are only used to predict outcomes in undeclared Southern Con./Lab. marginals). The upper

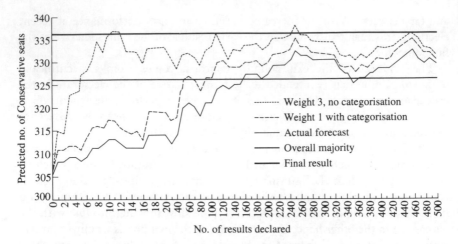

Figure 16.1   The impact of different updating procedures

dotted line traces what would have been the forecast if the exit poll had still been given a weight of three results, but across the country as a whole rather than separately within each forecast category. This allows an actual result in a particular category to be used to predict the outcome in undeclared constituencies in other categories (e.g. a result in a Con./Lab. marginal in the South would be used to predict outcomes in other marginals outside the South). This is essentially the procedure used by the BBC at all elections between 1974 and 1987. Finally, the middle line traces what would have happened if the exit poll had had a weight of one result, but with the categorisation retained.[24]

It can be seen that under both these alternative procedures the forecast would have moved more rapidly into line with the actual outcome than the procedure actually used. In particular, it can be seen that the most crucial decision made was the application of the exit poll weights separately within each category of seats. If this had not been done the forecast would have passed the 326 mark after just five results.

The reason for this finding lies in the regional variation in the time the first result was received. The first result from the Midlands was not declared until after seventeen other results had already been declared. The first result from London was the forty-second to be received. With the high incidence of marginals in both these regions the continued reliance upon the exit poll until these results were received had a particularly strong impact on the overall forecast.

We have already seen that the number of categories was inappropriately large given the exit poll data available at 10 pm rather than at 9 pm. Now it can be appreciated that this also had profound consequences for the process of updating the forecast. The fewer the number of categories employed, the more rapidly the forecast would have moved into line with the eventual outcome.

Mistakenly, the possibility of needing to change after 10 pm the number of categories on which the forecast was based, had not been considered in the planning for the programme. And the combination of the sudden late change in the forecast, the hectic scramble to get this forecast on air and the coincidence of the BBC's exit poll findings with ITN's, left little intellectual room and impetus for considering the need to do so at the time.

But even in the absence of action on the number of categories used the forecast procedure was still capable of being changed. The option was always available at any time to downweight or ditch the exit poll entirely, and indeed such action had been taken in rehearsals. So, given the manifest difference between the exit poll and the pattern of the results, why was this action not taken?

Despite Basildon, the general flow of the early results did not in fact provide sufficient evidence to suggest that the findings of the exit poll should be doubted and removed from the forecast. Firstly, the early results appeared to confirm the finding that the results in marginal seats were different from those in the rest of the country. So the more promising results for the Conservatives across the country as a whole did not give sufficient cause to reject the exit poll. Secondly, despite Basildon, on average the results in the early marginals proved to be more favourable to Labour than those that were declared later, such that the gap between the exit poll's estimate of what would happen and the pattern of the early results was too small to reject the poll. Thus by 12.30 am just thirty results had been declared, of which five were Conservative/Labour marginals. The average swing to Labour in these marginals was as high as 4.9 per cent, thanks to strong Labour performances in Exeter and Nuneaton. Even at 1.00 am when ninety-five results had been declared overall and the results were available for fourteen marginals, the median swing was still 4.7 per cent, with particularly disappointing Labour performances in Putney and Littleborough easily attributable to local factors. In any case, by this time the pace of the declarations had speeded up considerably so that simply keeping the forecast abreast of the results using the existing procedure left insufficient time actually to change the procedure.

There is one other small part to the story. The prediction for the special seats continued to be determined by the prior expert judgements rather than by any of the results. With few of them declaring early – just three[25] declared by 1 pm and none of these was a Con–SNP seat or a seat where by-election gains were being defended – there was little evidence to contradict the validity of the prior judgements. Thereafter, the fast flow of the results again gave insufficient time to make changes. Changes were however made well into the night, especially in the light of the SNP's failure to capture Galloway just after 3 am.

Lessons

Five important general lessons emerge from this chapter. Firstly, the 1992 election result thoroughly underlined the virtue of basing any exit poll based forecast on a poll of marginal constituencies rather than a nationwide poll. There was a significant difference between the behaviour of marginal constituencies and other seats in 1992; an accurate forecast of the national vote share would have led the forecaster badly astray. In contrast an accurate estimate of what was happening in marginal constituencies would have produced a forecast close to the actual outcome.[26] Of course, it does not follow that this difference in the behaviour of constituencies will repeat itself at future elections, but concentration on marginal seats does provide an essential insurance.

Secondly, however, in other respects there is still a need to develop the methodology of exit polls. Despite the methodological work undertaken by the BBC during by-elections to try to address the problem, it seems likely that its exit poll did not wholly avoid the problem of differential refusal. ITN's analysis exit poll, conducted by Harris, has also consistently underestimated the Conservatives' vote share at the last four general elections, suggesting that this is not a problem peculiar to NOP.[27] Further experimentation to try to reduce refusal rates would still seem potentially profitable. But in addition attempts need to be made to find improved methods to monitor and correct for its incidence. Monitoring age and sex alone appears to be insufficient.

Thirdly, exit poll based forecasts cannot, in the absence of inordinate resources, wholly avoid reliance upon the opinion polls. Certain types of marginal constituency are extremely rare, while in others local factors are likely to have a wholly disproportionate impact upon the outcome. Judgement of what is likely to happen in those seats is inevitably reliant to some extent on the evidence of the campaign polls – which in 1992 of course were badly astray.

Fourthly, the BBC's experience in 1992 underlined the need not to assume that what an exit poll says for most of the day will be the same as what it says at the end of the day. The requirement to produce a forecast at 10 pm places severe demands on the processing capacity of any organisation, but the need to maximise the amount of data available by that time is clear.[28] Equally, forecasters need to be prepared to adjust to the implications of a significant change in the results up to the last minute (and beyond!).

Finally, the 1992 experience made clear the dangers of continuing to place considerable weight on the exit poll in updating the seats forecast as the first results come in. Even when the exit poll is only moderately inaccurate, as on this occasion, a high weight can mean that it takes some considerable time before the forecast approaches the eventual outcome. Fears that the audience may be confused by rapid changes in the forecast need to be offset against the danger that the apparent implications of the early results are missed.

Should exit polls continue to be taken?

The 'scoop' is still many a journalist's dream, especially in today's competitive media environment. Conducting an exit poll offers the chance to be first with one of the biggest domestic news stories of all – even if the results are only available a matter of hours before the actual results start flooding in. Success – which means getting the headline right, if not the precise number of seats – can significantly enhance the credibility of a news organisation in the eyes of both fellow journalists and politicians. Failure can cast its shadow long after the event.

But can exit polls really be relied upon to get the headline right? Doing so means at least successfully identifying which is the largest party and whether or not that party has an overall majority. In 1992 both the BBC's and ITN's exit poll just succeeded on the first count, but clearly failed on the second. This was despite the fact that neither poll was wildly wrong. Look again at the figures in table 16.4. The BBC's poll was accurate to within a couple of percentage points and identified a narrow Conservative 'victory'. If this had been produced as a forecast of the outcome of a by-election in an individual constituency, the poll would have been deemed reasonably satisfactory. But in a national election, where each 1 per cent swing between Conservative and Labour makes a difference on average of around nine seats, and where the outcome is close to the boundary between an overall majority or not, the poll's performance was insufficient.

To get the headline right, national exit polls in Britain often have to be more accurate than by-election polls. Yet they are far more difficult to do. It is more difficult to choose a representative sample of polling locations. One has to translate votes into seats under an electoral system in which there is no guaranteed relationship between the two. Coupled with such problems as a high refusal rate which also trouble by-election polls, no organisation can conduct or commission an exit poll with a high assurance of even getting the headline right.

It thus makes little sense for any commissioning organisation to allow its professional reputation to rest upon the success of its election forecast. But because the competition between the various news media has encouraged a tendency to overclaim success when a forecast has proved right, it has left the door open for others to cast aspersions when things go wrong. An election forecaster's watchword should always be humility.

But if exit polls cannot be guaranteed to get the headline right, how else can they be justified? We would suggest two possibilities. Firstly, they can provide a valuable framework for understanding the implications of the early results. Formally, a British parliamentary election is simply 651 separate elections for the 651 members of the House of Commons. In practice we regard the election as a national election which determines who holds the reins of government. The challenge for the election broadcaster is to explain to the viewer the apparent implications of the early individual constituency results for the national competition for office.

An exit poll is a useful mechanism in meeting that challenge. It can provide a benchmark of expectations against which the early results can be interpreted. The viewer can be informed what the result in a particular constituency ought approximately to be if the exit poll is correct. If indeed the result is in line with the poll then the implication of the result is clear – the national outcome looks as though it will be similar to the seats forecast. But equally if it is not in line then the viewer will be aware that the national outcome looks as though it may be more or less favourable for a particular party.[29] Of course, an exit poll is not the only way of generating such a benchmark. One could simply rely for example upon the final opinion polls. An exit poll is however not only more up to date, but can also provide a depth of information on the likely geographical variation in party performance which few opinion polls can provide. Such information is crucial to generating an accurate seats forecast or making sensible inferences about the national outcome on the basis of individual early results.

The second justification we offer is that an exit poll can provide evidence for interpretation. No sooner are the results declared than politicians and commentators are rapidly claiming that the result has this or that implication or, perhaps most crucially, gives the newly elected government a mandate to do this or that. An exit poll can give the viewer evidence against which to test these propositions. In the early hours of the night, before results are in from all parts of the country, it may be a seats forecast poll's evidence on possible geographical variation in the results which may be useful. Later on it is the analysis exit poll, which may provide information on why people voted as they did, which can come into its own. Either way, this potential of an exit poll must be of interest to any broadcasting organisation which seeks to inform its audience.

So exit polls are still likely to be with us in future. But there is clearly a need for methodological development, combined with a wider understanding of how such polls are conducted and what they can, and cannot, achieve. Learning the lessons from the experience of the 1992 election is certainly crucial to the achievement of these ends.

Notes

We are grateful to Nick Moon of NOP for providing data and information and for commenting upon an earlier version of this chapter. Responsibility for the views expressed here, however, lies entirely with the authors, who do not necessarily represent the views of either NOP or the BBC. We are also indebted to Martin Range for his invaluable assistance in the computing undertaken for this chapter.

1 True, many aspects of exit poll questionnaire methodology can be tested in by-elections. But such important features as the choice of polling locations and assessing the relationship between seats and votes cannot.

2 As participants in both the design and the implementation of the BBC's methodology we cannot be considered independent assessors. For one such assessment see M. Collins, 'Pre-election and election polls in the 1992 campaign', BBC, 1992. Our involvement does however give us the advantage of acquaintance with many of the critical details of the exercise.

3 The BBC initially forecast a majority of 26 while the eventual outcome was a majority of 101.

4 Because the methodology adopted by the BBC in 1992 was similar to that used by ITN in recent elections, this confidence band was determined on the basis of ITN's forecasting record. It was clearly too narrow as it implicitly assumes that there is a 95 per cent chance that the poll will be within 1.5 percentage points of the correct Conservative and Labour figure (see also M. Collins, 'Pre-election and election polls in the 1992 campaign', BBC, 1992). Consideration of what a more accurate theoretically based set of confidence intervals for the complex survey design employed would be is, however, a major statistical exercise and beyond the scope of this chapter.

5 Letters to the Editor, *The Independent*, 5 May 1992.

6 Following the substantial underestimate of the Conservatives' performance in the 1987 poll, it was felt that the advantages of an exit poll were that it was immune to late swing and differential turnout. See N. Moon and R. McGregor, 'Exit polls: developing a technique', *Journal of the Market Research Society*, 34 (1992), 257–68. It should, however, be remembered that in 1983, when the BBC also used a quota sample poll, its forecast of the number of Conservative MPs was just one seat out. The BBC had previously utilised a (national) exit poll in February 1974.

7 Moon and McGregor, 'Exit polls'.

8 J. Curtice and M. Steed, 'Appendix 2: the results analysed', in D. Butler and D. Kavanagh (eds.), *The British General Election of 1992* (Basingstoke: Macmillan, 1992), pp. 332–4.

9 A few seats were three-way marginals in which Labour were less than 24 per cent behind the Conservatives and the Alliance, while the Alliance were also less than 15 per cent behind. These were assigned to the Conservative/Liberal Democrat category if the 1987 Alliance lead over Labour was greater than the Conservative lead over the Liberal Democrats. Otherwise it was considered a Conservative/Labour marginal.

10 For a description of earlier procedures see C. Payne and P. Brown, 'Forecasting the British election to the European Parliament', *British Journal of Political Science*, 4 (1981), 235–48; P. Brown and C. Payne, 'Forecasting the 1983 British general election', *The Statistician*, 32, 217–28; C. Payne, 'Statistical methods for election forecasting in the United Kingdom, 1970–90', in P. Norris, I. Crewe, D. Denver and D. Broughton (eds.), *British Elections and Parties Yearbooks 1992* (Hemel Hempstead: Harvester Wheatsheaf, 1992), pp. 138–58.

11 Throughout the analysis of the poll we used the mean of the estimated changes for each individual constituency rather than the overall change in the total votes cast in the constituencies. In forecasting the outcome in seats this mean is a more reliable guide than the overall change in votes cast in all constituencies because it is unaffected by differences in constituency size and turnout which can inflate or deflate a party's share of the overall vote without having any impact upon the number of seats won or lost. Indeed, the mean swing to Labour across the country as a whole since 1987 was 2.5 per cent compared with the overall swing of 2.1 per cent, and this difference is another reason why the Conservatives won fewer seats than uniform swing models suggested they should have. (See Curtice and Steed, 'The results analysed', pp. 324 and 350.).

12 Except that all Scottish and Welsh seats were included.

13 More specifically, wards were rank ordered according to the size of the Labour (Liberal Democrat) percentage lead over the Conservatives, and one ward was selected from each of the four quartiles produced by this rank order. In a few constituencies, however, a random selection had to be made because local elections were not widely fought on a partisan basis.

14 It should also be noted that, rather than interviewing at each polling station all day, each was covered for just three hours, the specific hours covered at each polling station being allocated at random. For further details of the strategy behind this 'time sampling' see Moon and McGregor, 'Exit polls'. It was impossible to have equal numbers of polling stations covered at each time point but the differences in the proportion covered were adjusted by weighting. This particular weighting had virtually no impact on the results in the Con./Lab. marginals, and slightly increased the estimate of the Conservative performance in Con./Lib. Dem. marginals. So this adjustment did not contribute to the error in the poll.

15 These figures are statistically significant at the 5 per cent level. One constituency (Ipswich) has been excluded from the analysis because its refusal rate of 40 per cent is clearly an outlier.

16 This particular weight also compensated for any failure by the interviewers to approach all whom they should have because the flow of voters was too fast for them to cope.

17 S. Thomsen, *Danish Elections 1920–79: A Logit Approach to Ecological Analysis and Inference* (Aarhu: Politica, 1987).

18 These are the combined figures for Great Britain from an analysis that was undertaken separately for England, Wales and Scotland.

19 See also Curtice and Steed, 'The results analysed', p. 324.

20 For further details of precisely how the estimated change in vote share figures are used to generate a seat prediction see Payne and Brown, 'Forecasting'; Payne and Brown, 'The 1983 British general election'; Payne, *British Elections*. In particular it should be noted that the technique does not depend upon simply applying the estimated change in party support uniformly within each group of seats and identifying who would win each constituency in that event. Rather, the probability that each party might win each seat is calculated, a probability which takes into account the closeness of the predicted outcome and the likely variance in party performance around the mean.

21 Indeed, but for the expertise and cool headedness under extreme pressure of Martin Range who was responsible for much of the necessary computing the 10 pm forecast would never have made it on air at all.

22 But we should note here that the forecast moved yet further in a Conservative direction after 10 pm. After 11 pm the estimated average swing had fallen to 5.8 per cent, which as we have already seen increased the estimate of the Conservative lead to 305. The final data were in fact not received until just after midnight after the first results were declared (and thus too late ever to be incorporated into the forecast) and showed yet a further movement in favour of the Conservatives, with the estimated swing falling to 5.5 per cent. On the basis of these figures the forecast number of Conservative seats would have been 306. Overall between 9 pm (by which time in fact only two-thirds of the data had been received) and the final data the estimated swing to Labour fell by 1.6 per cent!.

23 This includes the Conservative recapture of Langbaurgh which was not regarded as a special seat because the by-election swing to Labour had been small.

24 In addition a separate procedure, whereby the results of constituencies where the long-term political trend had been atypical were downweighted, has also been removed.

25 These were Yeovil, Montgomery and Portsmouth South. The Liberal Democrats safely defended the first two as anticipated and only narrowly failed to capture the third.

26 Thus the most crucial stage in producing an accurate 10 pm forecast is the production of an accurate exit poll in relevant categories of marginal seats. The translation of this information about votes into an estimate of the seats is not an important source of error.

27 Market Research Society, *Report of the MRS Inquiry into the 1992 General Election Opinion Polls* (London: MRS, 1992).

28 Particularly important is maximising the flow of data in the early evening. Not only is this a particularly popular time to go and vote but the sampling strategy adopted by NOP in 1992 meant that a disproportionate number of polling locations were covered between 6 and 8.30 pm. In total one-third of all the (unweighted) interviews were conducted during that period, and clearly the majority of them had not been processed by the time the 9 pm forecast was made; many were still missing at 10 pm.

29 The implication of this perspective is, however, that the way in which the seats forecast changes as a consequence of early results that differ from the exit poll, needs to be made reasonably transparent to the viewer.

17 The ITN exit poll

Glyn Matthias and David Cowling

ITN has commissioned two exit polls from Harris Research for each of the last four general elections. Each serves different purposes. The projection poll (comprising 16,500 voters in 1992), conducted among Conservative-held marginal seats (those which might change hands on election day), is used to project the composition of the new House of Commons. The analysis poll (comprising 4,700 voters in 1992) aims to give ITN the national share of the vote and to provide data on why people voted the way they did. In the past, the demarcation has been total. It has always been held that the share of the vote in the analysis poll could not give an adequate forecast of the House of Commons seats because that would presume a uniform swing in every seat in Britain, with no regard to regional variations or to different voting behaviour in various categories of seats (e.g. marginals).

To clarify the point beyond peradventure, the 1992 election analysis poll was at no stage programmed for predictive purposes. Even when it was clear there was a divergency between the findings of the two polls on the night, there was no way, practical or otherwise, that we could have switched the whole system to base the seat projection on a poll set up for a different purpose. After all, the logic has, in theory, to be that the marginal seats should be a more reliable basis on which to project the division of seats than a smaller national sample.

What was the divergence between the two polls? The national share of the vote from the analysis poll we broadcast at 10 pm on election night was Conservative 41 per cent, Labour 37 per cent, Liberal Democrats 18 per cent – a 4 per cent margin in favour of the Conservatives. These were based on results in by about 8 pm.

The final figures from the poll, in fact, showed a higher margin – 5.2 per cent – for the Conservatives, against an actual margin of victory of 7.6 per cent.

The share of the vote from the analysis poll also underestimated the Conservative margin of success; nevertheless, a seat projection based on it would have been considerably more accurate than the projection we did make.

Our projection put the Conservatives 41 seats short of an overall majority; a projection from the analysis poll, as at 10 pm, would have given us an overall Conservative majority of 7 – a creditable result you might think, but to some extent it was right because it was wrong. If you take the real share of the vote (the 7.6 per cent Conservative lead) and project seats from that, you get an overall Conservative majority of 43 – twice their actual majority.

Table 17.1 *Seat projection broadcast at 10 pm*

Con.	Lab.	Lib. Dem.	Other
305	294	25	27

Table 17.2 *Seats projections*

Actual result	ITN projection poll	Projection from analysis poll at 10 pm	Projection from real share of vote
Overall Con. majority +21	−41	+7	+43

These figures indicate that Labour did do better in their target marginals (i.e. the marginals were more pro-Labour than the national vote suggested). So the direction of the ITN projection poll prediction was correct – but flawed in the size of the swing it gave, predicting that Labour would win 23 more seats than they eventually did. How can we explain this margin of error?

The following are some of the main hypotheses:

1. The selection of polling stations may not have reflected accurately the demographic makeup of the population. The availability of the data from the 1991 census will help. There was some internal evidence from the returns that some of our sample polling stations require review.

2. We also reviewed the practice of what we call 'handsetting'. This is based on the belief, widely shared, that certain individual seats would perform differently from the national swing – that, in particular, the Liberal Democrats would do better in some of their target seats than their national share of the poll would indicate. A similar view was taken about certain SNP 'chances' and a number of other individual constituencies. In all, a decision was taken at ITN to 'handset' 41 seats, so that, whatever the national trend, those results were predetermined. With the benefit of hindsight, some of these were right, some were wrong. One result was to over-estimate the total of Liberal Democrat seats. It is also true, however, that without 'handsetting' the number of Liberal Democrat seats would have been seriously under-estimated.

    The elimination of 'handsetting' would have put the Conservatives closer to – but still short of – an overall majority, but at the undue expense of the Liberal Democrats.

Table 17.3 *ITN/Harris exit poll divergence from election result*

	Con.	Lab.
1979	− 0.5	− 0.2
1983	− 1.4	+ 0.6
1987	− 1.5	+ 0.5
1992	− 1.7	+ 1.1

3.   There may be a wider problem relevant to all polling in this election –
a problem identified by the Market Research Society Committee of
Inquiry in its report of June 1992. This identified a disproportionate
refusal to participate in polls by Conservative voters, which could have
reduced the Conservative lead over Labour by up to 2 per cent. The
report specifically points to the ITN/Harris exit polls over the last
four general elections as lending support to this thesis. Exit poll
interviewers try to interview every 'nth' voter as they leave the polling
stations. If that person refuses to take part, the interviewer has to find
the next person who most approximates to the 'refuser'. But, the
argument goes, if that substitute agrees to take part, they are more
likely to be non-Conservative.

The Market Research Society lists the differences between the share of the
vote in the ITN/Harris exit polls and the actual result over the last four
elections (see table 17.3).

There may be other reasons (e.g. an unrepresentative selection of polling
stations) than differential refusal, but it would appear that the discrepancies
against the Conservatives and in favour of Labour have increased over these
four elections. It is a question which must therefore be addressed. It does not,
however, explain the contradictory performance of the polling in the marginals
and the national polling in the analysis poll. The method of conducting the
polling is broadly the same in both cases, although, of course, the underestimation of the Conservative vote might be more critical in the marginals.

But the central issue remains: taking all the swings and roundabouts into
account, the purpose-built projection poll was less accurate than a projection
based on the share of vote in the analysis poll would have been. Is it still
sensible, therefore, to assume the House of Commons seats should not be
projected from the national share of the vote? Do the marginals still matter
enough? The fact is that if the polling in the marginals had been correct, in
other words if it had accurately reflected the real change in the vote in those
seats, the prediction would have been very close indeed.

The accuracy of the prediction method and calculations can be gauged if we
re-run the prediction with the real change in the share of the vote in the
selected marginal seats, instead of the estimations from the projection poll.

Table 17.4 *Marginal seats*

	Election result	Real change
Con.	336	329
Lab.	271	270
Lib. Dem.	20	25
Other	24	17

It can be seen that if the poll in the marginal seats had been correct, the prediction would have been within seven seats of the correct result for the Conservatives.

One important consequence of the inaccuracy in the seat prediction was that it delayed the moment when the election night programme could forecast a Conservative victory. It was a mystery to many viewers (including some of those watching in ITN) why it took so long. It was not until 01.21 that we forecast the Conservative overall majority, two hours after the Conservatives held Basildon, subsequently viewed as a key turning-point of the night.

The exit poll prediction is, of course, the starting point for our forecast; it is given greater weight at the outset to prevent a few early results having a disproportionate effect. It is then programmed to have less influence as more results come in. But it is a subjective judgement at what point the exit poll should be phased out of the forecast entirely. The exit poll is not programmed to drop out after a pre-determined number of seats – the decision to pull it out manually is a matter of timing on the night.

Basildon is the result which sticks in the memory, with only a 1.3 per cent swing to Labour. But a number of other key marginals declared in the following hour with much bigger swings to Labour – Pendle (a Labour gain with a 4.5 per cent swing), Hyndburn (a Labour gain with a 4.3 per cent swing) and Nuneaton (a Labour gain with a 6.5 per cent swing). These certainly confused the picture (the forecast is based on marginal seats and only changes when a marginal is declared). Chris Long, ITN's Head of Computer Development, carried out an instructive exercise which showed that if the exit poll had not been included in the computer prediction (instead, beginning with the result of the previous general election), the prediction would have moved to the final result very quickly.

Table 17.5 shows in greater detail how the forecast would have developed without the exit poll in the system. This method would have hit the eventual Conservative total with the declaration of the second marginal seat at 19 minutes past midnight. After 100 results it varies little from the correct result. This forecast, minus the exit poll, was run along the on-air forecast with the poll, and it was because of the disparity between the two that the decision was taken to pull the exit poll out of the on-air forecast soon after 1 am.

Table 17.5 *Election night*

Time	Seats declared* Initial prediction		Percentage swing to Lab.	Con. 366	Lab. 233
23.34	3	Basildon	1.3	352	247
00.19	16	Pendle	4.5	336	263
00.24	19	Hyndburn	4.3	331	268
00.28	25	Nuneaton	6.5	319	280
00.39	43	Putney	0.6	329	270
00.46	56	Lincoln	4.8	329	270
00.49	60	Delyn	3.0	333	266
00.59	84	Bristol East	6.8	328	272
01.00	88	Coventry SW	1.7	334	266
01.03	95	Wolverhampton NE	4.2	332	268

* Total number of seats already declared, i.e. Basildon was the fourth seat to declare.

We clearly have to reassess the weight given to the exit poll in the forecast. Of course, if the exit poll prediction were to revert to being more accurate, the problem would decrease proportionately.

So all in all, some radical reassessments are required before the next general election, in order to learn the lessons of 1992.

18 The impact of the 1992 general election on the image of public opinion surveys

Robert J. Wybrow

None of the final published polls in the 1992 general elections suggested anything other than a close-run result – a hung parliament – with Labour probably the largest party in terms of votes; the tally of seats was more problematical. Even Gallup's 0.5 per cent lead for the Conservatives (based on 2,478 respondents) and a wider, 2 per cent gap among the 'definite voters' were outside the normal accuracy achieved by the polling companies in national elections since 1970.

In view of this, it was decided immediately after the election to repeat a 1988 Gallup study to see what effect the polls' performance had had on the public. As Helene Riffault and the present author wrote in our paper on a 1988 joint Anglo–French study: 'such an image study is at the same time the source of our raw material and the consumer of our final product when survey results are published'.[1] Four months later, in August 1992, when it could be assumed that the public's memory of the election was diminishing, many of the questions were repeated to test their sensitivity to changing events.

The survey

Details of the three surveys are as follows:

  i)   30 June–5 July 1988, 956 adults.
 ii)   15–20 April 1992, 981 adults.
iii)   19–25 August 1992, 1,032 adults.

They were based upon questionnaires of about twenty-five questions conducted face-to-face. The main objectives were:

to collect factual information, such as the proportions of the public which had already been interviewed and the proportions which notice the publication of results of polls in the media;

to check on the level of awareness (or ignorance) of the characteristics of sample surveys;

and, above all, to measure basic attitudes towards the principle of opinion polling and the impact of the publication of results.

In addition, for the purposes of analysing the answers, the questionnaire included a number of questions about the various fields of interest of the

Table 18.1 *Awareness of poll results (%)*

Q. Over the past 2 or 3 months, have you noticed the results of a political opinion poll in a newspaper, magazine, on the radio or television?

		All aware	
	July 1988	April 1992	August 1992
General public	44	83	35
Information intake*			
Low	26	73	23
Medium	41	88	40
High	65	93	47
Social class			
AB	59	95	40
C1	46	90	38
C2	41	80	34
DE	36	74	32

* The notional range is from 0 to a maximum of 21 'days' (listening to news on the radio and watching news programmes on TV and reading about politics in a newspaper or magazine every day of the week).

Low has been defined on this scale as 13 or less, medium as 14 or 15, and high as 16 or more. They represent the following average proportion of the public over the three studies: low 39%, medium 31%, and high 31%.

Source: Gallup.

respondents (omitted in the third study), the level of their information intake and their political inclination.

A little under one in two in each of the studies – 47 per cent in 1988, 46 per cent in April 1992 and 43 per cent in August 1992 – said they had been interviewed at some time before the current study. As well as being asked if they personally had ever been interviewed, people were asked if any of their family or friends had. A little over one in four said that they knew a close acquaintance who had been interviewed – 27 per cent, 26 per cent and 29 per cent respectively. Among these people who had been interviewed in the past, the proportion knowing someone else who had been, rose to around two in five. We should not, however, be surprised by the sceptic who expresses disbelief of opinion polls in the form, 'I have never been interviewed and none of my friends have'. This person represented 50 per cent of the British public in the most recent of the three studies.

Awareness of and level of interest in poll results

During the election campaign the public was inundated, virtually on a daily basis, with individual polls and amalgamated polls-of-polls. In a separate

Table 18.2 *Interest in poll results (%)*

	July 1988	April 1992	August 1992
Q. How interested are you in the changing popularity of the political parties?			
Very interested	20	25	17
Fairly interested	39	36	36
Not very interested	26	23	30
Not at all interested	14	15	16
No answer	1	1	1
Q. When you come across the results of a poll in a newspaper or magazine, do you . . .?			
Read it with interest	31	28	27
Cast an eye over it	49	52	53
Turn to something else	19	18	19
No answer	1	2	1

Source: Gallup.

exercise in late March 1992, 73 per cent said that they had seen or heard the results of a nationwide opinion poll; two thirds (correctly) said that Labour was in the lead with nine in ten (correctly) saying that it was a small lead. Following the election the figure rose to 83 per cent. This compares with 44 per cent in the 1988 study and 35 per cent in August 1992. More than one in two (59 per cent) said they had seen 'many' such poll results (compared with only 6 per cent in 1988 and 7 per cent in August 1992).

As might be expected, the level of awareness of poll result was related to the amount of news information intake (newspapers, radio and television) and to the social class of the respondent.

Despite the near saturation of the British public with how the campaign was progressing, they remained interested in the poll results and only one in five were 'turned off'.

Thus, an election campaign does not appear to diminish the public's interest in the changing popularity of the political parties: around 30 per cent say they read poll results 'with interest'.

Level of information about survey techniques

If they read about the surveys, what do respondents remember about the polling information? According to the polling organisations' code of practice, any primary publication of poll results should be accompanied by information about how, by whom, and when the survey was conducted, and also indicate the number of people interviewed.

Table 18.3 *Awareness of technical details (%)*

Q. Have you noticed if, in general, as well as the results, they give any of the following information or not?

	July 1988	April 1992	August 1992
The company which did the survey	38	49	43
The number of people interviewed	35	45	44
The date of the survey	23	32	27
The wording of the questions asked	23	28	25
None of these	44	31	38

Source: Gallup.

Table 18.4 *Belief in sampling techniques (%)*

Q. From a survey of 1,000 or 2,000 people, do you think it is possible to give a reliable picture of British public opinion?

	July 1988	April 1992	August 1992
Is possible	41	27	32
Is not possible	51	63	60
Don't know	8	10	8
Net	− 10	− 36	− 28

Source: Gallup.

As might be expected, awareness of any of these details (according to the post-election study) was highest among ABs, among those who know somebody who has been interviewed and among people defined as being in the 'high' information intake – 81 per cent in each case.

On the specific question of how many people were interviewed in a survey, over half could not give an answer. The sample size mentioned by the highest proportion of people was 1,000 (cited by 18 per cent on average), with an average of 11 per cent saying 500 or less. At the other end of the scale, 6 per cent said that 2,500 or more people were interviewed.

Belief in surveys/sampling techniques

Thus far the results from the three studies had shown great consistency, with the notable exception of exposure to opinion poll findings. However, this similarity disappeared when the public's belief in surveys and sampling

Table 18.5 *The accuracy of opinion polls (%)*

Q. Do you think that the results of opinion polls published do or do not reflect British public opinion at present?

	July 1988	April 1992	August 1992
Do	46	26	34
Do not	36	60	47
Don't know	18	14	19
Net	+ 10	− 34	− 13

Source: Gallup.

techniques was measured. The proportion, for example, who accept the concept of using a sample of 1,000 or 2,000 people fell from 41 per cent in 1988 to 27 per cent (April) and 32 per cent (August) in the 1992 studies.

Even among those who claimed to read the results of opinion surveys 'with interest', 61 per cent were sceptics post-election (compared with 49 per cent in 1988 and 57 per cent in August 1992).

In 1988, among all the groups analysed, only two showed more people accepting than rejecting the concept of sample surveys: senior citizens and those people who had not been interviewed themselves nor knew anybody who had been. Now both these groups are very close to the national average.

Not unnaturally, there was an even bigger shift of opinion on the question as to whether or not opinion polls truly reflect current public opinion: from almost one in two (46 per cent) taking a positive view in 1988, down to as low as 26 per cent post-election.

Immediately after the election, one in two of those who said they read poll findings 'with interest' believed opinion polls did not reflect public opinion. In 1988 this proportion was 36 per cent, and by August 1992 the comparable figure had fallen back to 41 per cent.

Why did those who say the results did not reflect contemporary public opinion hold this view? Offered four possible reasons their replies are shown in table 18.6.

This scepticism, however, did not affect the public's attitude towards the anonymity of the responses or their awareness of who is actually interviewed. Only 15 per cent (14 per cent in 1988) thought the surveys always consisted of the same people, while 71 per cent (75 per cent in 1988) said they were not always the same. Similarly 65 per cent believed 'that the answers given by the people interviewed stayed confidential and anonymous', compared with 18 per cent who expressed concerns about the anonymity of the answers.

Table 18.6 *Why polls are not thought of as reflecting public opinion (%)*

	July 1988	April 1992	August 1992
It is impossible to measure the views of the British	44	35	36
Public opinion techniques are not good enough	20	19	22
The people interviewed do not tell the truth	12	31	25
The published results have been 'manipulated'	12	9	11
None of these	13	7	6

Base: All saying polls do not reflect public opinion.
Source: Gallup.

Suppressing poll findings?

Despite the public's obvious unease about the accuracy of opinion surveys in April 1992, a majority continued to believe that the results of such surveys should be published: 70 per cent, 59 per cent and 65 per cent respectively in the three surveys. On the other hand, those thinking the results should be kept solely for politicians was consistently less than one in three of the public: 21 per cent, 30 per cent and 26 per cent respectively.

In contrast to 1988, when politicians, on balance, were thought to pay too little notice to opinion polls, following the 1992 election the public thought that, if anything, too much notice was taken of them by politicians (the percentage saying 'too much' nearly doubled, from 22 to 42 between 1988 and April 1992, before declining to 30 per cent over the next four months).

In April 1992, all groups, with one exception, took the view that too much notice was taken of the opinion polls by politicians, peaking at 57 per cent among ABs.

The main role of pre-election public opinion surveys

Opinion polls are now a fact of life in pre-election periods in all democratic countries (and in many not so democratic countries). Some have expressed doubts about the possible negative influence of polling information on the electorate, and hence on the result of the election. Following the 1992 experience in Britain one in four held this negative attitude (27 per cent), though the most widely given answer was still 'it's one piece of information among lots of others' (36 per cent), while one in six said that polls can help electors to get a clear picture (17 per cent) or that they are of no importance (16 per cent).

Table 18.7 *Usefulness of surveys (% saying 'useful')*

Q. Here is a list of different types of surveys made among the general public. For each of them please tell me if you think it is useful, not particularly interesting or a bad thing to interview people in Britain about?

	July 1988	April 1992	August 1992
What people think of problems of society, such as unemployment, drugs, health, family life etc.	89	86	86
What people think of products	83	80	82
What they think of the actions and policies of the government	74	71	71
What they think of the services of supermarkets	71	68	71
The television programmes people like	71	59	60
How people intend to vote in coming elections	56	44	49
What they think of political personalities	48	42	42

Source: Gallup.

Basic attitudes toward surveys

Political surveys comprise a small proportion of the questioning conducted each year in Britain. There does appear, however, to have been a small knock-on effect on purely commercial topics, people being slightly less likely to see such surveys as useful.

There were still substantial majorities, despite the decline, who saw a use for market research surveys. As might be expected, the biggest drops had been for two of the three political items – particularly voting studies – and the popularity of television programmes. One in five (19 per cent) of the general public thought it a 'bad thing' to conduct surveys on 'how people intend to vote in coming elections', rising to around one in four of the ABs.

Finally, respondents were invited to react to a number of stereotypes about the surveys: three of them were positively and three of them negatively oriented.

Majorities agreed with all three positive statements and disagreed with two of the negatives, while a plurality disagreed with the third negative statement.

Again there was a worrying increase in the proportion of people agreeing with the statement 'I don't believe that people who are interviewed say what they think': up from 30 per cent to 40 per cent, then dropping slightly to 37 per cent – the biggest shift of opinion. This attitude was highest among the elderly, the DEs and those people who were either unaware of survey results or not interested in them even when they did see them.

Table 18.8 *Attitudes towards opinion surveys (% agreeing)*

Q. On the subject of public opinion in general, here are a number of things people have said about surveys. Can you tell me, for each one, whether you agree or disagree with the statement?

	July 1988	April 1992	August 1992
It is pleasant to be asked my opinion	87	86	87
It's good to be able to show what we think of people who govern us	86	80	84
It is useful and interesting for me to know of the opinion of the people of Britain in order to compare what I think with what others think	68	62	64
Those who publish the results are trying to influence me	31	33	34
I don't believe that people who are interviewed say what they think	30	40	37
It is wrong to try and interview just anybody, you should only question people who are well-informed and competent	17	13	12

Source: Gallup.

Other issues

Mention has already been made of other questions asked about opinions polls and a few more are worth mentioning. The first of these relates to the question in a 1992 post-campaign survey: 'When you finally decided which way to vote, did you take notice of what the opinion polls were saying?' The 13 per cent who said they had, included 14 per cent of Conservatives, 18 per cent of Labour voters and 9 per cent of Liberal Democrats. This compares nationally with 9 per cent in 1987, 5 per cent in 1983 and 3 per cent in 1979.

Similarly, Gallup has been asking the general public whether or not opinion polls should be banned during election campaigns. Majorities have always opposed such a ban, though a substantial minority (38 per cent) in June 1987 thought there should be a ban. A more recent survey (August 1992) still showed almost one in two (45 per cent) opposed to a ban, but the supporters had risen to a new high of 42 per cent.

Who wants to ban opinion polls? Whereas almost one in two Conservatives (46 per cent) were against a ban, with 42 per cent for it, Labour supporters were reversed, with 47 per cent wanting a ban and 41 per cent opposed. Support for a ban also tended to be greater among people aged 45 or over.

Results from two other questions asked at the same time show a somewhat

Table 18.9 *Banning opinion polls (%)*

Q. It has been suggested that opinion polls should be banned during an election campaign. Do you think the publication of opinion polls should or should not be banned during an election?

	May 1983	April 1987	June 1987	April 1991	March 1992	May 1992
Should	30	29	38	28	31	41
Should not	53	59	51	58	58	48
Don't know	17	12	11	14	11	11

Source: Gallup.

puzzling picture: the level of influence attributed to opinion polls in general elections has remained fairly static but their perceived influence in by-elections has fallen. In 1983 42 per cent thought that opinion polls had 'a lot' or 'a fair amount' of influence on people in general elections, while 31 per cent said it was 'little' or 'none at all'. By August 1992 the figures were 45 per cent and 50 per cent respectively. When it came to by-elections, 37 per cent in 1983 said 'a lot' or 'a fair amount', with 55 per cent saying 'little' or 'none at all'. The August 1992 position was 27 per cent and 65 per cent respectively.

Again there are significant differences between the party supporters on the question of the influence of polls in general elections: whereas 55 per cent of Labour supporters thought it was at least 'a fair amount' of influence, the figure was 42 per cent among Liberal Democrats and 37 per cent among Conservatives. The differences were less marked on the by-election question.

In early June 1992 opinion polls were compared with short and long-range weather forecasts, horoscopes and race tipsters, coming third compared with second six years ago and losing credibility at the same time.

Thus, from a position six years ago when 54 per cent thought that public opinion polls were at least 'fairly good' in saying what was happening, 56 per cent said they were either 'not very good' or 'no good at all'.

Finally, in June 1992, people were asked, 'You often read the results of opinion polls in the newspapers or hear them on television or radio. Do you think the opinion polls are normally right or wrong?' By a margin of two to one, 54 per cent against 25 per cent, the public's verdict was that the opinion polls were normally wrong. Four years previously the position was almost the reverse, 26 per cent and 43 per cent respectively. But when the question was repeated in mid-August 1992, the position for opinion polls had improved slightly, to 46 per cent and 31 per cent respectively.

Table 18.10 *Credibility of different 'guides' (%)*

Q. How good do you think the following are in saying what is happening: very good, fairly good, not very good or not good at all?

	Weather forecasts for the next day or so	Weather forecasts for the next month or so	Public opinion polls	Race tipsters in newspapers	Horoscopes in newspapers or magazines
June 1986					
Very good	15	2	6	2	3
Fairly good	55	31	48	19	13
Not very good	20	36	24	16	19
No good at all	7	21	10	23	53
Don't know	3	10	12	40	11
June 1992					
Very good	20	4	2	1	2
Fairly good	62	36	33	16	10
Not very good	12	37	31	13	16
No good at all	5	14	25	29	58
Don't know	1	10	8	41	15

Source: Gallup.

Conclusions

It is clear that the polls' poor performance in the 1992 election increased the credibility problem which lay just below the surface among a significant and vocal minority of the general public; and a growing number want to ban such surveys. Opinion polls are likely to suffer as a result for some time, creating a potential reluctance to be interviewed not only on a purely political study but potentially feeding into commercial studies as well.

The findings, however, from the more recent surveys show slight improvements in the public's image of public opinion surveys, not yet back to the levels of 1988, but the shift is noticeable. The possible single exception is the proportion who want to ban polls during election campaigns. The perceived success of the polls in the two referendum exercises in Denmark and France and in the US presidential election could help their British compatriots.

Note

1 Hélène Riffault and Robert J. Wybrow, 'The image of public opinion surveys in Britain and France', *International Journal of Public Opinion Research*, 1, 4 (Winter 1989).

Part VI
Reflections

19 Majorspeak: observations on the Prime Minister's style of speaking

Max Atkinson

A gap between sound and sight?[1]

A catalogue of John Major's talents would be unlikely to feature his effectiveness as a public speaker very near the top of the list. Even some of his own colleagues and supporters sometimes seem to have trouble remaining attentive during speeches by their leader. For example, in one section Mr Major's statement to the House of Commons on his return from the Maastricht Summit conference, Foreign Secretary Douglas Hurd was to be seen sitting by his side, apparently much more interested in the workings of his watch than in paying attention to a key speech on his own area of responsibility. At about the same time in the same speech, another cabinet minister could be seen rubbing his eyes and trying unsuccessfully to conceal a yawn. During the general election, the specially created set for the Prime Minister's rallies placed him in the centre of a circular auditorium. This meant that some members of the audience were not only visible behind him while he was speaking, but could also on occasions be seen to be yawning or looking drowsy, even during sound bites selected for prime-time news coverage.

If verbal effectiveness is not widely regarded as one of Mr Major's main strengths, the opposite may be true of his visual image. Some time before the general election, an opposition politician told me, off the record, of his fear that the Prime Minister's engaging smile might win him as many as a million extra votes. His appearance in shirt sleeves, chatting to British troops during the Gulf War, had been seen by Conservative campaign managers as a public relations triumph, and was used as a model for the informal 'meet the people' style rallies during the early part of the election campaign. The image of Mr Major as a cricket-loving, football-supporting ordinary chap from humble origins was also featured in party election broadcasts by the Conservatives. Making a virtue out of 'ordinariness' was also apparent in the Prime Minister's decision to campaign on the streets from a traditional soap box. Indeed, in terms of the scenes in which Mr Major is to be seen appearing most at ease, he is perhaps the first Prime Minister since Harold Wilson to have mastered the informal 'man of the people' image that is thought to have such mass appeal in the television age.

There is, however, an important difference between Wilson and Major. Wilson, as well as looking like a man of the people, was also able to sound like one, whereas the same cannot always be said of John Major. In other words, compared with Wilson's informal colloquial style of speaking, Major tends to come across as rather stilted and formal, and has acquired a reputation as a dull, boring and uninspiring speaker. It would therefore seem that John Major's public image is characterised by an intriguing tension or contradiction between the visual impression that comes across when he is seen but not heard (informal and folksy), and the audible impact of his speech (formal and official).

If audiences arrive at similar subjective impressions of a speaker, there must be a range of observable and describable features of the way he speaks that gives rise to that particular impression. In other words, underlying every general impression, there will be objective characteristics of the talk that recur often enough in a speaker's repertoire to create and consolidate a particular view in the minds of hearers. The remainder of this chapter therefore looks at some features of Mr Major's speaking style that may underpin the kinds of impressions touched on above, first in the context of scripted speeches, and second with reference to the more discursive unscripted talk of the kind that takes place during interviews. It ends with some speculative remarks on the relationship between style of speaking and public image.

Scripted Majorspeak

The effective delivery of scripted set piece speeches, whether from hard copy or teleprompter, involves a range of speaking patterns which diverge from the way people speak in everyday conversation. As has been discussed in more detail elsewhere,[2] most of the variations in speaking patterns associated with addressing large gatherings can be seen as being sensitive to the problems that arise for listeners as they move from participating in small-scale conversation to larger gatherings. These include the difficulties audiences may have in hearing, remaining attentive, understanding and interpreting an extended stream of talk, delivered by a speaker who may be a long distance away, and in a situation where there is no scope for requesting clarification of any points not fully understood.

In response to such potential problems for listeners, an effective speech will be delivered with greater volume, at a slower speed, and will be punctuated with more frequent and longer pauses than is found in everyday conversation. Intonational variation, stresses on particular words or phrases and gestural behaviour will also be more marked or exaggerated than in conversational talk. However, as in conversation, regular eye contact with the audiences remains important, as is evidenced by the development and use of teleprompting technology to make it appear as though the speaker is looking at the audience.

Closer examination of Mr Major's report to the House of Commons on Maastricht mentioned earlier shows that it falls short on a number of these points. There was very little variation in tone or emphasis, either within or between sentences. Most of the time, his eyes remained firmly fixed on the text, with only very occasional fleeting glances away. On average, pauses only occurred every fifteen words, which contrasts with the average of at least every seven words recommended by some top American speech writers.

It might be said, of course, that it is unfair to take a parliamentary statement as representative of his scripted speaking style, as it may have been written by civil servants, and at such short notice that there was no time for rehearsal. And indeed, compared with such Commons statements, Mr Major's set piece speeches during the general election showed distinct signs of improvement. As one might expect, they were more powerfully and creatively scripted. The eye contact problem was improved by the use of a teleprompter, rather than paper-based scripts. There was a little more variety in stress and inflection, but still room for a good deal more. For example, the shifts in intonation sometimes sounded forced, rather than natural, reminiscent in some cases of the recurring line from the satirical Secret Diary of John Major in Private Eye: 'I put on my special stern voice'. Compared with the Commons statement, the words were delivered in slightly shorter bursts, pauses occurring on average every thirteen words.

If a number of key elements of effective oratory are absent from or underplayed in a particular speaker's performance, there may be two kinds of negative consequences for the audience. The first is the problem of understanding, and the ease or otherwise of following a developing argument. The second has to do with the audience's impression of the speaker's commitment to and enthusiasm for the argument he is putting across.

As far as the problem of understanding is concerned, one reason why audiences are likely to find frequent short pauses helpful is that they partition the talk into readily digestible segments. The pace of delivery thereby achieved is well matched to the pace at which audiences can comfortably make sense of what is being said: it allows them to take in one short piece at a time, rather than forcing them to make sense of a long string of words delivered without a break. Frequent pausing thus makes it less likely that audiences will lose the thread, and more likely that they will be able to follow the developing argument. Intonation and stress also help to amplify and clarify the meaning of the words being spoken. At one level, then, a failure by a speaker to pay attention to these aspects of vocal delivery is likely to make it more difficult for an audience to follow, and therefore less interesting to listen to.

At a second, and from a political point of view perhaps more important, level, these features of delivery play an important part in the communication of emotion, passion, commitment and sincerity. Lack of variety in intonation, stress, phrasing, gestural activity and so on, is likely to be associated with lack of emotion, passion and commitment to the messages being communicated. Indeed, it is no coincidence that where an official statement is being made which is explicitly intended to be heard as 'official' and on behalf of someone else, rather than personal and on behalf of the speaker, the person reading it is likely to read it out in a deliberately monotonous and unexpressive way. For example, the way the Queen reads out of the Queen's Speech at the opening of parliament seems designed to make it clear that she is not the author of it, but is merely reading it. A more extreme example is the way science fiction film and television producers depict talking robots, their machine-like character being conveyed by stripping out almost any variation in pace, tone, emphasis, etc.

This is not to suggest that Mr Major's style of public speaking is so devoid of variety in its delivery as to sound as neutral or lacking in personal expression as that found in fictional talking robots. However, if one thinks of a continuum of styles extending between two extremes, with a totally flat neutral sounding robot at one end, and the manic passion of Adolf Hitler at the other, it is arguable that Mr Major is a good deal closer to the neutral end than is advisable for a politician. This is not, of course, to recommend that politicians in the television age should model their oratory on Hitler. It is, however, to suggest that the more 'downbeat' or 'deadpan' their delivery, the more difficult will it be for the wider public to judge what their politicians feel passionately for and against.

Unscripted Majorspeak

When it comes to looking at the way Mr Major speaks when not using a script (e.g. in interviews, at press conferences, etc.), some of the same features of delivery as those outlined above are still present. However, a new element emerges, which is perhaps at the heart of the earlier mentioned clash between the informal and formal dimensions of his image. This is a tendency to make recurrent use of certain ways of speaking, word selection and sentence construction which, taken together, tend to sound somewhat formal, stilted or even archaic.

One example is his habit of avoiding elided forms such as 'it's' rather than 'it is', or 'we'll' rather than 'we shall'. Mr Major is much more likely to use the non-elided forms: 'that is' rather than 'that's', 'cannot' rather than 'can't', 'should not' rather than 'shouldn't', etc. In spoken English, the elided forms tend to be preferred except where special emphasis or clarity is required, whereas there is (or at least used to be) a fairly widespread restriction against the use of elided forms in written English. Mr Major, however, seems to make much more use of the non-elided forms than is usual in spoken English. Initial investigations suggest that this tendency is not only noticeable to casual listeners, but is also interpreted by most of them in much the same way, namely that it sounds formal, stilted and even 'hyper-correct'.[3]

The impression that Mr Major's unscripted speech comes across as more than usually formal is further enhanced by his penchant for using words that are more usually found in written or 'official' English than in everyday common use. Whether or not he has ever actually said that he was 'not inconsiderably displeased', such phrases are readily recognised by the audiences of professional impersonators as characteristic Majorspeak. Nor, given that genuine samples of idiosyncratic word selection can be found without looking too hard or too far, is this really surprising. For example, in an interview with Sue Lawley, shortly after becoming Prime Minister, he spoke about 'calling in at a local hostelry with whomsoever I happen to be'. If the word 'whomsoever' is mainly to be found in legal and bureaucratic documents, so too are others like 'hence' and 'moreover', which also feature in his standard repertoire. In the party election broadcast which showed him retracing his early life in South London, he talked about how the people of Brixton would respond to his early speeches from the soap box with a good deal of 'badinage'. Here, then, was a clear and highly visible example of the clash between the informal sight and the formal sound referred to earlier: in a sequence designed to present him as coming from an ordinary background, he could hardly have used a less ordinary word.

If speech is characterised by words and usages that are more commonly associated with written rather than spoken English, it tends to sound formal, bureaucratic and even stilted. As such, it tends also to conceal or understate the expression of emotional feeling and passion. In other words, unscripted talk of this kind is likely to have a similar impact on listeners as does scripted talk when delivered with a minimum of variation in pace, intonation and stress.

Speaking style and images of the speaker

The implication of the above is that Mr Major's style of speaking, both in scripted speeches, and when talking more discursively without a script, is characterised by a relatively low level of those features normally associated with the expression of strong feelings (passion, commitment, etc.). In the context of British politics, this is very unusual for a political leader. In the context of European politics, however, and especially in those countries with a less adversarial tradition than the UK, it may well be more usual, and perhaps even the norm. It could therefore be that Mr Major's style is much more in line with that of other European political leaders, and that he may in that sense be the first 'Euro-style' British Prime Minister.

For a leader whose speaking style is low on those elements which convey passion and emotion, there remains a potential problem that goes beyond merely being seen to be rather dull or boring. Put simply, the more a speaker refrains from deploying those features of talk that convey feeling and conviction, the more difficult will it be for others to gauge what he really means and what he really stands for. It may therefore be no coincidence that, since the general election, there has been much comment in the media, and even among some Conservative politicians themselves, to the effect that Mr Major's views have turned out to be very different from what they had been expecting before he became leader. There have also been complaints that he appears to lack a philosophy or long-term vision.

This is, of course, in marked contrast to the way Mr Major's predecessor is commonly perceived. Indeed, one of the virtues often cited by those who compare him unfavourably with Mrs Thatcher is that she never left anyone in any doubt about what her convictions were, or how strongly she felt about them. Underlying these very different impressions of the two Prime Ministers are two very different styles of speaking.

Notes

1 This paper is based on observations of video tapes from news and current affairs television programmes before and during the 1992 general election. The discussion of Mr Major's style of speaking is therefore confined exclusively to what is available to the public through television and radio audiences, and makes no claims about the way he speaks in private. Indeed, it is worth noting that people who have met him privately, including some of his political opponents, often report that they find him charming and easy to get along with.

  The original conference presentation was illustrated with reference to selected videotaped excerpts. No attempt has been made to reproduce such audio-visual material here, but readers interested in obtaining further information are welcome to contact the author.

2 See J. M. Atkinson, 'Understanding formality: the categorisation and production of "formal" interaction', *British Journal of Sociology*, 33, 1 (1982), 86–117; Atkinson, *Our Masters' Voices: The Language and Body Language of Politics* (London: Routledge, 1986); J. M. Atkinson and P. Drew, *Order in Court: The Organisation of Verbal Interaction in Judicial Settings* (London: Macmillan, 1979).

3 These observations are based on responses collected from individuals who have attended courses on public speaking and presentation skills over the last two years.

Questions and discussion

John Pearce:

I wonder if one of the lessons of the 1992 election which comes out of the three presentations is that parties are not always in charge. Neither of them were in charge of the consequences of 'Jennifer's Ear' and in the final few days it was almost inevitable, I think, given the state of the opinion polls, that the issue of a hung parliament was going to take off.

Lord Wakeham:

In the first few days when I arrived at Central Office, I was presented with a provisional plan which pretty well identified every day, every press conference, every morning, every subject, who was coming and who was not. And the very first thing I did was to say to both Chris Patten and Sarah Hogg, who was close to the Prime Minister, 'Look, this is no good. We can't have this programme, we have to reduce it and have fewer messages and fewer messengers'. I was quite clear that we would not be at all flexible if we had stuck to that original plan. So I agree that there were events occurring which one couldn't control. I sought in my modest way to persuade the Conservative Party that the right way forward was to change the subjects we were going to discuss quite quickly. At times our campaign did look a bit ragged because we did things at the very last minute, but that was the price you pay for flexibility, but I think the flexibility was the right course.

Robin Cook:

It is the whole purpose of an election campaign to try and get the media to follow your strategy rather than you following the media's strategy. It is perfectly true that we lost control on 'Jennifer's Ear' and that it did not work out the way we had planned it. On the other hand, had we been planning to lose control of an issue the issue we would have picked was health. (Laughter).

Your point on the hung parliament touches a raw patch, frankly. I *do* think it would be extremely helpful if we could have *rational* discussions about scenarios for a hung parliament now the Lib. Dems at their Conference appear to want to think of how they might cooperate with us. But the problem for both of us in talking rationally and lucidly about the potential of hung parliaments, is that immediately the media, or John Wakeham, turn round and say, 'You are admitting you cannot win'.

Des Wilson:

We hoped that the Sunday morning papers would all have one headline – 'Balance of power' – and that our party election broadcast that Sunday night would snatch that moment with Ashdown addressing the nation at a moment of crisis. That would have been the ideal scenario. What happened was that the newspapers on the Sunday morning were not quite saying that and it was at that point, I think, that we all felt it was starting to slip back to the Conservatives.

Now, our party election broadcast was made, except for the last piece of Paddy talking to camera, which we did not record until that day. And one thing I have to admit is that we should have read the situation in the newspapers that morning more sensitively and changed our final message. In the end we half went for the original scenario of addressing the nation in a crisis and half slipped back from that and I think that as a result our last election broadcast was not strong enough. That is really where it went wrong from our point of view.

Lord Wakeham:

In the latter part of the *campaign* the issues of a hung parliament and of PR were deliberately used by *us*. Not as an issue which we thought was important, but as a way of getting John Major over. We detected a greater interest in these matters amongst journalists than the public at large but reckoned that if he came out strongly on these issues the chances were that television news was going to lead on it and so we would be able to get in. He was very happy to do this, to lead on this issue, to talk about these issues, not believing that many people actually were frightfully concerned at the grass roots about it. The significance of it was that he came over as a strong Prime Minister, as a strong leader, and he got well up on the news bulletins for doing it.

Des Wilson:

We felt it starting to slip and on the Tuesday night when Paddy got back from his tour I had to say to him that I *knew* that it was slipping away. 'There was no poll evidence', I said 'but I *know* it is.' And he said, '*Why* is it happening?' and I said, 'Because candidates all over the country are saying the same thing. They're getting on the doorstep "but if we vote for you it will put Labour in". The other thing is that our *own* polling showed that Neil Kinnock's rating was really incredibly low. His standing was a really serious drag for Labour. We believe that we probably went from a potential 22–23 per cent a week to ten days out, to where we eventually ended up. In fact we are *sure* of that and I have not heard anyone really argue against it.

Peter Kellner:

Do Robin Cook and John Wakeham agree with Des Wilson that the fear of a Labour victory had an effect at the end? And if they do, do they think there would have been any difference to the margin had the opinion polls been showing consistently narrow Conservative leads rather than narrow Labour leads during the three weeks up to and around April 7th/8th?

Robin Cook:

Obviously if the polls had not shown Labour winning then presumably the mere fact of Labour winning would not have been so powerful. On the other hand, if the polls had shown Labour behind then we would have looked like not being able to win and we might have paid a penalty because we did not look like winning! I am bound to say that we cannot contrive a campaign that is so clever that we arrange for an opinion poll in which we lose so that we win on the day.

There *was* a Kinnock factor. It would be totally dishonest to deny it. But I do think it was greatly overrated and in fact, the interesting feature of the election is that the ratings for Neil Kinnock over the period of the election improved dramatically while John Major's ratings declined. It is therefore very difficult to see how you can use the 'Kinnock factor' to explain how in that last week, over a period in which he greatly improved his ratings, the situation slipped away from us.

Lord Wakeham:

As far as I was concerned, in an election campaign where you are talking about trust the fear of a Labour government is obviously a factor. I did not notice it significantly change very much, except on one occasion, which was after the Sheffield rally, but whether that was just among our own supporters who found the triumphalist nature of that occasion rather frightening, I do not know.

Justin Fisher:

What role do the panelists think the non-partisan election campaigns played – by that I mean the NALGO 'credit card for health' campaign and the business groups' 'recession, what recession?' ads. in the press?

Robin Cook:

It may have had an impact but I think either way it was very marginal.

Lord Wakeham:

I believe that at one time the NALGO budget for advertising was more than the Conservative press advertising budget, which is quite interesting. When I arrived at Central Office, Chris Patten was determined not to spend anything other than the minimum amount of money on press advertising. He was quite unconvinced that it was actually worth the money. But as the campaign went on it was extremely hard to see how you could sustain that with the newspapers. If some party went and won an election without any press advertising it is an awful change in the scene which nobody would like to contemplate if they were running a newspaper. We discussed it over again and again and with some reluctance we did have a modest press campaign at the end of the day.

David Cowling:

Would you have won the election if Mrs Thatcher had been in power?

Lord Wakeham:

In my view, if Mrs Thatcher had still been Prime Minister we would have won, but the reason why is that she would not have been removed by the back benchers if they thought she was going to win. It was only the fundamental fact that they thought they were going to lose that we ever got to that crisis: therefore, if she had been still the leader we would not have been facing that issue. (Laughter.)

Robin Cook:

I think John is practising a tautology on us. The fact of the matter is that they took her out because they thought that she would lose the election and I am bound to say I think their judgement was right. We would have won the election had she stayed. It was a frequent talking point in the tea room as one of the moral dilemmas of our time, if we had a vote in the Conservative leadership would we be for or against her?

I think there are two factors here. One factor is Thatcher's personality which would, I think, have contributed to us winning. Secondly, there is the quite separate factor of Thatcher as a *former* leader. The Conservatives took on a *new* leader. For a year after he replaced her we had a real problem with the BBC who kept discussing things in terms of how John Major's government differed from Thatcher's government rather than how Labour policies differed from

Conservative policies. That was a very serious problem. It does actually reverse the conventional wisdom that a party has to get a leader in place a long time before a general election to lay that leader in. The wisdom now is that if you can replace your leader just a year before a general election you have probably done a clever thing.

Des Wilson:

I do not think that the question of whether Thatcher could have won is relevant. Labour was always going to lose this election and this is really the crux of the matter. Between 1987 and 1992 Labour had not yet convinced the people of the country that it was fit to govern. It was not a question of whether Thatcher or Major was heading the Conservative campaign but that Labour could not win, because of the distance they had to cover and the trust they still had to win over.

Index